THE FALL OF SPIRITUALITY

THE FALL OF SPIRITUALITY

The Corruption of Tradition in the Modern World

JULIUS EVOLA

TRANSLATED BY
JOHN BRUCE LEONARD

Inner Traditions
Rochester, Vermont

Inner Traditions
One Park Street
Rochester, Vermont 05767
www.InnerTraditions.com

Text stock is SFI certified

Copyright © 1971, 2008 by Edizioni Mediterranee
English translation copyright © 2021 by Inner Traditions International

Originally published in Italian under the title *Maschera e volto dello spiritualismo contemporaneo* by Edizioni Mediterranee, Via Flaminia 109 – 00196 Rome, Italy

First U.S. edition published in 2021 by Inner Traditions

All rights reserved. No part of this book may be reproduced or utilized in any form or by any means, electronic or mechanical, including photocopying, recording, or by any information storage and retrieval system, without permission in writing from the publisher.

Cataloging-in-Publication Data for this title is available from the Library of Congress

ISBN 978-1-62055-977-2 (print)
ISBN 978-1-62055-978-9 (ebook)

Printed and bound in the United States by Lake Book Manufacturing, Inc. The text stock is SFI certified. The Sustainable Forestry Initiative® program promotes sustainable forest management.

10 9 8 7 6 5 4 3 2 1

Text design and layout by Debbie Glogover
This book was typeset in Garamond Premier Pro with Leftheria Pro, Gill Sans MT Pro, and Futura Std used for display fonts

Contents

	Julius Evola and Modern Spiritualism by Hans Thomas Hakl	ix
	Preface to the Third Edition (1971)	xxxvii
	Preface to the Second Edition (1949)	xxxviii
	Preface to the First Edition (1932)	xl
I	The Supernatural in the Modern World	1
II	Spiritualism and "Psychic Research"	13
III	Critique of Psychoanalysis	30
IV	Critique of Theosophism	61
V	Critique of Anthroposophy	80
VI	Neo-mysticism—Krishnamurti	95
VII	An Excursus on Esoteric Catholicism and "Integral Traditionalism"	111

VIII	Primitivism—The Possessed—The "Superman"	131
IX	Satanism	154
X	Initiatic Currents and "High Magic"	168
	Conclusion	189
	Index	195

Editor's Note Regarding This Edition

The Fall of Spirituality is a translation of Julius Evola's *Maschera e volto dello spiritualismo contemporaneo* (Mask and Face of Contemporary Spiritualism), which appeared in its third version in 1971, only a few years before the author's death. The text presented here contains updates based on the corrected fourth edition of 2008,* including the introductory essay by Hans Thomas Hakl, "Julius Evola and Modern Spirituality."

For this English edition, names of persons mentioned in the text have been expanded to their full form, and more complete bibliographic citations have been provided in the notes. Whenever possible, corresponding English bibliographic references and sources have been given. All explanatory translations of foreign terms (e.g., from Latin, Greek, or German) that appear in square brackets within the text itself have been supplied by the editor; all footnotes in square brackets are likewise the editor's work.

**Maschera e volto dello spiritualismo contemporaneo: Analisi critica delle principali correnti verso il "sovrasensibile,"* fourth corrected edition, edited by Gianfranco de Turris (Rome: Edizioni Mediterranee, 2008).

Julius Evola and Modern Spiritualism[1]

Hans Thomas Hakl

I. THE DEVELOPMENT

The question of how one might distinguish "authentic" schools of wisdom—those with "real" access to "transcendent forces"—from the schools that are merely pseudo-organizations has always been a highly contentious topic among esotericists. For Julius Evola, this question was one of central importance from an early point in his life. At the beginning of the 1920s, in the midst of his so-called philosophical phase, Evola came into contact with the teachings of Count Hermann Keyserling and his School of Wisdom (Schule der Weisheit) in Darmstadt, Germany. Even by that time, Evola had already developed serious demands when it came to esoteric groups. Above all, he required that genuine training had to take place in the form of self-realizations (*autorealizzazioni*) that have their basis

---

[1]. Translated from the original German by Michael Moynihan. The direct quotations from Italian (i.e., quotes by Evola and Evola's translations of Paul Tillich) have been translated by Joscelyn Godwin.

in the absolute autonomy of the personality, as opposed to their being accomplished in a *participation mystique* (Levy Brühl). Evola's requirements in this regard can be traced back to the situation of his deceased friend Carlo Michelstaedter[2] and, as Evola clearly stated, Keyserling's School of Wisdom did not live up to them.[3]

Evola's verdict on the teachings of Rudolf Steiner and the Anthroposophical Society at this time was even more harsh.[4] He specifically attacks Steiner's clairvoyance, which he contrasts with the intellectual intuition of Scholasticism. Unlike Steiner's "spiritual science," intellectual intuition concerns not only "psychic" regions but also penetrates into the highest, purely spiritual realm of ideas. Evola further criticizes the anthroposophists' belief in progress, their ideology of reincarnation and karma, and their concepts of morality, humility, and grace, which are related to Steiner's Christocentric worldview.

As the result of the adaption of the *Tao Te Ching* that he published,[5] Evola also became acquainted in about 1924 with Decio Calvari, who was the head of an independent Theosophical lodge in Rome. In Calvari he definitely found an interesting conversation partner, and one who introduced him to Tantrism, but the Theosophical Society itself did not escape Evola's criticism,

---

2. See Michelstaedter, *La persuasione e la rettorica* (Genoa: Formiggini, 1913; rpt. Milan: Adelphi, 1982; English edition: *Persuasion and Rhetoric,* trans. Russell Scott Valentino, Cinzia Sartini Blum, and David J. Depew [New Haven: Yale University Press, 2004]).
3. Evola, "E. Keyserling e la 'Scuola della Sapienza,'" *Ultra* 18, nos. 5–6 (Dec. 1924): 280–91; rpt. in Evola, *Il Mondo alla rovescia: Saggi critici e recensioni 1923–1959,* ed. Renato del Ponte (Genoa: Arya, 2008), 13–25. A very similar article by Evola about Keyserling appeared in the newspaper *Il Mondo,* March 4, 1924.
4. Evola, "Che cosa vuole l''antroposofia' di R. Steiner," *Ignis* 1, nos. 6–7 (June–July, 1925): 185–96.
5. My referring to this as an "adaptation" and not a "translation" is deliberate, as it was essentially an Italian version of Alexander Ular's philosophically toned German translation of the text. A Chinese person named He-Sing assisted Evola. A comparison between the Italian version and that of Ular demonstrates that Evola closely followed the German translation, although he did add a detailed commentary.

although some years would go by before he fully formulated his critique in a comprehensive way.⁶ Instead of a genuine *teo-sofia* (wisdom of god), Evola found Theosophy merely to be a "system of intellectual concepts and imaginations" (*un sistema di concetti e imaginazini*). Moreover, he condemned the mediumship of Madame Blavatsky, the society's founder, as well as the conceptions that theosophy promoted of karma and reincarnation.

Evola's rejection of the Theosophical Society was reinforced by his reading of René Guénon's very sharply worded book *Theosophy: History of a Pseudo-Religion,*⁷ wherein Guénon leveled the accusation that the teachings of Helena P. Blavatsky were devoid of any coherent doctrine whatsoever and had simply been constructed out of smoke and mirrors, so to speak.

Another book by Guénon, *The Spiritist Fallacy,*⁸ was particularly important for Evola's efforts to determine convincing criteria for authentic spiritual groups. In this book Guénon very clearly laid out the danger that emanated from spiritism, especially since it presented itself as being "scientific" and experimentally verified. For Guénon, however, spiritism was just as much of a "pseudo-religion" as theosophy. In *The Spiritist Fallacy,* Guénon uses the term *neo-spiritualism,* which Evola also adopted, in reference to what the French esotericist termed the "pseudo-religious" worldviews that emerged in the first half of the nineteenth century in the United States and subsequently spread into Europe. He saw them as errant religious endeavors that received

---

6. Evola, "Critica della teosofia," *La Torre* 10 (June 15, 1930); rpt. in Evola, *La Torre* (Milan: Il Falco, 1977), 372–80, and in *L'Italia Letteraria,* vol. 2, no. 39 (August 30, 1931). Evola had, however, already included theosophy in his 1925 critique of anthroposophy (see n. 4 above).

7. Guénon, *Le Théosophisme, histoire d'une pseudo-religion* (Paris: Nouvelle Librairie Nationale, 1921). English edition: *Theosophy: History of a Pseudo-Religion,* trans. Alvin Moore Jr., Cecil Bethell, and Hubert and Rohini Schiff (Hillsdale, N.Y.: Sophia Perennis, 2003).

8. Guénon, *L'Erreur spirite* (Paris: Rivière, 1923). English edition: *The Spiritist Fallacy,* trans. Alvin Moore Jr. and Rama P. Coomaraswamy (Hillsdale, N.Y.: Sophia Perennis, 2003).

their main impetus from the modern faith in science and not from any inwardly experienced spirituality. Guénon's touchstone for a genuine spirituality was the "pure metaphysics" that he had derived from his own study of Eastern religions, together with what he would have received directly from his esoteric teachers.

It was these and similar criteria that Evola firmly had in mind when he and Arturo Reghini founded the magical order known as the UR Group in 1927. In his editorial preface to the first issue of the journal *UR,* which featured monographs by members of the group, Evola already made clear what, in his view, is the crucial matter for those who would involve themselves in authentic esoteric groups. This concerns the "problem of all problems, and the anguish of all anguishes: *What am I?*"

In this search for the innermost core of the I, however, one must renounce all of the "false" consolations of philosophy and religion. One can no longer play hide-and-seek with oneself or in front of oneself, for the imperative is much more "to expose the game and no longer play it; to foil the lure, give up the illusion; shatter the compromises and be at daggers drawn with oneself . . . with nothing to lean on, nowhere to go. And a chilling breath speaks the hard words: 'Do not believe, do not love, do not hope.'"

Evola then goes on to speak of the

> *absurdity* of claiming that the anguish that is tormenting you can vanish while you remain what you *are.* . . .
>
> *You must be transformed.* You must be *integrated* and elevated. What really faces the I is not a "problem" but a *task.* The solution is strictly identical to a state to be *realized* by transforming your being. "Know yourself" means "*Realize, create* yourself."
>
> This "realization" is then understood as radically *positive*—nothing conceptual, moral, or sentimental about it, utterly independent of any specific human belief, faith, or philosophy—and a pure matter of *experience.*

But this is an experience that radically alters the I, because the I becomes one with the experienced object, and thus it becomes wisdom and creates power. And for this "way of metaphysical accomplishment, this self-realization above all that is proper to man," there is a "*science,* precise, rigorous, methodical, transmitted as one flame to another, from initiate to initiate in an unbroken chain."[9]

This "science" must also lead to (high) initiation, which according to Evola brings with it a complete transformation of consciousness and of state, creating something out of the human being that goes beyond the human. This also entails the achievement of a continuum of consciousness beyond sleep and even beyond (bodily) death. What becomes Evola's actual criterion for the authenticity of an esoteric group, then, is the spiritual power necessary to prepare the way for such an initiation and to transmit it.

Evola had become acquainted with Guénon's conception of the Integral Tradition in the early 1920s through Arturo Reghini, and he felt an increasing connection with it. It was therefore within the context of the Integral Tradition that the concept of initiation began to take on a more concrete shape for him. In his primary work on the traditional worldview, *Revolt Against the Modern World,* Evola devoted a chapter to this topic, although he shifted his emphasis to the subject of royal initiation.[10] Now Evola regards only traditional schools of wisdom as being authentic, and it was only within such schools that an effective initiation could take place. By the same token, wisdom schools that do not represent a traditional ideology automatically become neospiritual pseudo-organizations for him.

In 1928 the UR Group changed its name to KRUR for legal reasons, and it dissolved entirely in 1929. Evola then founded the magazine *La Torre,* which published ten issues between February 1 and

---

9. "Ai Lettori," *UR: Rivista di indirizzi per una scienza dell'Io* 1, no. 1 (1927): 1–4.
10. Evola, *Revolt Against the Modern World,* trans. Guido Stucco (Rochester, Vt.: Inner Traditions, 1995), 60–67.

June 15 of 1930. Although *La Torre* was more politically and culturally oriented than *UR* had been, Evola nevertheless published three essays in it dealing with the general situation regarding "spiritualism" in Italy, spiritism,[11] psychoanalysis, and theosophy.[12] Evola had originally planned to write a total of seven essays on this theme, but since the magazine barely lasted for six months, four of those essays had to be canceled. The most important of the essays that did appear is the first one, which discusses spiritualism in Italy, because it most clearly expresses why Evola repeatedly warned so vehemently against modern esoteric currents.

Above all, Evola was aware of the spiritually dissatisfied state of modern people, for whom materialism and rationalism are insufficient but can also no longer believe in the salvation promised by traditional religions. As a result, they turn, far too trustingly, toward anything that sounds plausible and promises a "new spirituality." This was all the more true with respect to the modern esoteric or occult currents—spiritism being a prime example—that claim to be based on new scientific findings and refer to experimental evidence in their bid to attract seekers. But instead of finding any genuine spirituality in such groups, the seekers end up in a mixture of materialism, religious longings, and notions of progress, all of which is further elevated by the conviction that some personally experienced "scientific" evidence has proved the veracity of the new faith. In Evola's view, however, everything remains fully in the tangible material realm, without a trace of transcendence to be found. There is also no real support, but at best the feeling of belonging to the group.

For Evola, though, the real danger lay somewhere else entirely—

---

11. Evola had offered an earlier critique of spiritism in his article "Il superamento dello spiritismo," which appeared in the biweekly *Il Lavoro d'Italia,* April 11, 1928.
12. These articles are "Panorama dello spiritualismo italiano," *La Torre* 8 (May 15, 1930) [rpt. (op. cit., n. 6 above), 301–11], "Critica della Psicanalisi," *La Torre* 9 (June 1, 1930) [rpt. (op. cit., n. 6 above), 321–28], and the previously cited "Critica della Teosofia" (see n. 6 above).

and was all the more threatening because it remained largely unrecognized. It arises in the unsuspecting game one plays with the "supernatural," because, as he says, "The evocation of the supernatural is dreadful. It works destructively. And the preferred object of its destruction is the I."[13] Evola even considers the labeling of this destructive force as "diabolical," as the Catholic Church does, to be entirely appropriate, just as he sees a real and present danger that "the soul could be lost." The locus of attack for these forces is the personality as a physical and spiritual unity of the person, which can easily split apart and fragment. Evola further emphasizes that people in the modern world usually lack a unified and clearly structured personality in the first place, which only heightens the danger of an ultimate fragmentation. After such a disintegration it is almost impossible to reconstruct an integrated personality. And without that integrated personality, there can be no initiatic training.

As Evola writes, the situation is exacerbated by the enormous thirst for sensations and sheer desire for the supernatural, which are hallmarks of our age. Should the opportunity arise to experience the supernatural, a genuine enthusiasm would immediately surge through people, and they would surrender to the phenomena with utter naïveté and abandon, clueless as to what actually lies behind it all. Here Evola is referring to an aspect of nature that is completely ignored today. Nature is not just beautiful scenery and something that science measures and weighs; there is also an occult background to nature that consists of forces, against which we moderns are defenseless. The ancients called these forces genii, elementals, nature deities, demons, and so on. Although they are indeed invisible, they are nevertheless a part of nature. Their opportunities for gaining access to the human personality come most easily when the threshold of consciousness is lowered, as in a trance state.

With regard to demons, Evola refers directly to the ideas of the

---

13. Evola, "Panorama dello spiritualismo italiano," 302.

well-known German Protestant theologian and religious scholar Paul Tillich, who was also a friend and colleague of Mircea Eliade. Already in the third issue of *La Torre*,[14] Evola had selected, translated, and published some characteristic excerpts from Tillich's book *Das Dämonische* (The Demonic).[15]

Tillich views the demonic as a force that is both creative and destructive. If the creative aspect is victorious over the destructive, then the outcome bears a "divine" stamp. If, by contrast, the destructive aspect is victorious, then the demonic aspect has succeeded.[16] A few lines from the Tillich material published by Evola will attest to how forceful and direct the influence of this Protestant religious scholar was on Evola's ideas about contemporary "spiritualism."

> The demonic is accomplished in the spirit, but the destructive forces that dominate in the demonic are directly visible in the sub-spiritual. . . . The demonic achieves plenitude only in the spiritual personality, and thus the latter is the object most chosen for demonic destruction. . . . And the state of "obsession," with which the demonic quality realizes itself in the person. . . . The "obsession" is the attack on unity and liberty, against the center of that which is personal.

And here is another statement from Tillich, one that Evola printed in italics and therefore seems to have identified with: *"Against the demonic heteronomy, there is the heroic autonomy."* And further: "The psychic place from which the demonic erupts is the unconscious." The following thought from Tillich also seems to have been

---

14. Paul Tillich, "Conoscenza del Demonico," rpt. (op. cit., n. 6 above), 104–6.
15. Tillich, *Das Dämonische* (Tübingen: Mohr, 1926).
16. The first sentence from Tillich that Evola included in his selection of excerpts is "Demonry is an eruption of the creative principle into things, in the sense of a destruction of the form." Thus, the old form is destroyed. The new form can now be closer to the transcendent (which is oriented upward) or to the demonic (which is oriented downward).

tailor-made for Evola: "Demonry is not the simple awakening of the will to power or the erotic energies, but an ecstatic eruption of them that transports, constricts, and destroys the spirit."

And as a surprising conclusion to these Tillich excerpts, I would like to quote the following passage: "In the practical sphere two demonries surpass all others in their significance and symbolic force, and constitute its appearance in our time. One is the demonry of the autonomous economy—capitalism—and the other is the demonry of popular sovereignty—nationalism." In light of this, one might even wonder whether Paul Tillich's influence on Evola extended into the political sphere.

When Evola warns against "spiritualistic" organizations and currents, then, he does so expressly because it is the unity of the personality for each of their followers that is at stake. This is the reason why he repeatedly puts emphasis on the work toward a *super*consciousness, which is anchored in the higher-than-human realms, and why he warns of the uncontrolled opening of the *sub*conscious, where the aforementioned dark, natural forces are active in subhuman realms.[17]

This brings us straight to the second essay in *La Torre,* which contains Evola's first comprehensive critique of psychoanalysis. Some might be surprised that Evola counts psychoanalysis among the neospiritualist currents, but the categorization is thoroughly

---

17. This provides an interesting glimpse into the views of G. W. F. Hegel, one of the authors most studied and cited by Evola during the latter's philosophical phase. In the third part of his *Encyclopädie der philosophischen Wissenschaften im Grundrisse* (Encyclopedia of the Philosophical Sciences in Basic Outline; 1830), where he deals with the philosophy of the spirit, Hegel discusses parapsychological topics such as animal magnetism and clairvoyance, and he even mentions shamanism. Hegel makes it clear here that he does not view the states of consciousness that arise through such practices as being a higher form of consciousness, but rather he sees them as lying under the conscious personality, and even as pathological. Since it is clear that Evola studied this work, an early influence upon him from Hegel concerning the supernatural is certainly possible. See also the very interesting article by Glenn Alexander Magee, "Hegel on the Paranormal: Altered States of Consciousness in the Philosophy of Subjective Spirit," *Aries* 8:1 (2008): 21–36, esp. 32.

understandable. Like such neo-spiritualist currents, psychoanalysis can be seen as a path to "perfection," whereby the person undergoes a self-analysis and through doing so makes subconscious processes conscious and usable. The analyst can also be seen as someone who takes over the role of the spiritual master.

This essay allows us to clearly see how Evola's views changed over the years with respect to the doctrines of Freud and Jung. In the third edition of *Maschera e volto dello spiritualismo contemporaneo* (Mask and Face of Contemporary Spiritualism; retitled *The Fall of Spirituality* for the present English version), which Evola revised himself for publication in 1971, there is hardly a kind word to found about either of these famous psychologists of the unconscious. But in Evola's 1930 essay on psychoanalysis from issue nine of *La Torre*, he took a somewhat different position. Although that earlier essay contains no shortage of critical commentary, Evola nevertheless seems to have still considered it possible that psychoanalytical doctrines could develop in a positive way. And if what Yvon de Begnac reports is true[18]—namely, that Evola was so enthusiastic about Sigmund Freud when he visited Mussolini in 1922 that he expressed his belief that Freud's world should become the "true world of thought"—then indeed this enthusiasm must have cooled considerably by 1930. What is also astonishing to see on display here is Evola's impressive level of erudition, for in 1930 there would have been very few Italians who have even heard of Carl Gustav Jung.

The critical positions that Evola takes against psychoanalytical doctrines are clear.[19] First, there is the problem that psychoanalysis makes the subconscious paramount, thus severely restricting the developmental possibilities for the conscious personality. Second,

---

18. De Begnac, *Taccuini Mussoliniani* (Bologna: Il Mulino, 1990), 646.
19. The term *psychoanalysis* should be understood here as one that also encompasses the analytical psychology of C. G. Jung. At the time when Evola's original critiques were written, the more specialized designation for Jung's work had not yet come into common usage.

through the artificial opening up of the subconscious, but without any concurrent strengthening of the I, there arises the danger that the "demonic" is allowed access to consciousness of the person. Already in his 1930 essay, Evola was further lamenting the fact that while psychoanalysis probed into the realm of the subconscious, it knew nothing of a superconscious and supramundane world. Another psychoanalytical premise that Evola found completely unacceptable was the claim that results originally obtained solely from investigating the psyches of sick people could then be used to shed light on the psyches of those who were mentally sound.

At the beginning of this introduction, I discussed the third essay that Evola wrote for *La Torre,* which contained his critique of the Theosophical Society. Incidentally, the topics that Evola addressed in the *La Torre* essays were discussed by him again, in an equivalent manner, a year later in the weekly paper *L'Italia letteraria.* All of this material appeared in essentially the same form—with some passages even verbatim—in the first edition of Evola's foundational work on the topic of neo-spiritualism, *Maschera e volto dello spiritualismo contemporaneo,*[20] which I will now consider in greater detail.

II. *THE MASK AND FACE OF CONTEMPORARY SPIRITUALISM*

As we have seen, Evola had already done a considerable amount of preparatory work for his book on neo-spiritualist currents that would appear in 1932. With regard to the book's contents,

---

20. Turin: Bocca, 1932. An interesting recent doctoral dissertation that considers the esoteric concept of "transmutation" in this work by Evola, but also within the larger Italian historical, political, and cultural context, is Roberto Bacci, *La trasmutazione della coscienza nell'esoterismo italiano del periodo fascista: Spaccio dei maghi (1929) di Mario Manlio Rossi e Maschera e volto dello spiritualismo contemporaneo (1932) di Julius Evola* (Dissertation, Brown University, 2012).

the first five chapters consisted of revised versions of his earlier essays on the demonic, spiritualism, psychoanalysis, theosophy, and anthroposophy, all of which we have discussed above. In addition to this, several new chapters were included: one on "neo-mysticism" and Krishnamurti; one on the question of whether a return to traditional Catholicism was possible (taking into account the views of authors such as Henri Massi and René Guénon); and one on modern magical orders, which also discussed the occult ideas of Gustav Meyrink, Éliphas Lévi, and Giuliano Kremmerz. However, we need not discuss these chapters in any detail here, as they appear in the present volume in an essentially similar, albeit expanded, form.

In his intellectual autobiography, *Il cammino del cinabro* (The Path of Cinnabar),[21] Evola discusses *Maschera e volto* in great detail, which is an indication of the importance that he attached to this particular work. He mentions two motivations that led him to write the book. The first—and less important—motivation was his desire to clearly establish once and for all that he was neither a theosophist nor a Freemason, as he had been wrongly accused for years by those who wanted to discredit him politically. His second motivation was by far the more important of the two. As we have already discussed, Evola wanted to warn people of the dangers that were present for anyone who carelessly engaged with the "supernatural" and to provide them with criteria that would serve as a genuine orientation for such pursuits. With these goals in mind, Evola did something that was otherwise rare for him: he set aside his elitism and endeavored to write the book in a more accessible style. It was only in this way that he might reach a wider audience and enlighten them in regard to the "demonic" danger that is ubiquitous in neo-spiritualism.

---

21. Evola, *Il cammino del cinabro* (Milan: Scheiwiller, 1961). The quotes cited and translated here, however, derive from the 2nd expanded edition (Milan: Scheiwiller, 1972), 11ff.

Evola writes:

> I drew on the doctrine according to which the human personality, with its normal faculties and their corresponding experience of the physical world and of nature, occupies an intermediate position; it is situated between two different regions, the first being inferior and the other superior to it: on the one hand, the subnatural and subpersonal; on the other, the truly supernatural and superindividual. But these domains should not be understood in merely theoretical and abstract terms, for they refer to real states and powers of being. . . . Hence the dual possibility of a descending self-transcendence (downward, toward the prepersonal, the subpersonal, and the unconscious) and of an ascending self-transcendence (upward, toward that which is effectively above the boundary of the ordinary human personality—which in some respects is also defensive and protective).

However, since the majority of the groups that fall into the category of contemporary spiritualism clearly evinced a "downward" tendency, and therefore one could only expect them to facilitate contacts to obscure forces that would further weaken the already frail spiritual cohesion of modern people, Evola felt compelled to write the book.

The fact that Evola revised and expanded the book for two subsequent editions (1949 and 1971) is a further testament to his commitment, but it also shows that the book must have met with sufficient interest from the reading public. This underscores the enduring practical value of the work, if only as a clear analysis by someone who understood the topic from more than just a theoretical standpoint.

For the 1971 edition Evola further expanded the book with a chapter on Satanism, which also contained a fairly positive assessment of Aleister Crowley. Since I have already published an article in 2005 on the relationship between Evola and Crowley,[22] I will take the opportunity here to mention some interesting information that was not yet available to me at that time. In 1949 a German judge in Heidelberg by the name of Dr. Heinrich Wendt, who can be described as an extremely knowledgeable specialist in the "history of initiation systems, past and present"[23] and also someone who kept in contact with numerous esotericists, sent a copy of Crowley's *Book of the Law* to Evola and solicited the latter's opinion on it. In a letter dated December 18, 1949, from Wendt to Dr. Herbert Fritsche, who had taken over the patriarchate of the Crowleyan Gnostic Catholic Church after the death of Arnoldo Krumm-Heller eight months earlier, Wendt reported that Evola's reply had been as follows:

> Regarding the "Book of the Law" my findings are not so favorable. If its origin story is true, then this is certainly not a matter of a conscious intervention from "above," but rather concerns influences (wandering and even "syncretic" ones) from the intermediate world. Fifty percent of the text consists not of "mysteries" but of dross; in the remainder, various things are interwoven and Crowley's personal "complexes" must themselves have played a role in it.[24]

At the conclusion of the lengthy section that he dedicates to the book in *The Path of Cinnabar,* Evola laments that his intention to present clear criteria for discrimination in the field of neo-spiritualism had not met with success. He had hoped to establish his position once and for all. But "the exponents of profane culture

---

22. Hans Thomas Hakl, "La questione dei rapporti fra Julius Evola e Aleister Crowley," *Arthos* (n.s.) anno IX, vol. 2, no. 13 (2005): 269–89.
23. Herbert Fritsche, writing in *Merlin: Archiv für forschenden und praktischen Okkultismus, Grenzwissenschaften, Schicksalskunde und esoterische Tradition,* series 3 (1950), 64.
24. Reproduced in *Gnostika* 37 [vol. 11] (Dec. 2007), 57–58.

had not the faintest idea of the essential difference in rank" and were unimpressed by his arguments. Moreover, he had made new enemies; namely, among the theosophists, anthroposophists, spiritists, as so on, whom he had criticized so severely. But, as he remarks sardonically, they lacked the intellectual level necessary to understand him; they were too accustomed to the trivialities of their own beliefs. "The right way—keeping one's distance both from spiritualist meanderings and from the trivia and conventionalities of official culture, while following the method and criteria of serious information and objective criticism thereof—was the least one could expect."[25] Unfortunately, this had the consequence of limiting the circulation of his text.

The first edition of Evola's *Maschera e volto* was also read and reviewed by René Guénon, the founder of the Integral Tradition.[26] Guénon describes the book as one of Evola's best and praises the author's objective in writing it. But in doing so he also remarks that Evola had tried more to draw attention to the psychological dangers of neo-spiritualism and did not go into the falsity of the corresponding spiritualistic theories enough. Guénon also emphasizes that Evola "agrees almost completely" with what he himself wrote on the subject. He does not, however, consider Evola's views on the "magical" schools to be justifiable—which is not surprising given Guénon's negative attitude toward anything connected with magic.[27] Guénon also finds himself unable to concur with Evola's "mild" assessment of Rudolf Steiner.

On the other hand, Guénon was quite pleased with the chapter on the esoteric significance of Catholicism, especially since Evola had shown a contempt for Christianity in his earlier writings. In Guénon's

---

25. Evola, *Il cammino del cinabro,* 122ff.
26. The review appeared in the October 1932 issue of Guénon's journal *Études Traditionnelles*. It is reprinted in René Guénon, *Articles et Comptes Rendus,* vol. 1: *Le voile d'Isis/Études Traditionnelles 1925–1950* (Paris: Éditions Traditionnelles, 2002), 111.
27. For example, in his book *Perspectives on Initiation* (trans. Henry D. Fohr [Ghent, N.Y.: Sophia Perennis, 2001], 259), Guénon writes: "magic in its proper sense is nothing but one of the most inferior applications of traditional knowledge."

opinion, the fact that current representatives of the Christian Church deny any higher meaning to their own faith should not be grounds for others to do the same. Despite Evola's reservations about the original Christianity, which he saw—à la Nietzsche—as being only characterized by humility and an expectation of Grace from above, he nevertheless referred to Guénon's views on the subject. According to Guénon, all higher religions in their esoteric aspect come from the same transcendent root. Christianity must therefore also have a traditional core, even if this is no longer visible today.

On the occasion of the publication of a recent French translation of *Maschera e volto* by Philippe Baillet,[28] the prominent Guénonian journal *Études Traditionnelles* published an extensive review of the book.[29] The reviewer, A. Delarocque-Colombière, only agrees with Guénon's positive assessments with respect to some individual chapters and has a major objection to Evola's central concept of the "personality," which he regards as too vague and therefore at risk of being confused with the everyday self. Similarly, he reproaches Evola for always referring to the I (*Moi,* in the French translation) rather than to the Self (*Soi*). He is also dismayed that Evola does not—like Guénon—simply dismiss psychoanalysis as a "satanic fallacy" but manages to find "something positive" there, if one could just make a few corrections to it. The fact that Delarocque-Colombière adopts the same negative attitude of his master Guénon concerning magic is only to be expected.

III. EVOLA'S LATER WORKS ON NEO-SPIRITUALISM

Evola's efforts to draw attention to the problem of neo-spiritualism were not limited to the essays collected in *Maschera e volto*. In

---

28. Evola, *Masques et Visages du Spiritualisme contemporain,* trans. Philippe Baillet (Puiseaux: Pardès, 1991). An earlier French translation of the book by Pierre Pascal was published in Canada in 1972 (Montreal: Les Editions de l'Homme).
29. Delarocque-Colombière, "A propos d'un livre de Julius Evola," *Études Traditionnelles* 515 [vol. 93] (Jan.–Feb.–Mar., 1992): 28–42.

addition to writing a considerable number of newspaper and magazine articles,[30] he also returned to the subject at various times in his later books. At least three of these instances are worth mentioning.

As the first example, I would like to refer to a substantial and extensive essay that Evola contributed to the second revised edition of the UR/KRUR monographs, which deals with the question of the unconscious and looks at the analytical psychology of C. G. Jung in particular.[31]

In the essay Evola very sharply attacks this "pseudo-spiritual variety" of psychoanalysis because it also engages with issues that, in his view, belong exclusively to the sphere of the "initiatic sciences." The very concept of the "unconscious" is completely opposed to that sphere, because psychoanalysis has endowed the unconscious with the traits of an "autonomous being" that stands in contrast to the conscious personality. Jung teaches that the conscious personality emerged from the unconscious in an evolutionary process. Evola is unwilling to accept such a notion, which echoes the biological theory of evolution that he fully rejects. For Evola, the "development" of the personality could only have originated from a spiritual impulse, born of the highest consciousness that has sunk into deeper, ever more unconscious layers of matter. The individual personality of the human being should therefore be placed hierarchically above the subconscious (Evola's preferred term) and not the other way around.

For Evola, however, the worst aspect of Jung's doctrine is that he draws conclusions from the dream images of psychotic people—images that spring up from the unconscious—based on symbols and myths that belong to the superconscious realm, such as can be found

---

30. For example, six magazine articles by Evola, specifically on the topic of psychoanalysis, are collected in the pamphlet titled *L'infezione psicanalista* (Quaderni di testi evoliani 7; Rome: Julius Evola Foundation, n.d. [1978]).
31. EA, "Esotericism, the Unconscious, Pyschoanalysis," in *Introduction to Magic,* vol. 3, trans. Joscelyn Godwin (Rochester, Vt.: Inner Traditions, 2021), essay XII.2.

in texts of ancient wisdom like the *Tibetan Book of the Dead*. It is therefore misguided to equate Jung's process of individuation, which allows a psychologically unstable person to become healthy, with that of initiation, which implies a complete transformation of being away from that of the ordinary person. A successful individuation is merely the prerequisite for being able to set out on the initiatic path in the first place.

As a second example, I would like to refer to an essay that appears in Evola's book *L'arco e la clava* (The Bow and the Club), in which he deals with the concept of high initiation from a theoretical standpoint.[32] As we have seen, Evola was firmly convinced that initiation was the most essential criterion for an authentic school of wisdom. This is why he is concerned in this essay with pinpointing the differences between the concept of initiation as understood by himself and the Integral Tradition versus the way in which it is understood by theosophists, anthroposophists, and other neospiritualist groups, as well as in academic disciplines such as ethnology and religious studies. The basis for this essay was an earlier article of his from 1965, "Über das Initiatische" (On the Initiatic), which appeared in the German journal *Antaios*, published under the nominal (but not actual) editorial direction of Mircea Eliade and Ernst Jünger.[33]

In the second edition of *L'arco e la clava,* Evola added an essay on

---

32. "Sul concetto di iniziazione" (On the Concept of Initiation), in Evola, *L'arco e la clava* (Milan: Scheiwiller, 1968), 93–115. In the second edition of this book (Milan: Scheiwiller, 1971), Evola included three further essays, one of which also pertains to our topic and is titled "I centri iniziatici e la storia" (Initiatic Centers and History).

33. *Antaios,* 6, no. 2 (1965): 184–208. Reprinted in Evola, *Über das Initiatische: Aufsatzsammlung* (Sinzheim: Frietsch, 1998), 105–29. This volume also includes two essays by H. T. Hansen (= H. T. Hakl) that discuss Evola's relationships with Mircea Eliade and Count Karlfried Dürckheim, respectively. On the background of the journal *Antaios,* see also Hans Thomas Hakl, "L'effetto, pur non esteso, è stato profondo come quello d'una sonda: Breve storia della rivista *Antaios,* curata da Mircea Eliade ed Ernst Jünger (1959–1971)," in *Cenacoli: Circoli e gruppi letterari, artistici, spirituali,* ed. Francesco Zambon (Milan: Medusa, 2007), 247–70.

"Initiatic Centers."[34] In it he emphasizes that an initiation is usually given by a master in a hidden and inaccessible initiatic center. Evola does not claim that such centers no longer exist in Europe, but he stresses that they have become increasingly rare over the course of history and it is almost impossible to come into contact with one today. He adds anecdotally that he once had a friendly argument with the well-known Swiss traditionalist Titus Burckhardt about this topic. Burckhardt, who was initiated into a Sufi order, said that for an honest seeker there were still ways open to a traditional initiation, whereby he was alluding to Sufi lineages in North Africa. These traditional schools allegedly had the potential for powers that went far beyond the merely human. Evola then asked him, somewhat polemically, why such schools had not intervened in situations like that of Tibet, where Communist China was destroying the old traditional monasteries. Could they do nothing to stop the general process of involution?[35]

Perhaps this is also the place to point out the differences between Evola's views and those of Guénon (which were also echoed by the latter's students Frithjof Schuon and Titus Burckhardt), with respect to what constitutes a "regular" initiation. For Guénon and his students, this is only possible if the student also lives exoterically within the framework of one of the major world religions and strictly adheres to its tenets. Esoteric training on its own is inadequate. Evola is much less strict and even sees the possibility of a self-initiation outside of any affiliation to a group or religious community as conceivable, although such an achievement would be extremely rare.

As a third example, I can refer to Evola's book *Ride the Tiger*, which is intended to provide a "guide to life" for those people who, although tradition-bound themselves, have to live as *"uomini differenziati"* (differentiated men) in a modern world devoid

---

34. Evola, *L'arco e la clava*, 2nd rev. and exp. ed. (Milan: Scheiwiller, 1971), 226–31.
35. Evola, *Il Cammino del Cinabro*, 207.

of tradition.³⁶ Chapter 29 of the book is titled "The 'Second Religiosity,'" a phrase that derives from Oswald Spengler and his famous work *The Decline of the West*.³⁷ Spengler understands this as a characteristic phenomenon that occurs time and again in dying cultures, manifesting in the form of mysticisms, irrationalisms, and quasi-religious currents; it is thus parallel with what we have described here as "neospiritualistic." Spengler and Evola do not interpret such phenomena as the beginning of a return to any original and genuine spirituality but rather as the symptoms of a final dissolution. In this context Evola quotes Guénon, who states that the ways upward (to transcendence) were first blocked by positivism and materialism, whereas now, with the neo-spiritualist movements, the ways downward into the subhuman (or in Paul Tillich's terminology, "demonic") realm are opened as well.

Guénon specifically dealt with this question in his book *The Reign of Quantity and the Signs of Times*, devoting an entire chapter to it titled "The Fissures in the Great Wall."³⁸ He understands this great wall as the spiritual one that surrounds people and protects them from destructive, demonic forces. This wall, which naturally also represents a kind of "prison," would, however, already have some cracks in it. Man could escape from it, but then he would be confronted with powers against which he is entirely unsuspecting and knows no way to defend himself. These are all points with which Evola is in full agreement.

A very important component of this chapter from *Ride the Tiger* is Evola's clear treatment of the topic of initiation and the

---

36. Evola, *Cavalcare la tigre* (Milan: Scheiwiller, 1961). English edition: *Ride the Tiger: A Survival Manual for the Aristocrats of the Soul*, trans. Joscelyn Godwin and Constance Fontana (Rochester, Vt.: Inner Traditions, 2003). References that follow are to the English edition.
37. Evola, *Ride the Tiger*, 208–17. The definitive edition of Spengler's two-volume work was published in German in 1923.
38. Guénon, *The Reign of Quantity and the Signs of the Times*, trans. Lord Northbourne (London: Luzac, 1953), 205–10.

present-day possibilities (or lack thereof) for attaining it. He writes:

> [O]ne must assume a priori that [initiation] is not even a hypothetical possibility in an epoch like the present, in an environment like the one we live in, and also given the general inner formation of individuals. . . . Anyone who sees things differently either does not understand the matter, or else is deceiving himself and others. What has to be negated most decisively is the transposition to this field of the individualistic and democratic view of the "self-made man"; that is, the idea that anyone who wants can become an "initiate," and that he can also become one on his own, through his own strength alone, by resorting to various kinds of "exercises" and practices. This is an illusion, the truth being that through his strength alone, the human individual cannot go beyond human individuality, and that any positive result in this field is conditioned by the presence and action of a genuine power of a different, nonindividual order.[39]

Finally, a brief remark based on Evola's last major interview, which was conducted by Gianfranco de Turris and Sebastiano Fusco on December 27, 1973. Here Evola confirms once again that he sees hardly any opportunities for initiation at the present time.[40] Thus, he has no desire to stir false hopes.

As a conclusion to the forgoing survey of Evola's nearly lifelong literary efforts to warn of the dangers of neo-spiritualism and to indicate other ways to transcendence, I will attempt to summarize below the characteristic standpoints of Evola and the Integral Tradition, versus those of neo-spiritualism.

---

39. Evola, *Ride the Tiger,* 214.
40. "Testimonianze su Evola," appendix 1 in Evola, *L'iniziazione nel mondo moderno,* ed. Gianfranco de Turris (Rome: Edizioni Mediterranee, 1985), 332–54; esp. 336ff.

Evola/Integral Tradition	Neo-spiritualism, New Age
elitist	open to all
hidden	strong public presence
belongs to a single tradition	eclectic
origin largely unknown	origin largely known
the spiritual path is consistently the same	the spiritual path can be very diverse
traditional, unchanging, ahistorical	modern, progressive, evolutionary
focus on superconsciousness	subconscious is also incorporated
one should remain in a fully conscious state	trance states are also feasible
spiritual knowledge comes via intellectual intuition	knowledge comes from beyond the rational, e.g., from the unconscious, the "astral" world, spirits, etc.
initiation causes an ontological change of state	initiation leads the person "upward" gradually
builds upon the foundation of a strong personality	the weak can also "join in"
uniformity is paramount	multiform
the path is amoral	the moral "good" is striven after
ascesis and discipline	ideal of well-being
spiritual growth through suffering	avoidance of suffering
orientation is strictly toward transcendence	orientation is also toward the emotional realm and toward astral and other "higher" worlds
self-made delusions must be dismantled	not necessarily the case; self-made delusions can also be intensified if they convey something "useful"
high degree of personal commitment	not necessarily the case
knowledge comes only through one's own realizations	secret wisdom can also be taught
opening is only toward the "above"	opening is also toward the "below"
high initiation is exclusively for men	initiation is for everyone

While these classifications may not always be so clear in actual practice, this comparison provides enough reference points to make Evola's ideas and concerns more perceivable.

IV. SOME CONCLUDING REMARKS ON EVOLA'S ESOTERIC METHODOLOGY

In drawing the distinction between traditional, "authentic" spiritual orders and neo-spiritualist groups, Evola is never concerned with neutral criteria but rather with absolute valuations. His intent is to show what he thinks is authentic and correct, and what should be rejected, by referring to both ancient and recent wisdom literature of the East and West. This is what sets his work completely apart from modern academic research on esoteric groups.

Scholarly studies on this topic strive to be as neutral and objective as possible and to examine all groups in an unbiased way. Such investigations must therefore remain on an "external" quantitative and descriptive level; the groups under consideration cannot be interpreted in terms of a subjective or qualitative evaluation. The problem with this approach is that while a "seeker" may be provided all sorts of interesting information about a certain group, no answer with regard to the key question—the question of which specific esoteric group is capable of providing an "authentic" initiation—is forthcoming. The great success of scientific research in the modern age essentially rests on the fact that it strictly holds to a rational-empirical methodology; in doing so, however, it excludes from the outset any questions that go beyond this. As a result, the scientific approach also lacks the tools needed to comprehend or handle such questions. In addition, the problems that the esoteric and initiatic realms deal with cannot always be fully expressed in verbal or logical terms.

Religions and esoteric traditions, by contrast, have recourse to convey their "truths" through symbols and myths. The Integral Tradition, which assumes a common, transcendent origin for all high cultures and religions, also asserts that "authentic" symbols and myths are universal and are always understandable, independent of a given historical epoch. However, the prerequisite for such understanding is that the recipient of the symbolic message has developed the "correct" awareness to perceive it. Armed with such an awareness, he could also discern the original meaning and deeper spiritual background of symbols and myths from ancient or completely foreign cultures. Evola calls this the traditional method, and he applies it in his research and in his writings. The traditional method places less emphasis on historical facts than it does on spiritual content. It concentrates on the timeless, universal, and cross-cultural meaning, the *"quod ubique, quod ab omnibus et quod semper"* (that which is everywhere, by everyone, and always [true]).[41] This method—which was also used to a certain extent by Giambattista Vico, Johann Jakob Bachofen, and Numa Denis Fustel de Coulanges—also enables one to apprehend the complexity and ambiguity of symbols and myths. Whereas the logical mind arrives at knowledge through a process of separation or division (i.e., analysis), the traditional method works "holistically." A unified whole is grasped "all at once" as opposed to being understood slowly in a temporal and analytically sequential process. Since this whole extends beyond the logical-empirical realm, it can contain opposites within itself as well as "invisible" aspects that can be "sensed." (Here one might draw an analogy to how a piece of music is perceived, although Evola would view the accessible meaning of myths and symbols as being much more precise.)

Nevertheless, the traditional method is neither irrational nor arbitrary. If one has the requisite "synthesizing" intuition (the requisite "consciousness"), it is just as "objective" as the scientific method. It thereby allows a clear evaluation of spiritual paths and groups. The knowledge gained through the traditional method is indeed a knowl-

---

41. See Walter Heinrich, *Sul metodo tradizionale* (Rome: Julius Evola Foundation, 1982).

edge *sub specie interioritatis* (of an interior kind), yet it has a universal character since the gift of intuitive knowledge is "potentially" given to all people. It is also not the case that the individual symbols and myths must always exhibit an identical external form in order to betoken a certain "higher" truth. An intuitive knowledge grasps this truth even if it is clothed in different vestments. So long as those vestments are "consistent," they awaken exactly the right associations that point to the "higher" truth.

Now it seems that one can, to a certain extent, "learn" to apprehend such "truths" and to "train" the intuition that is needed for that process. A decisive factor here may be a kind of "familiarization" process: through a recurring engagement with the aforementioned universal symbols and myths, their "inner" truth suddenly flares up, and from that point on they are "forever" understood. This understanding does not come in a logical-deductive sense but is instead borne of a deep conviction that one has recognized their innermost meaning. The previously unrecognized "truth" has suddenly become part of one's own personality; one is identified with that truth and can therefore implement and "use" it in further cognitive processes. In comparison with such a dramatic experience, a logical-deductive conclusion seems but pale and superficial. The danger here, of course, is that the traditional method can easily lead to a sort of fanaticism.

One of the likely reasons for the relative success of Evola's esoteric writings—also outside of Italy—is his skill in linking together universal symbols and myths in such a way that the requisite intuition for apprehending their inner meaning makes itself felt relatively quickly for perspicacious readers of his work. This may be an indication that Evola himself possessed this intuition to an extraordinary degree and also knew how to incorporate it into his writings. In particular when one reads a text of his several times over, the underlying "higher truths" seem to be "induced," so to speak, in the reader. This is similar to the situation that one experiences with alchemical texts, which invite the reader to study them several times to understand them in the right way.

The question as to what extent this synthesizing knowledge may be related to the intuitive knowledge of antiquity, the "intellectual intuition" (*intellectualis intuitio*) of Nicholas of Cusa, or to Henry Corbin's *imaginatio vera* (true imagination) and the Islamic *ta'wīl* (esoteric interpretation), is probably a matter best left to academic specialists; in any case, it falls outside the scope of this introduction.

I would also point out that the contrasting terms *emic* and *etic*, which are often used by sociologists and academic researchers into esotericism, do not apply here when we are speaking of the traditional method. An emic perspective is the view of a culture—or, in our case, an esoteric group—through the eyes of an "insider" who utilizes the special terms and symbols as they are understood and used within the group itself. An etic perspective, on the other hand, is the viewpoint of an observer from the "outside" who can only understand in his own "external" way the special terms and symbols used within this group. By contrast, the "traditional method" used by Evola is ahistorical, universal, and cross-cultural, and it is available as well to both "insiders" and to those who exist outside the group. However, it does require a "higher" intuitive knowledge. This, in turn, is not necessary for the emic view of internal symbols and terms within an esoteric group, since that view is based solely on familiarity with the respective customs. It remains at the level of normal internal group communication and specifically is not ahistorical, universal, or cross-cultural.

It goes without saying that it is impossible for academic esoteric research at universities to accept "higher" intuitive knowledge as a scientific instrument. Since the study of esotericism is a recent scholarly discipline, the methodological, philosophical, and sociological studies first have to establish a foundation. The rejection of the "traditional method" within the discipline is therefore justified. Evola himself would say that the scholarly efforts represent no more than a "horizontal" accumulation of knowledge, to which only a further vertical axis of transcendence is capable of giving meaning, value, and weight. For him, the research into and evaluation of esoteric topics and groups is in any case inconceivable in the absence of such "vertical" intuitive knowledge.

This is the reason why Evola dared to make unequivocal judgments in his research, even when he had only a small amount of reliable information, whether of an esoteric or historical sort, at his disposal. Yet even scholars working in the conventional academic contexts have conceded time and again that his intuitions have proved to be useful. One example of this relates his book *The Hermetic Tradition*,[42] which, with its particular hermeneutics of specialized alchemical expressions, served as an inspiration to both Mircea Eliade and C. G. Jung. Other examples pertain to comparative religious studies. As Silvio Via, an orientalist at the University of Naples, puts it, Evola seems at times to have achieved "more reliable restorations of the message of Lao Tse" through "fortunate intuitions" than many academic translators of the Chinese wisdom classic the *Tao Te Ching*. Similar observations can be made with regard to Evola's interpretations in the areas of Tantrism, early Buddhism, and Zen Buddhism. But in any case, Evola's intuition seems to have been concentrated on areas whose spirituality corresponded to his own inner being. To return to the musical analogy we mentioned above, not every conductor can intuitively grasp and interpret every composer to the same extent.

HANS THOMAS HAKL received a Doctor of Law degree in 1970 and, together with partners, created a large international trading company as well as the publishing house Ansata in Switzerland, which specializes in the esoteric. After having sold his shares in both companies in 1966, he founded and

---

42. Evola, *The Hermetic Tradition: Symbols and Teachings of the Royal Art*, trans. E. E. Rehmus (Rochester, Vt.: Inner Traditions, 1995).

is still editor of *Gnostika,* the most widely acknowledged German publication dealing with esotericism in an academic way. Hakl has collaborated in several international journals and dictionaries on the occult and religion and is the author of *Unknown Sources: National Socialism and the Occult* and *Eranos: An Alternative Intellectual History of the Twentieth Century.* His writings have been translated into English, French, Italian, Czech, and Russian.

Preface to the Third Edition (1971)

This book, updated and expanded in the current third edition, is written for all those interested in contemporary "spiritualism" or who wish to orient themselves to its principal currents. Precisely for this reason, the point of view adopted for the purposes of this orientation will not be as absolute as that which characterizes other works by the author. The defense of the human personality—a task, failing whose realization, any true "spiritualistic" aspiration will be lacking in its main presupposition—can be taken as the fundamental guiding principle of the present work.

Nonetheless, whoever knows how to see, to separate the essential from the accessory, will easily be able to recognize that there is no contradiction standing between these two points of view. The first—the point of view taken in the present critique—can indeed work to clarify the sense and the rightful place of the second one: that taken by works on specialized esoteric arguments or works affirming "integral traditionalism." What is more, the very sequence of the present essays will furnish a natural passage from one plane to the other.

J.E.

Preface to the Second Edition (1949)

This book, whose first edition appeared in 1932 and is now revised and augmented, occupies a position midway between works I have written for a specialized public—for example, *The Hermetic Tradition* and *The Yoga of Power*—and general critical works on epochs and civilizations, such as *Revolt against the Modern World*.

This book speaks to all those who are interested in contemporary "spirituality" and want guidance with regard to its principal currents. For that very reason, the point of view taken here to provide such orientation will not be as absolute as that adopted in my other works, but more comprehensive. Its fundamental and ruling principle will be the defense of the human personality: a task without fulfillment whose truly "spiritual" aspiration will lack its primary requirement.

Anyone who can see and separate the essential from the accessory will easily recognize that there is no contradiction between the two points of view. The one—as assumed in the present critique—can also serve for defining the meaning and the proper place of the other: that of the works of initiatic character and which affirm the "integral tradition." For the rest, the very sequence of the present essays will furnish a natural passage from one level to the next.

Some readers may be surprised to find here some positive evaluations of Catholicism and Christianity (no less in the present edition than in the first). This does not prejudice what we have said on the subject elsewhere, in a different spirit and with a different purpose. We take the opportunity here to raise some points on which one cannot insist too much. 1) One should not confuse being *beyond* a tradition with being *inside* it, as is the case with the individualists, the "critical minds," and the modern freethinkers. 2) One must be able to recognize under what conditions a limit petrifies (as Dante well knew when, in his ciphered language, he spoke of the "Rock that petrifies"), and under which it can, on the contrary, protect. 3) To apply what is valid for the "more than human" to the human individual, especially that of today, is to fall into the most dangerous of deviations and misunderstandings, something for which we want to take no responsibility.

Thus even for those who have been following my work for some time, this book may be far from useless. For the wider public, on the other hand, it may be of help in discriminating between the negative and the positive in the new "spirituality," and to discern the paths by which this positive element could be properly integrated. Yet it remains for each one to discover up to what point his mentality, his qualification, and his vocation allow him to pursue such paths.

J.E.
BAD ISCHL, 1948

Preface to the First Edition (1932)

This volume is not intended for a limited group of specialists, but for all those interested in any way in modern "spirituality" who would like to develop a criterion by which they can judge its nature.

Those who have read my previous works will find here a point of view that is in some respects less absolute and more comprehensive, but which does not contradict the point of view appropriate to those other works, serving instead to define its proper place and its true meaning.

For example, the reader will see that some of the present comments on the Catholic tradition, suitable for this book, do not contradict what they may have found on the subject elsewhere and in a different spirit, for example in *L'uomo come potenza*. This serves to underline what can never be overemphasized: that one should not confuse being *beyond* traditions with being *inside* them, as is the case with the so-called liberal spirits or modern individualists. To apply what is valid for the "more than human" to the human individual, especially that of today, is to fall into the most dangerous deviation and misunderstanding, for which we want to take no responsibility.

And this is why, even for those who have been following my work for some time, this new book may prove useful and worthwhile.

J.E.

Karthaus, October 1931

I
The Supernatural in the Modern World

> *It is a propitious moment for the equivocal enterprises of all the false mysticisms which mingle materialistic sensuality with spiritualistic confusions. For the spiritual forces are invading everything. . . . It can no longer be said that the modern world is lacking in the supernatural. All sorts and varieties of it can be seen appearing; and the great evil today is no longer materialism and scientism, it is an unbridled spirituality. But the true supernatural is none the more recognised. "Mystery" envelops everything, and is installed in the sombre regions of the ego it ravages, at the centre of the reason it drives away from its domain. Everybody is ready to reintroduce it everywhere, except in the divine order in which it really resides.*[1]

Thus wrote the Catholic Henri Massis in an uneven and by now somewhat dated work, but these are words that still carry weight

---

[1]. Henri Massis, *Defence of the West,* trans. F. S. Flint (London: Faber & Gwyer, 1927), 185–86.

today. Indeed, even today, many and thriving are the groups, sects, and movements that devote themselves to the occult and to the "supernatural." Such currents, enlivened by every new sharpening of the crisis of the Western world, gather adherents in substantial numbers: spiritism alone can count millions of them. Exotic doctrines of every kind are imported, and the more these display characteristics of strangeness and mystery, the more they exert a fascination. Well might it be said that every concoction finds its place in the vessel of "spiritualism"—adaptations of yoga, varieties of a spurious mysticism, "occultism" at the margins of Masonic lodges, neo-Rosicrucianism, naturalistic and primitivistic regressions of a fundamentally pantheistic kind, neo-gnosticism and astrological divagations, parapsychology, mediumism, and such like—not to speak of the aspect of pure mystification in all this. In general, it is enough that something deviates from what one conventionally called normal; it is enough that it presents the characteristics of the exceptional, the occult, the mystical, and the irrational, for a substantial number of our contemporaries to become interested in it, with much greater ease than ever before. Finally, even "science" has gotten involved: in some of its branches, like psychoanalysis and "deep psychology," it has often wound up in promiscuous evocations at the border regions of the I and the conscious personality. A paradox has, moreover, become apparent in all of this: it is precisely certain that representatives of those "positivistic" disciplines who, to justify and organize themselves, gave themselves over to a systematic denial of any vision of the world containing supersensible elements—precisely these people, in a separate sector, today frequently indulge in primitive forms of neospiritualism. And so the reputation that they have acquired for seriousness in their fields of competency is taken as a validation of these forms and transmutes into a dangerous instrument of seduction and propaganda. A typical case is that of the physicists William Crookes and Oliver Lodge, with respect to spiritism. And thus broad segments of the Western world are exhaling a spiritual chaos that makes them strangely similar to the Asiaticized world of Hellenistic decadence. Nor are we lacking in our own messiahs, in various versions and forms.

First of all it is necessary to orient ourselves and to see what the principal causes of this phenomenon are. As its most conspicuous trait, one might point out a general impulse toward evasion. In one of its aspects, the role of neo-spiritualism is doubtless analogous to everything, which the man of today attempts to employ in his evasion of the surrounding world, of the suffocating forms assumed by civilization and the culture of the modern West, and along this path he comes, in extreme cases, even to the use of drugs, to anarchist bombings, to the pandemic of sex, or to diffuse and varied forms of neurotic overcompensation.

At the same time, there are motivations here that one must recognize as partially legitimate. It is not by accident that the beginnings of neo-spiritualism are contemporaneous with the affirmation of the materialist-positivist vision of man and of the world, in its squalor and in its soullessness, as well as rationalism, the pretense that abstract reason might banish or regulate everything that belongs to the deepest strata of being or of the psyche. At the same time, we must indicate the dearth of the forms of a traditional civilization in the superior sense, capable of effective openings toward the heights. We are speaking above all of the religion that has come to predominate in the West, Christianity, and of the fact that it itself has ceased to appear as something living, has ceased to offer points of reference for a true transcendence, and has reduced itself rather, in Catholicism, to confessional devotionalism and petit-bourgeois moralism—so much so that one has come to speak of the "death of God" and to formulate the need for a demythologization of religion, which would reduce religious content to social practice (as, for example, in so-called atheistic Christianity).

But supposing that positive religion has thus failed in its higher function, supposing it has offered little to those who sought, more than a "faith" and a moralistic bourgeois and social domestication of the human animal, albeit dimly, a liberating spiritual experience: supposing all this, still it is clear that nothing apart from intolerance and rebellion could come from the subversive maxims of the latest ideologies, according to which the beginning and end of man are to be found on this earth, and the goal is a society of production of mass well-being—a society destined, moreover, to become insipid and boring and to be paid for with multiple conditionings and mutilations of the personality.

Barring the effects of fundamentally degrading processes, there subsists in the depths of human nature the need for "something else" and, at the limit, something supernatural. In every human being this can be suppressed only to a certain point. In the most recent times, the vice grip has closed, by way of the factors we have just mentioned. Thus, there arises in many an impulse, which faithfully seeks its fulfillment and its outlet in everything that neo-spiritualism claims to offer, to a certain degree in a new way, through ideas that seem to grant access to a vaster reality, not only theoretically but above all as a lived spiritual experience. In the most recent times one has come to recognize, albeit sporadically, the "extranormal" as the manifestation of energies, laws, and possibilities beyond those admitted in the late positivistic period; and this fact constitutes another factor in the particular orientation of the impulse toward evasion, which we intend to deal with here.

A final, not irrelevant factor in all of this is the awareness, no longer constrained to a specialized superior culture, of doctrines of a predominately Asian origin, which promised more than the positive Western religions, especially in their most recent drained and enfeebled forms, have been able to offer.

This, in short, is the "situational" conjunction that underlies the diffusion of neo-spiritualism. This neo-spiritualism, as we have noted elsewhere, generally displays the characteristics of what Oswald Spengler has called the "second religiosity," which manifests itself not at the center of an organic, qualitative, and spiritual civilization in its luminous original period but rather at the margins of a twilight civilization in dissolution; specifically, it appears as a phenomenon that is peculiar to what Spengler termed "the decline of the West."

In light of this, it is necessary to establish some fundamental points of reference, which permit a discriminating stance in confronting the varieties of neo-spiritualism and any other similar current.

In this connection, we must underline that we are above all interested in the part of this spiritualism that does not reduce itself to theories but that, often without knowing or willing it, includes tendencies favoring the conjuring of forces from "the other side," bringing individuals and groups into contact with these through the cultivation of extranormal modalities of consciousness.

The premise, obviously, is that these influences and these modalities exist as truly as the forms of physical reality and the ordinary psyche. One way or another, this has always been recognized by every normal and complete civilization; it has only been denied for a few decades by Western "positivism." Nowadays, however, one must go further than a simple recognition in psychological, or, better, psychologistic terms, as happens, for example, in the domain of psychiatry and generalized psychoanalysis. So far as our own concerns here go, this "spiritual" must be understood in ontological terms, which is to say, precisely as reality. Otherwise, the problem of the danger of the "spiritual" (or of spiritualism) and of the "extranormal" is either not posited at all or else ends up taking on a quite banal character. One might then speak of fetishes, of paranoias, and of the chimera of unbalanced and "cracked" minds, regarding all of which there is not much reason to be alarmed.

Here we must refer to the personality in the proper sense. Contact with the "spiritual" and its emergence can represent a fundamental risk for man, in the sense that it can result in an impairment of his internal unity, of his belonging to himself, of his power of clear presence to himself, and of clear vision and autonomous action, which precisely define the essence of the personality.

In its current form, the personality finds itself right at home, on solid ground in the world of tangible and measurable things, of logical thoughts with a clear-cut form, of practical action, and more generally of whatever has relation to the physical senses and to the brain. In the world of the "spiritual," on the other hand, the personality runs a continual risk, it returns to the problematic state, because in that world there no longer exist any of the supports to which it is accustomed and of which it has need, as long as it is a personality conditioned by a physical body.

It is no accident that many of those who cultivate "spiritualism" today are beings without a pronounced personality (the large percentage of women in these ranks is significant), while those who show signs of a strong and conscious personality limit themselves to "positive" things and harbor an indefatigable repulsion against the supersensible, for which they are ready to create any kind of alibi. We must understand that this reaction is nothing but the unconscious manifestation in them of an instinct of spiritual defense. The weakest personalities, in which such an instinct is lacking or is attenuated, are most disposed to accept and to imprudently cultivate ideas, tendencies, and evocations, whose danger they do not realize.

Such people believe that anything transcending the world to which they are accustomed constitutes ipso facto something superior, a higher state. The moment the need for "something else" acts in them—the impulse toward evasion—they take any road whatever, without realizing how often they thus enter into the orbit of forces that are not above but rather below man as a personality.

This is the fundamental point: to see as clearly as possible the situations in which neo-spiritualism might effectively have a regressive character, notwithstanding every appearance and every mask, and in which the "spiritual" might not be a "supernatural" so much as an "infranatural"—and to see this concretely and existentially, apart from every confusion, every doctrinal and intellectual deviation.

To have an idea of the influences with which we might be dealing when this opening that is downward and not upward, this shift that is descending rather than ascending, occurs, it will be necessary to indicate what the word *nature* must mean, in a broad and complete sense. When one speaks of "nature" today, one generally refers to the physical world, known via the physical senses of every awake person and measurable by the exact sciences. In reality, this is only one aspect of nature, an image formed in relation to the human personality, and indeed at a certain phase of its historical development, as an experience belonging to that development rather than to other possible phases and forms of existence. Man perceives nature in such definite forms of physical reality because he has detached himself from nature, because he has freed and separated himself from it so much that he finally feels it as something external, as the "not-I." Nature in itself is not this appearance in space: it is instead grasped at that point where this sense of exteriority is attenuated and where the state of lucid waking consciousness attenuates to the same degree, to be replaced by states in which objective and subjective, "inside" and "outside," are confounded. Here begin the first dominions of an "invisible" and "psychic" world, which, to be such, do not cease to be "nature"—indeed, they are eminently "nature," and not at all "supernature." With objective scientific investigation into material or energy, man basically moves in a sort of magic circle that he himself has drawn. The only one to leave this circle and to reach nature will be the man who retreats from his formed personal consciousness into the subconscious, via the road that commences with dark, organic sensations, with the emergence of complexes and psychic automatisms in their free state (released, that is, from cerebral control), and which then continues by descending into the depths of the physical subconscious.

Some recent research has furnished certain elements for identifying this process of regression, even from a positivistic point of view.

With experimentally induced local anesthesia, a state arises just as in the psychic functions, when the layers of the cerebral cortex are progressively neutralized, from the newest and most external to the most internal and ancient, until the entire action of the brain has been paralyzed and one passes into the sympathetic nervous system—which, as has been demonstrated, is still connected to certain forms of consciousness. The first things to disappear are the concepts of space, time, and causality; that is, the concepts that uphold the waking experience of nature and the logical concatenation of thoughts in the conscious personality. In relation to the deeper strata, ordinary consciousness itself, distinct from the "I," diminishes, and we stand on the threshold of subconscious functions, in an immediate relation with vegetative life. This precisely is the end of the "person" and the threshold of the impersonal, of "nature."

Leaving aside popular superstitious assumptions and folkloristic and poetic appropriations, those entities to which antiquity gave the name of *genii,* spirits of the elements, gods of nature, and so on, cannot be reduced to mere fables. Certainly, all of this involved "imaginations"—namely, forms produced in certain circumstances by a faculty analogous to that which acts in dreams through the sympathetic nervous system—that, however, originally dramatized the dark psychic experiences of contact with forces, of which the forms, beings, and the visible laws of nature are but manifestations.

Similarly, the phenomena of so-called natural clairvoyance, which is to say somnambulistic clairvoyance, are tied to the neutralization and exclusion of the brain and to dependency on a reduced state of consciousness, which in certain beings subsists thanks to special circumstances; that is to say, these phenomena are tied to the sympathetic nervous system. The principal plexuses of this system, and especially the solar plexus, are then transformed into a sensorium and assume the functions of the brain, which they exercise without the help of the instrument of the physical senses in the strict sense, on the basis of stimuli and sensations that do not come from the outside but instead from within. Naturally, depending on the case, the products of this activity have a more or less direct character; that is, they are more or less intermixed with the forms that they use to translate themselves and to become conscious, and these forms are more or less informed by the spatiotemporal element proper to the brain.[2] But, however great the amount of dross, there is in these phenomena an indisputable margin of objectivity, which is sometimes confirmed even in a lucid form, through the correspondence of the data provided in this manner with other data that are controllable on the basis of the physical perceptions sifted and organized by the waking consciousness.

This already provides a point of orientation. There exists a whole "psychic" zone, "hidden" with respect to ordinary consciousness, which is in its way real (and not mere "subjective illusion" or "hallucination") but should not be confused with the "spiritual" in the sense of value, and still less with the "supernatural." It would be more apt here to speak instead of the infranatural; and he who opens himself to this world passively, "ecstatically," in reality regresses, he forces his internal level to descend from a higher degree to a lower degree.

Every positive measure for a man's true spirituality must be clear, active, and distinct consciousness: that which he possesses when he objectively scrutinizes external reality or exterior form in terms of logical reasoning, mathematical deduction, or when he makes a decision in his moral life. This is his conquest, which defines him in the hierarchy of beings. When he passes instead into states of nebulous mysticism or a pantheistic disintegration, when he proceeds into that phenomenology—however sensational it may be—which arises in the conditions of regression, psychic collapse, or trance, he does not ascend but instead descends along the ladder of spirituality, passing from more spirit to less. He does not go beyond "nature," but he gives

---

2. Cf. Arthur Schopenhauer, *Parerga und Paralipomena: kleine philosophische Schriften* (Berlin: Hahn, 1851), I, 231–33. Schopenhauer already saw this point clearly.

himself to it once more; indeed, he makes himself the instrument of the underworld forces that are enclosed in its forms.

Only after having seen this point very clearly can one formulate the idea of another, antithetical spiritual direction—a direction that can serve as a measure of what might be valid in "spiritualism" and which can be proposed to him who, having a particular vocation and qualification, seeks "transcendence," something higher than that which the modern vision of man and of the world offers: the space for a superior liberty beyond the conditionings and senselessness of today's existence, beyond the residual forms of the religious confessions. In principle, we must posit the necessity of a path leading to experiences that, far from "reducing" consciousness, transform it into superconsciousness; which, far from abolishing the distinct presence that conserves itself so easily in a healthy and awake man among material things and practical activities, raises this presence to a higher degree in such a way as to integrate rather adulterate the principles that constitute the essence of the personality. The road toward experiences of this kind is the road toward the true supernatural. But this road is neither comfortable nor, for many, alluring. It presupposes precisely a contrary attitude to that of the enthusiasts for "spiritualism" and of whomever is driven solely by a confused impulse toward evasion: it presupposes an attitude and a will of ascesis, in the original sense of this word as distinct from the assumptions of a monastic devotional order that practices mortification.

It is not easy to bring the modern mentality back to considering and adjudicating in terms of interiority, rather than based on appearance and "phenomenon" or sensation. Still more difficult, after the devastation wrought by biologism, anthropology, and evolutionism, is to bring it back to the sense of what was once and nominally remains a Catholic teaching: the dignity and the supernatural destination of the human person.

Now, this is precisely the fundamental point with regard to the order of things with which we are dealing. Indeed, only he who possesses such a sense can recognize that in everything immaterial there exists two distinct, indeed antithetical, domains. One, corresponding to the forms of consciousness that are inferior to the level of a normal human being's waking state, is the natural order, in the broadest sense. The other order alone is the supernatural. Man finds himself between the one and the other of these two domains, and whoever escapes a condition of stasis or of precarious equilibrium might gravitate toward the one or toward the other. According to the aforementioned doctrine of the dignity and supernatural destination of man, such a one does not belong to "nature," neither in the materialistic sense of evolutionism and Darwinism nor in the "spiritualistic" sense of pantheism and similar conceptions. As a personality he already rises from the world of mystical souls of things and elements and from out of the depths of an undifferentiated "cosmicity," and his vision of clear physical things, crude in their outlines, objective in their space, as well as his experience of well-defined and logically linked thoughts, already expresses almost a kind of catharsis and liberation from the world, despite the limitation of horizons and possibilities that derive from it.[3] When, on the other hand, he returns, he abdicates and betrays his supernatural destination: he gives way to his "soul." He takes, consciously or unconsciously, the descending path, whereas if he were but faithful to his end, it would eventually be given to him to go beyond any conditioned state, however "cosmic" it might be.

---

3. Buddhist teaching is related to this view, according to which the "gods" (understood as "natural" powers), if they want to attain "liberation," must first pass into the human state and therein attain "awakening." This is further corroborated by the hermetic teachings regarding the superiority of man over the gods as the "lord of the two natures" and also regarding the continual danger in which he finds himself. It should be noted—and in what follows we will examine this closely—that against the ideal of "liberation," identical to that of the complete realization of the supernatural destination of man, the concept of "nature" embraces also cosmic and nonhuman states, which nonetheless fall within the conditioned world.

This schematic framework is sufficient for an initial orientation vis-à-vis the various currents of "spiritualism." The development of this critique of each of these will go on to clarify and gradually integrate these views so as to let us see, at the same time, what their positive points of reference might be.

II
Spiritualism and "Psychic Research"

Spiritism has constituted the avant-garde of the new spiritualism. It has sounded the call to revolt against materialism and was followed immediately afterward in this by theosophism; even now, these two currents contain the great majority of those who are passionate about the invisible. It is not irrelevant to note the fact that both these movements were born in Protestant Anglo-Saxon countries and that certain women—the Fox sisters for the one, and Helena Petrovna Blavatsky and then Annie Besant for the other—played a fundamental role in their origins.

Spiritism was the first current to bring the general public's attention back to an order of phenomena that, to tell the truth, were well known to antiquity but were later denied and considered as the fixations and imaginations of superstitious minds, because they departed from the framework of the "positivist" vision of the world that coalesced in the previous century. The entire worth of spiritism begins and ends there.

Spiritism did not limit itself to drawing attention to the reality of these phenomena but instead sought in every possible way to favor them and to provoke them, discovering the so-called mediums and proposing for itself the task of developing latent mediumistic faculties. It also sought an explanation for these phenomena; and insofar as it relates them to the action of "spirits" (broadly, the "spirits" of deceased humans) and claims to furnish, by this route, a kind of experimental proof of the survival of the soul, or even of the soul's immortality, the resulting position is spiritism properly understood.

The examination and the production of both these phenomena, and of those others that have an extranormal character, without an obligatory theoretical and interpretive superstructure, and above all under rigorous scientific control and with an attitude similar to that which is assumed for the exploration and the classification of "natural" phenomena in the strict sense, instead constitute the object of so-called psychic, metapsychic, or parapsychic research. This research, inaugurated in a more recent period and now under way at numerous institutes and societies, has reclaimed and integrated the positive aspect, as we deem it, of spiritism, in the sense that thanks to its assessments, it is no longer possible to doubt the reality of the extranormal. However, for this research as well, its entire worth begins and ends there.

Moreover, limiting ourselves to the order of phenomena on which spiritism especially focuses its attention, and to that part of psychic research that is not mere study but rather a favoring and cultivation of mediumship (even if it is with the simple intent of obtaining an ever broader material for investigation), it must be said that we are faced with a current that as a whole typically presents the aforementioned aspect, by which "spiritualism" constitutes a danger for the spirit. Mediumship might be defined as a method for favoring or emphasizing the disintegration of the internal unity of the person. Having partially freed a certain group of subtler elements from the body, man, as medium, becomes the organ for the manifestation in our world of forces and of influences of an extremely diverse, but always subpersonal, nature. The medium cannot control these forces and influences in any way, since his consciousness either grasps only certain effects, or else slips directly into sleep, trance, or catalepsy.

Nor are matters otherwise with the rest—that is, on the one hand, the spiritists who await the manifestation of the dead, and, on the other hand, those who scientifically control the séances. The last of their concerns is to have a proper sense and a judgment about the spiritual conditions that favor these manifestations. For the first group, all of this has value passively as "revelation," and what essentially counts for them is the "sensational" and whatever seems to confirm their "spiritistic" hypotheses, thus satisfying their sentimental needs. For the second group—that is, for the "psychic researchers"—man has validity as a producer of "phenomena"; the phenomena are appreciated insofar as they are unusual and controllable, and one gives little thought to what happens from the internal point of view. They would also have no scruples in using all kinds of methods, hypnotic procedures, and special substances to artificially provoke or intensify mediumship, so as to produce "subjects" fit for their experiments and their findings.

Now, in this random opening, which occurs in the person of the medium at these points of access with the invisible, if something should stir and impose itself, the danger is far from being limited to an attack on the medium's spiritual unity. Neither the common man nor the "optimists" today have any idea of the dark and impersonal forces that linger at the borders of the reality from which they have been excluded. The medium, by making himself the instrument for the manifestation that they crave, literally has the function of being a center of psychic infection for his environment. He acts as a medium; that is, a channel, through which those forces might exert an action on our world and on our minds, which remain defenseless before them. The often negligible and harmless manifestations that are obtained in these "séances" are only a portion of all that escapes through the half-closed doors of the "lower regions." If only one had the intelligence to apprehend certain occult laws that act within the web of common experience, one could identify otherwise grave effects both for individuals and for collectives, in relation to the conditions created involuntarily and inconsiderately in these séances, be they of a "spiritistic," "scientific," or pseudo-initiatic type. To mention just one case in passing, it would be as interesting as it is alarming to disclose the part that evocations of this kind had, in a period even before the birth of contemporary spiritualism and of spiritism, in the processes of infiltration and degradation that occurred in certain secret societies, which then played a leading role in revolutionary European subversion.

If one considers that the number of those who actively practice spiritism in Italy is in the thousands, and worldwide in the millions, one might form an idea of the spiritist danger, not only in the realm of superstitious credence and intellectual deviance, but above all in the realm of an insensible action of corrosion of those barriers that, by closing men off from the beyond, permit them a certain residual margin of security and autonomy.

Moreover, every saturation with "lower" influences, which is produced in life though these or other means, acting between the weft and weave of consciousness, is today more worrying than it has ever been, because our day almost entirely lacks the counterpart to those influences in an opposite sense; that is, effectively supernatural influences, which the great traditions knew how to invisibly attract and graft onto our intentions, thoughts, and actions. From the Renaissance onward, Western man has desired to be "free": he has been indulged in this desire, he has been let go, the spiritual has withdrawn—and he has been abandoned to himself, which amounts to saying: he has been excluded from those connections with the higher realm by which he might arm himself for his internal defense.

Now, with regard to spiritism in particular, one might think these comments to be somewhat exaggerated. Many will even deny the danger altogether, until they find themselves standing before something that belongs to the domain of the "sensational": mysterious illnesses, inexplicable accidents, mental aberrations, catastrophes in their lives, and so on and so forth. Today we are so far gone that the only thing we consider serious any longer is what threatens our fortune, our bodily existence, or, at least, our physical health and our nerves. One pays no mind to the rest. That which concerns the spirit is a private matter; it falls onto the plane of opinions and "moral" judgments, not onto the plane of reality. Ideas of the kind, in their primitivism, are precisely what is necessary to confirm the aforementioned state of defenselessness of today's man in the face of subtler forces.[1] Possession in the broad sense—no longer belonging to oneself—is one of the most widespread forms in which the action of the aforementioned influences on the human personality is manifested and realizes itself. Something is substituted for the free person, something that, without giving any warning of its constrictions, obstructs or perverts every higher aspiration. The personal principle, impaired, recedes "ecstatically" (we will later consider the sense of this word more closely) into the promiscuous and collective principle—and the collective, the psychically formless, reveals a typically destructive irruption. Evidently, one can no longer speak of mediums in the strict, spiritistic sense, nor only of those who form a new kind of cult around these mediums. It is a broader action, one whose starting points can nevertheless be identified in hotbeds of this kind. Now, the modern world has no need of pushing further in this direction. And any man of keen vision can see how many things converge here, almost as if they were the elements of the same plan; in perceiving this, one also gains a means to understand the direction and the effective meaning of certain phenomena.

The considerations we have set forth at the outset apply both to militant spiritism as well as to that branch of psychic research that deals with the same phenomena, not limiting itself to observing and

---

[1]. It is not without reason that the Inquisition condemned not only him who was a "support" for phenomena akin to spiritist ones but also those who denied the existence of such phenomena altogether: these latter persons fell under the suspicion of being instruments of the same "lower" influences on another front, precisely by encouraging the "concealment" of such influences.

recording them wherever they occur but tending also to produce and multiply them, thus endorsing and validating mediumship. Yet in the second case there is an almost automatic limitation of the danger. Indeed, when the scientific attitude, with its inherent suspicion and methodical doubt, is really maintained, it acts more often than not as a negative and paralyzing factor on mediumship and on the production of "phenomena," since these require an ad hoc psychic atmosphere for their full execution: the result is like a vicious circle, proceeding from the inadequacy of its method with respect to the material to which it would apply itself.[2]

It now remains to us to examine the hypotheses and the speculations of the two tendencies. We will have to limit ourselves here to a few essential points.[3]

As mentioned, mediumistic phenomena count for the "spiritists" as an experimental proof of the survival, or even very immortality, of the souls of the dead. Setting aside the dogmas of faith, they believe that by this route they can confute the agnosticism and the materialism of the moderns, since they place themselves on their own ground of "facts," of tangible evidence.

However, we must be very cautious before saying that it is the personality of the dead that operates in mediumistic phenomena, or even only in some cases. In reality, both the spiritists as well as the "psychic researchers" have absolutely no means at their disposal to ascertain the true causes of these phenomena. Hypothetically, mediumship and the other analogous states in which "subjects" arise, are

---
2. The inhibiting effect we have mentioned becomes disastrous when at the séances there are not only people intent only on supervising and preventing tricks but also people who are, so to speak, "carriers" of the true supernatural. Then the effect is frequently a true and proper hysterical and convulsive crisis of the medium, which cannot help but bring things to mind that sometimes occur in rites of exorcism.
3. For a corresponding point of view in this regard, we also refer the reader to the work of René Guénon, *L'erreur spirite* (Paris: Rivière, 1923) [English edition: *The Spiritist Fallacy*, trans. Alvin Moore Jr. and Rama P. Coomaraswamy (Hillsdale, N.Y.: Sophia Perennis, 2003)].

states of reduced or paralyzed consciousness; they are states in which the power of vision and the internal control of the I do not accompany the shifting in level through which the causes of such phenomena and extranormal manifestations are aroused. While one falls into a trance, the others remain "outside" to look on, or to feel moved or enraptured, or else are equipped with exceedingly precise recording instruments, awaiting the manifestation of something that, in its course materiality, cannot ever assume a definitive face. Now, an exceedingly wide variety of causes can produce the selfsame phenomenon (for instance, the phenomenon of levitation might be the work of a medium, a saint, a sorcerer, or an initiate and a yogi). And the lack of a solid doctrinal basis, the presence of suggestions and of sentimental predispositions (above all in the restricted and human sense that everything modern possesses), guarantee not only that the whole thing will reduce itself to hypotheses but also that the hypotheses in question will be among the most naive and one-sided—when one is not dealing, that is, with affirmations disguised as a true credo, which is no less intolerant than those religious credos that it claims to supersede by means of "experimental proofs."

As for "psychic research," or metapsychic research, in particular, the inadequacy of the method must again be indicted: it adopts the same attitude that positivistic science has toward physical or biological phenomena, not least of all because in most of them there is the tacit conviction that one is dealing here not with the "spirit" or the supersensible in the proper sense but rather with an order of "natural" laws that are not yet well known, just as not so long ago the laws of electricity and magnetism were not well known. To guarantee the ruling out of "tricks" and of mystifications—this is the positive contribution of such investigations.[4] Leaving aside professional malfeasance, the source of the methodological misunderstanding here

---

4. Leaving aside those cases in which the attitude of control and the obstinacy in wanting to will these phenomena into existence forces the mediums to do unconscious "tricks" when they are not able to produce them spontaneously.

is to be sought in the perceptible aspect of these manifestations. If this aspect were not present—and if the "spiritualists" did not insist so much on the "positivistic" validation of their theses—one would never have dreamed of applying the "experimental" method to this order of things, just as no sane mind would apply it, for example, to the products of genius or of aesthetic creation (naturally, before the overbearing demands accomplished even here by a certain materialistic psychology and by psychoanalysis). It is really singularly obtuse to fail to comprehend that, if one is really dealing with the "spiritual," adequate knowledge cannot come from external recordings and assessments but only and uniquely by identifying oneself with the same process, by following its genesis and its development actively, until one finally reaches the eventual sensible manifestation, which is nothing other in each individual case than a part that takes its own meaning from the whole.

It is often debated in metaphysics whether certain extranormal phenomena should be explained through unknown faculties of the mediums and of other subjects, or if one should rather refer also to external, extra-individual agents. But this question loses a large deal of its relevance when one brings the unconscious or the subconscious into consideration, because by definition this belongs to the subpersonal realm; it is the psychic region in which the individual and the non-individual are separated by a permeable barrier, and this region might extend itself to contain even zones populated by every sort of influence, by "errant thoughts" and even by forces that do not always have any correspondence in the world of incarnate beings and sensible reality. In the most recent metaphysics, the strictly "spiritistic" hypotheses of earlier times are viewed as being primitive and outmoded. But with this, one falls into the opposite excess, because in the case of a particular class of mediumistic manifestations there is reason to believe that within the influences we have spoken of there might also be "spirits" of the dead, with the caveat that the term *spirit* be given the ancient sense, according to which they are far from equivalent to "souls." "Spirits" are the vital energies, qualified both in a mental sense (memories, complexes of ideas, etc.) and in the "organic" sense, as well as in the dynamic sense (impulses, complexes of the will, habits, etc.); energies, which the soul, if it survives death, leaves behind, precisely as it has done with the physical body, whose elements pass to a free state. These vital elements pass to a free state in a way that is similar to the remains of the cadaver; that is, they are devoid of their essential unity of being, around which they were organized in the form of a "second personality" or even—more often and more simply—as mnemonic complexes, monoideisms, and entity-tendencies and kinetic virtualities that have become impersonal. After entering this free state, these elements come to incarnate themselves in the medium and, through this channel, to produce certain varieties of extranormal phenomenology, which the most naive take as experimental proofs of the survival of the soul.[5] In reality, we are not dealing here with the soul in the true and traditional sense of the word but rather with residual vital forms that are themselves destined to die out in the more or less short term.[6]

There is more. There are cases in which certain nonhuman forces incarnate in these residues, preserving something of a semblance to the deceased in the guise of a kind of "double"; they

---

[5]. This view is also sufficient to account for other presumed proofs of personal survival adduced by the spiritists: hauntings, spontaneous apparitions, premonitions of relatives or their communications at the moment of death, and so forth. It is only that here other conditions come into play, conditions that change from case to case, and that render the manifestation of "spirits" possible without a true medium.

[6]. Hence the notion of Hades in the Greco-Roman traditions, Niflheim in the Nordic traditions, pitṛ-yāna (opposed to the "way of the gods"—devayāna) in the Hindu tradition, and so forth—all places of a larval existence, an existence of reabsorption. In Christianity itself, Gehenna, referred to in the gospels as the "damned" (in Hebrew Gei-Hinnom, the *geenna* of Fire), originally designated the place in which the refuse of the city was destroyed, and it is said: "Fear him, which after he hath killed hath power to cast into hell [Gehenna]; yea, I say unto you, Fear him" [Luke 7:4].

animate and move them, causing the apparitions and phenomena that can be misleading, but which, at the same time, have the most sinister character when one discovers the true nature of the forces that resurrect such larval and automatic residues. Yet it is these cases that have predominately given spiritism the incentive to become a new macabre religion, without realizing how much mockery and seduction manifest themselves in phenomena of this kind—mockery and seduction that could be defined, without exaggeration, as being Satanic.[7] And yet reasons for suspicion are not lacking in this sphere, even for those who limit themselves to the viewpoint of simple metapsychical observations. One example will suffice. The study of the relationship between mediumship and fraud has led to some very interesting results. Through this study, it has been verified that in many cases mediumistic fraud in no way emerges from the medium's intention as conscious falsifier. This of course could happen, too, just as it could happen that, as has already been mentioned, the experimenters themselves might sometimes impel the medium, through their insistency, to a semiconscious invention. But in these latter cases, fraud arises as a fact that is itself already mediumistic and spiritistic, as a manifestation in the medium of an influence that one can no better characterize than with the well-known expression "spirit of deception."

Not long ago we expressed the caveat: if the soul survives death. This, in reality, is not so frequent and general as the nonmaterialists commonly think; they are laboring under certain recent Western religious beliefs, which are either mutilated or taken literally, or, finally, forged with certain special pragmatic aims in mind.

Without trying to get to the bottom of all this here, we will mention only the puerility involved in positing the problem as a dilemma—"either mortal or immortal"—and likewise the simplism

---

7. On this, Gustav Meyrink has written a number of very suggestive pages in his novel *The White Dominican* [for bibliographic details, see chap. X, n. 2].

of both the "materialistic" solution and "spiritualistic" solutions. The recurrent idea in the traditional teachings, whether implicit or explicit, is rather that there are some who die with or after the death of the body, and there are some who survive, passing into different states. And among those who survive, there is finally a small portion who attain the privileged condition of true immortality. No outcome can be predicted for man in general: the outcome varies from person to person and depends on what each man is. In general, he survives who already in life, in one way or another, has operated either an actual or virtual separation of his spiritual principle from the conditions imposed on the consciousness by the body or by the sensible experience of waking—which, in theological terms, would be equivalent to saying that he survives to the degree to which he has, already on earth, effectively directed his soul toward the supernatural end. As for the various possibilities that await the survivors (not to be confused with the immortals!) in the post-mortem, they depend both on their "knowledge," rather than intellectualistic achievements, and on the inclinations that one's internal conduct has impressed on the soul in life, and on one's initiative, on the comportment and the direction of which the soul itself is capable on the verge of death—in extremis—or in the face of situations, tests, and experiences that are no longer of this world. On this last point, whoever is interested can refer to the Lamaist teaching contained in *The Tibetan Book of the Dead* (Bardo Thodol), which furnishes a genuine science, superior to any particular religious confession in the Western sense, of the states of the post-mortem, and gives the logic of the different destinies proceeding from the spiritual actions to which the soul is called in these states.[8]

---

8. This teaching has been summarized in appendix 1 of my book *The Yoga of Power: Tantra, Shakti, and the Secret Way*, trans. Guido Stucco (Rochester, Vt.: Inner Traditions, 1992); cf. also our compendium *Introduction to Magic*, vol. 2, trans. Joscelyn Godwin (Rochester, Vt.: Inner Traditions, 2019).

With respect to those who have not reached a condition to survive, after death they decompose into their psychic and vital elements, into their "spirits," and not a single residue of true conscious spiritual unity remains. Hence, in certain traditions, there is the idea of the "second death," and the invocation "May you escape the second death," or else the curse "May the second death take you." Turning therefore to spiritism, it must be said that in general it is "spirits"—that is, the aforementioned de-individualized psychic residues, or "larvae," masks and facsimiles of personalities, vitalized by lower influences in the way which we alluded to earlier—that lend themselves to enthusing spiritist circles or to strengthening them in their faith, or to giving material to the collectors of "phenomena" and to the metapsychic archives. As for the other possibility, that it might actually be the freed souls of the dead that are the source of such activity—this is so rare, that one can almost rule it out from the start. Those souls sojourn in spiritual regions (i.e., states) so transcendent that they no longer have any relation with the world of bodies and with the affairs and feelings of men. And when, in order to perform some "mission," they abandon these states in favor of some manifestation within the conditions of space and of time, the last place in which this manifestation should be sought is among those phenomena that occur in the séances of the metaphysics and spiritists: capricious, confused, and aimless phenomena, devoid of any greatness, not infrequently mocking, much more often of an inferior rather than superior intelligence, or simply equal to what one might expect, not from a transfigured soul, but from a person of average culture in this world. Guénon rightly notes that the nature of such phenomena should leave no doubt as to the nature of the forces that produce them. Aside from the mixture of organic repercussions and other elements or images provided by the irrational and infraconscious part of the conjurers and mediums themselves, we are not dealing with souls transfigured by death or by truly supernatural influences, but with subhuman forces and errant psychic complexes, with greater or lesser relation to the "lower" element of nature; or they are larvae and residues that no longer belong to the ascended souls; or, again, the decomposition products of the souls that did not even survive. This is what can result from a vision conforming to reality.

In the latter case, it is the literal sense that we can say that sometimes it is the dead who operate in the order of things about which we are speaking. And one might add, in a likewise literal sense, that the medium follows the road of the dead: with trance and other related states, he evokes the first degrees of that reduction of consciousness and of that progressive dissociation of the spiritual unity, such as is succumbed to by those who really die. Along this road—the road to Hades—he encounters the residues of the dead, who are traversing that road in the other direction in their attempt to manifest themselves in the world from which they were excluded upon the destruction of their bodies. In the psychic order, such residues play a role similar to that of the products of putrefaction, which transform themselves into so many hotbeds of infection for living organisms. The Ancients, the Orientals, and even certain so-called primitive peoples knew more about these things than all the spiritists and all the presidents of the "Society for Psychical Research" put together. For this reason, conjuring the dead was almost always condemned as a serious crime. They sought to permanently remove from the living the spiritual remains of the dead; that is, they endeavored to "placate" or bind them. This alone was the secret reason for many traditional funerary rites, which cannot be reduced to mere "ceremonies" but which exerted, at that time, were an effective and necessitating action on the psychic forces that passed to the free state with the breakdown of the physical organism. Commerce, not with those residues but with the souls of the dead, with the aim of hearing "revelations" from them, was considered an absurdity. Even in our time, a lama, when informed by Alexandra David-Néel that the English believe in things of this sort, retorted, "And these are the men who conquered India!"⁹

All of this might be instructive regarding the error and the danger presented by mediumistic practices, not just for oneself but also for others. Even when they do not have anything to do with the "dead" (which is to say, in the majority of cases), things are no different: in these openings practiced at random, it is necessarily the first thing to arrive that will manifest itself. Moreover, there are laws—ignored today, but no less real—of "sympathy" and of "analogy": as the eventual possibility of contact with the transfigured souls of the dead is conditioned by the possibility of elevating oneself to essentially superindividual states, thus in states of subconsciousness (such as mediumistic states) only those forces and influences can be attracted, which in the cosmic order correspond to the dark subsoil of the subconscious and the prepersonal in man. All of this, let us repeat, cannot do other than work destructively on that which is formed personality and spiritual unity. In the order, then, of a broader action, which we have just mentioned, it can only resolve itself into a factor of disorder, imbalance, and deviation in the collective psyche.

On an ancient Etruscan tomb painting, near to an altar, which was considered the outlet of lower forces, one finds a depiction of a man armed with a sword. He is the symbol of an attitude directly contrary to that of the medium.

In antiquity there existed an art for creating, on the basis of the aforementioned laws of analogy, internal and external conditions to attract and consciously direct a determinate order of influ-

---

9. Alexandra David-Néel, *Magic and Mystery in Tibet* (New York: Kendall, 1932), 234. The ancient cult of the ancestors is a topic that requires its own consideration, insofar as it was not a simple expression of piety. Here we will mention only that such cults essentially had in view a unity of the living and of the dead, under the sign of the generative force of the race (the genius), which they sought to keep alive and present: a force of superindividual character, as appears above all in the aristocratic, patrician forms of this cult, where the genius was identified with the "archegete Hero" and took on a "divine," luminous character. But the idea of dark, lower forces often subsisted in the common Roman conception of the Lares.

ences, among the variety of those that populate the "behind" or the "inside" of visible reality, of the phenomenal world. Among the spiritualists of today, nothing is known of this art (though some echoes of it can be perceived in the Catholic ritual and sacramental tradition). The spiritists take the path of superstition and sentimental consolations, and the researchers take the path of "scientific" research, and none of them realizes the insanities that they might avoid, the many things they might come to know, if they were to radically change their attitude and method; if they returned to the study and comprehension of the traditional teachings; and if, before searching for "spirits," they sought the spirit and forged themselves as spirit.

But let us return for a moment to metaphysics, so as to bring two points into relief. The first is that in the vast documentation of phenomena that it has gathered, we remain forever on the plane of by-products of the extranormal, insofar as we are dealing with phenomena of a "spontaneous," sporadic, irrational, unintentional character—certainly this is so in the case of so-called ESP ("extrasensory perception," including psychometry, telepathy, clairvoyance, precognition, etc.), and yet even more in the case of phenomena called "paraphysical," which have objective effects in the field of the physical world, that do not admit of any normal explanation. This is obvious enough, because whoever truly has the power to produce phenomena of a different, intentional, and voluntary character, on the basis of a spiritual qualification—let us say, an initiate, a true yogi, or even a saint, since such a qualification appears to be almost without exception the constant counterpart to such power—would not ever permit it to so much as enter his mind to put himself at the disposition, as a "subject," of profane parapsychological research. This research, therefore, cannot rely on anything other than spurious, scattered, and random material that lacks any specific orientation. In the field of metaphysics, when one refers to the extranormal faculties of the subject alone, or even to his contacts with an undefined something,[10] the impossibility of examining these phenomena as they are willfully and freely produced, is generally recognized without exception, and is considered an insuperable handicap for "experimental" research.

There is more—and this is the second point to emphasize: it has been verified that the process of extrasensory perception and of other parapsychic faculties is, in its essential part, unconscious; that the manifestations are tied at least to a "reduction of consciousness" (recently, this has been underlined, for example, by G. N. M. Tyrrell and by J. B. Rhine) to a borderline state between dream and waking, somewhat akin to the trance of the medium: so much so that in certain attempts to experimentally activate those faculties one has sought recourse to the hypnosis of the subjects. All of this tells us that, in this field, we are dealing with a type of the extranormal that, from the standpoint of the values of the personality, has a regressive and subpersonal character. Thus there have been quite a few researchers, such as L. L. Vasiljev and W. H. C. Tenhaeff, who have formulated the hypothesis of "phylogenetically regressive" states: a regression of the subject into the condition of the primitive psyche corresponding to the level of savage populations, with extranormal faculties that have been lost—it is supposed—in the successive development of the human psyche, of logical thought, and so on. Since in metapsychics, with regard to "paraphysical" phenomena, one does not yet know how to rationally explain the phenomena along the lines of "extrasensory perception," including precognition, hypotheses have been formulated that sometimes border on spiritualism. It is not so much a question of the "collective unconscious" so dear to Jung, which basically does not lead beyond the psychological domain but is a kind of "universal consciousness" that includes a complete knowledge of present, past, and future events. In this connection, certain authors—namely C. A. Mace and H. H. Price—have even

---

10. [Evola uses the Latin *quid* in the original.]

spoken of a psychic aether (which quite closely recalls the Hindu notion of the ākāsha), the more scientific designation used in recent metaphysics, which has accepted a similar hypothetical explanatory principle, being, however, a "PSI field": something of simultaneously physical and psychic character that would resume and transcend the conditions of space and of time. It is due to contact with this "field" that the subject is rendered capable of extrasensory perceptions. It has been noted, however, that in this case one might as well speak simply of the "supersensible," the admission of which would impose the necessity of rather disturbing revisions in the current scientific and established conceptions regarding space, time, nature.[11]

But all this is only of theoretical interest. Whether or not we admit the existence of this supersensible something, it is important to point out that even in those cases where one might partly believe that contacts have been made with it by certain subjects—even then, according to what we have already noted and which metapsychics has also recognized, in the observed cases these contacts are established in the subconscious or in the unconscious, in conditions of a more or less reduced consciousness, along similar lines to what occurs in mediumship and hypnosis—therefore, they occur along a descending rather than ascending path, for a lowering of the personal psychic level rather than a raising of it to that of a superconsciousness.

The limit we have mentioned above has therefore been confirmed.

---

11. For these various hypotheses, the corresponding problems, and also for an exhaustive and up-to-date survey of everything that has been ascertained until now regarding the extranormal phenomena of metapsychics, cf. Milan Ryzl, *Parapsychology: A Scientific Approach* (New York: Hawthorn, 1970).

III
Critique of Psychoanalysis

It is not by chance that, after spiritism and psychic research, we move on to consider psychoanalysis. Psychoanalysis, as a general impulse, could have provided a beginning for overcoming the behavior that is characteristic of both of those two currents.

Indeed, in principle, this discipline no longer proposes a simple verification or provocation of psychic phenomena; to the contrary, it would proceed to the depths (hence the occasional designation "depth psychology," Tiefenpsychologie), in order to explore the subterranean zone of the soul and the forces that dwell and act therein.

Psychoanalysis, to be sure, no longer considers unusual manifestations like those in mediumship or metapsychics (though there have been only a few recent sporadic attempts to apply psychoanalysis to this field, too). Instead, it took shape in the study of neuroses, hysteria, and other psychic disorders, originally developing as a new branch of modern psychotherapy. This specialized field, however, was soon transcended. Psychoanalytic conceptions have been abusively generalized, with their validity extended well past a particular clinical casuology,[1] so far as to include man and the life of the soul in general. From here, psychoanalysis rapidly trespassed into domains that have nothing to do with medicine and with psychopathology and

---
1. [Evola uses the phrase *casuologia clinica* in the original.]

exerted itself to discover a more or less neurotic phenomenology in cultural and social phenomena and manifestations of every sort, even in morality, art, sexology, religion, and mythology—indeed even in sociology and politics. However, rather than the adoption of a serious and rigorous "depth psychology," this has specifically meant an abusive application of the hypotheses and principles that the psychoanalysts have formed with respect to pathological cases: hypotheses and principles that are—let us state it already from the outset—precisely as obsessive as those "complexes" that they seek to discover beneath the ordinary waking consciousness of neurotics. Thus, psychoanalysis finds a way of proceeding to aberrant and contaminating interpretations (but presented as "realistic" analyses that arise thanks to some new, keener insight) of a quantity of phenomena that are traced back, in their roots, to the shallows of the unconscious. For this reason, there are some who have spoken in this connection of a "delerium of interpretation," a delerium in the psychiatric sense of mania and "obsession": the mania of suspecting and discovering, wherever one looks, a murky and obscure background. This holds, too, for the individual analyses of the dreams, impulses, tendencies, as so on, of persons who consider themselves to be normal.

We will leave aside psychoanalysis as simple psychotherapy. It is claimed that the latter has achieved numerous successes, and continues to do so today. But among psychologists there are some who ask themselves if these successes, irrespective of what part of them is due to the suggestibility of their subjects (a problem that arises in nearly all psychotherapy), might have been accomplished by procedures that do not share the dogmatic presuppositions of psychoanalysis. However, we are not interested in the therapeutic field but instead in the anthropological one—that is, the psychoanalytic theory of man and psychoanalysis as a cultural phenomenon—above all, we are interested in what the "climate" of psychoanalysis, its suggestions, and its "ethics" might provoke in a direction not dissimilar to that of the dangers we have already indicated for neo-spiritualism. We shall refer mainly to the so-called orthodox school of psychoanalysis, which is to say, to the principal ideas of its founder, Sigmund Freud. Only secondarily, in the development of one particular point or another, will we consider the views of other psychoanalysts such as Alfred Adler, Carl Gustav Jung, and Wilhelm Reich.

Let us note first of all that psychoanalysis was not, in fact, the first field to discover the unconscious. The idea of a zone that, although still psychic, is not illuminated by the light of clear consciousness, had already gained precedence in modern psychology, especially after the research into hypnosis and personality dissociation. Moreover, all of this was known to traditional ancient doctrines. To cite only a single example, the doctrines of yoga and Buddhist practice (with their notions of the samskāra and the vasāna) recognized in the unconscious itself (better to say: in the subconscious) other broader and deeper stratifications. Nor was the imperative toward an "exploration of the depths" and the accompanying methodology any less precise, intended as they were to throw light on zones of the psyche and, in general, of being that usually fall outside the field of more peripheral waking consciousness.

But the modern discovery of the subconscious has not been without a certain polemical application, which was directed against the intellectualism of the epoch that immediately preceded it. In fact, the psychology of this period was based on the fiction of a life of the soul centered solely on conscious phenomena, even if these, in general, tended to be given a material basis. Apart from purely philosophical theories, such as those of Eduard von Hartmann, the first formulations of a more comprehensive psychology were rather vague and spiritualistic, such as that of William James regarding the subconscious in the varieties of religious and mystic experience, or of Frederic W. H. Myers on the "subliminal" (= that which lies beneath the threshold of consciousness). Other more technical formulations followed and, rather than the subconscious, one now began to speak of the unconscious. Here is what Gustave Le Bon has to say in this regard:

> The conscious life of the mind is of small importance in comparison with its unconscious life. The most subtle analyst, the most acute observer, is scarcely successful in discovering more than a very small number of the unconscious motives that determine his conduct. Our conscious acts are the outcome of an unconscious substratum created in the mind in the main by hereditary influences. This substratum consists of the innumerable common characteristics handed down from generation to generation, which constitute the genius of a race. Behind the avowed causes of our acts there undoubtedly lie secret causes that we do not avow, but behind these secret causes there are many more secret still which we ourselves ignore. The greater part of our daily actions are the result of hidden motives which escape our observation.[2]

Already here an anti-intellectualist reaction can be detected, which, however, clearly misses the mark with respect to any healthy and normal humanity. Another point to highlight in this modern discovery of the subconscious is the tendency to hypostasize it, to conceive of it as a distinct entity—a tendency that goes so far as to create a genuine dualism in the human being. This already appears whenever one speaks of the "unconscious" instead of the "subconscious" or "preconscious." In fact, the unconscious, as such, does not represent a reduced degree of consciousness, but another domain altogether, which in principle excludes the possibility of any direct knowledge. This splitting and substantialization of a part of the human being, which is characteristic of psychoanalysis, had already

---

2. Gustave Le Bon, *Psychologie des foules* (Paris: Alcan, 1909) 13 [English title: *The Crowd: A Study of the Popular Mind* (London: Unwin, 1910), 31].

taken on a dynamic character in schools like those of Emile Coué and Charles Badouin. If one speaks now of the unconscious and at other times of the subconscious, one proceeds, in any case, a step further in the dualistic direction, because this principle is considered as an entity that has its own laws and which almost always ends up victorious when it comes into conflict with the I. According to these schools, there is only a single way to influence the subconscious, and this is through suggestion, ceasing to employ one's will and using instead one's imagination. This means counterposing a method of conscious autosuggestion to the passive suggestions are obeyed in a large part of the ordinary life of the soul. Woe to it if the will directly confronts the unconscious and the imagination! Not only will it get the worst of this encounter, but the energy of its effort will actually strengthen its adversary (the "law of converted effort").

From this, one can already see the dangerous road that has been taken. If, as we have mentioned, long before being "discovered" by the moderns, the "subliminal" was known to the explorers of the soul in other times, they did not make it into a principle in itself. According to the very expressive symbolism of certain medieval texts, the conscious and subconscious represented the two parts of a broken sword that was to be re-welded, so as to reawaken the original state of a superior human type. The modern schools—let us state it from the outset—do nothing other than exasperate the fracture and invert the hierarchical relation between the two principles.

To return to the doctrine of Freud, its defining characteristic is, in the first place, to be found in its locating in the unconscious the main driving force of the psyche, in mechanical and deterministic terms. The impulses, instincts, and complexes of the psychic subsoil supposedly have a "cathetic energy" (the technical term is *Besetzungsenergie*) that must be discharged; if this does not occur, the whole human being will suffer the consequences to a greater or lesser degree. Hence, also, the characterization of the unconscious as the id, and the fundamental opposition between the ego (*das Ich*) and the id (*das Es*).³ Already from a lexical analysis of Freudian psychoanalysis we can therefore clearly see the inversion of values that characterizes it: the id, the unconscious, is the subject, the *agens* [Lat. "agent"]; the ego becomes the object, that which is acted upon. Therefore, psychoanalysis not only sees in the id the primary force of the human person, but it conceives of the relationship between it and the ego as being one of pure causality, as something similar, in psychic life, to the necessitation or coercion that one might externally suffer from on account of a physical force. The Triebe, the impulses, dynamisms, and "complexes" of the id, "impel" and act in this way. As has been said, these are forces that, in one way or another, must have their manifestation, they must resolve their "charge."

In the second place, Freudianism is characterized by its seeing the fundamental stem of the unconscious in the *libido,* in that impulse to pleasure (Lustprinzip), which manifests primarily in sexual pleasure. And here the whole mythology of the "complexes" comes into play that every man, more or less ineluctably, knowing it or not, harbors in himself, beginning with the famous Oedipus complex and proceeding to all the others, which are fabricated by a more or less imaginative interpretation, always with a sexual tone, of the life of a child (or else of certain customs of savages, such as is undertaken in the book *Totem and Taboo*). These complexes are translated into atavistic constellations of the human unconscious, both individual and (especially in the theories of Jung) collective.

The characteristic position of Freudianism is the disavowal, in

---

3. The term *Es* [= id] is derived from forms of the German language in which the impersonal pronoun *es* acts as the subject of phrases expressing states, movements, and sensations that are experienced as having a more or less compulsory character. A typical example one might adduce is the phrase *es treibt mich* [lit. "it drives me"], as "I feel driven" or "transported," because from the verb *treiben,* meaning "to impel or move," comes the term *Trieb,* meaning "impulse, force of instinct/inclination," used in psychoanalysis to designate the mode in which the Es manifests itself and acts. See Sigmund Freud, *Das Ich und das Es* (Leipzig, Vienna, and Zurich: Internationaler Psychoanalytischer Verlag, 1923).

man, of the presence and of the power of any sovereign spiritual center, which is to say of the I as such. In the face of the unconscious, the I is overthrown. The I, in its acceptation as a principle capable of recognizing true values and of giving autonomous norms, would be an illusion, possibly itself produced by some "complex." That which generally acts in man at the conscious moral level is the so-called superego, which is defined by the "introjection" of all prohibitions, taboos, and limitations existing in the environment (i.e., by taking these things on as a second artificial nature), through an action of censure, blockage, and repression of the demands of the unconscious. A kind of conformist—and at the same time hysterical—puppet thus takes the place of the true self. And, as has been indicated, even the manifestation of a "complex" might play a part in its construction—a complex (such as a Narcissus complex or an "autistic" complex) derived from earliest infancy, from the phase of infantile eroticism, when the child (according to the suppositions of psychoanalysis) satisfied its own libido without having recourse to other people, thereby attaining a sense of self-sufficiency and, we might almost say, of autarky. In a transposed form, this complex might be a fundamental aspect of the brink and limit of the ego that Freud calls the ego ideal (*Ich-Ideal*): the "introjected" values and the external norms are affirmed absolutely, despotically, through a libido sui generis. And this might in turn produce the illusory sense of the autonomy of the ego, and an opposition between the ego and that which man effectively is, in relation to other and more authentic expressions of the libido and the id.[4] On the other hand, nothing is left to the conscious principle in all of this except the role of a kind of agent or *executor* for the instinctual part of one's being. Just as the dyad of superego and unconscious (or libido) is supposed to define the fundamental structure of man, the

---

4. The *Ich-Ideal,* or "ideal ego," in its pretense to sufficiency, collects all the needs from the environment that the ego cannot satisfy: thus, the ego, discontent with itself, can find in the "ideal ego," differentiated from it, the satisfaction that it does not find in itself. The feeling of guilt would be nothing other than an expression of the tension between the ego and the "ego ideal."

contrast between the one and the other is supposed to provide the key for an interpretation not only of typical neurotic facts but also of multiple behaviors that are considered normal.

As has been said, the "charges" of the unconscious must be discharged. Thus, the only alternative is to guide the relevant impulses so that their expression, although going against the rules of the environment and the social order (which the superego had already overcome) does not lead to undesirable or perhaps disastrous consequences. In this connection, a modus vivendi is offered through their transposed and vicarious satisfaction: diverting the impulses from their immediate objects by directing them toward other objects, ends, or persons that take their place and that are not likely to create serious conflict. This is the process of "transpositions" or "sublimations." Thus, whoever is battling, let us say, with an incestuous complex can "discharge" by diverting the charge of the libido, for example, onto the homeland conceived as a "Mother." In large part these processes of substitution are carried out in the unconscious; the individual is not aware of them and believes he is obeying noble sentiments and higher purposes, until psychoanalysis opens his eyes. If, on the other hand—either on account of the barriers of the environment, or the inhibitory action, even unconscious, of the superego and the "social anxiety" experienced directly by the individual—one opposes oneself to the impulses and represses them, they reenter into the unconscious, barricading themselves therein, either enriching it with new complexes or else reawakening other latent ones, which are present both as an archaic inheritance and as the articulations of the infantile libido.[5] Situations

---

5. A well-known cornerstone of Freudian psychoanalysis is the so-called polymorphous infantile perversion thesis, which, if it were true, would even be agreeable as a reaction against the cloying bourgeois attitude of the cult of the child, which sees in every infant a "little angel." For Freud, the child brings together, albeit in an unconscious and embryonic form, so many variants of the libido so as to make every perverted adult seem disfigured and unilateral in comparison. And this supposedly belongs to the legacy of the "unconscious" that everyone carries within themselves and which is susceptible to reactivation in so-called regressions.

of this kind poison conscious life with varying degrees of neurosis. Eventually, what Freud calls the "Nirvana principle" intervenes: one seeks refuge in evasions that allow one to escape intolerable tensions (psychoanalysis makes a similarly grotesque use of the metaphysical Buddhist concept of nirvāna, presuming perhaps to clarify the genesis of this concept sexologically). In many other cases, however, these tensions are simply juggled about, so that the impulses of the psychic subsoil are satisfied despite everything by acting out at those moments when, as in the experiences of dreams, the conscious ego's faculties of control and censure are reduced or suspended. In yet other cases, they actively intervene so as to provoke an exclusion of consciousness and memory,[6] if not psychophysical disorders. More normally, they wait for the right moment to assume a mask, "move" in the desired direction, and discharge their energy in one way or another, possibly through the aforementioned procedure of sublimation.

Besides all this, there are the possibilities offered by "crowd states." Following Gustave Le Bon, Freud observes that in these states the individual, feeling himself to be part of the mass, sheds his "social anxiety," and with it the sense of his own responsibility and his own powerlessness in the face of the environment, which allows repressed impulses to break out in their original form.

In this context, mention can be made of the psychoanalysis of Alfred Adler (which he called *Individual psychologie* [Individual Psychology]). Adler assumes a different reference point; this constituted by the *Geltungstrieb* [need for recognition]—that is, the individual's impulse to be validated, to assert himself, but with anal-

---

6. According to Freudianism, there is nothing, or almost nothing, random in dreams. In the images and actions of the dream, impulses, which are repressed in waking life, manifest themselves or satisfy themselves. The insignificance or incoherency of these images or actions serve as camouflage, so as to elude their "censure" and to facilitate their being smuggled in. In other cases it happens that the dream, or a part of it, is not even recalled; memory, that is to say, is inhibited. These are processes that, according to psychoanalysis, are repeated to varying degrees in the diurnal life of the soul and then culminate in the experiences of neurotics.

ogous unconscious mechanisms that intervene when the individual is impeded by the conditions of the environment, by his situation, or by his weakness. At that point the famous "inferiority complex" is born, which acts as a sophisticated alibi for self-justification; or else one resorts to "supercompensations"; that is to say, to transposed and vicarious hysteroid affirmations of the same impulse, meant to hide from oneself one's own impotence in one situation or another, and to avoid taking action. As a humorous example of how far this line can be taken, a female disciple of Freud and Adler psychoanalyzed the claim—which she regards as absurd—of male superiority and masculine despotism in the history of civilization. The basis of all this would be a neuropathic, hysterical event. It is a neurotic "supercompensation" due to an unconscious "inferiority complex" deriving from the fact that, unlike the woman, man is not able to give himself continuously to the sexual act. To compensate for this sense of painful inferiority in the face of woman, man creates the pretense of a superiority in other fields, and he hysterically constitutes himself as the "stronger sex" and dominatinator.[7]

Returning to the general anthropology of Freudianism, it is already apparent from what has been said that Freudianism recognizes no ethical conflicts in the proper sense. Every conflict of the soul loses any ethical character and reveals itself as the effect of a hysteroid event. When the conscious personality opposes and combats the impulses of the other part of itself, this is not in any way the manifestation of a higher law but instead a kind of family conflict or a clash between complexes, because, as has been indicated, when the ego thinks it is acting for itself as an autonomous and despotic legislator, it is merely suffering the effects of a self-sadistic variety of the "autistic" complex: even in cases where it faces a catastrophe or death itself so as to hold steady, in truth it has been played, it has

---

7. Sofie Lazarsfeld, *Wie die Frau den Man erlebt: Fremde Bekenntnisse und eigene Betrachtungen* (Leipzig and Vienna: Verlag für Sexualwissenschaft Schneider, 1931).

been moved; it does not act, but it is the id that acts in it. Wherever there is no conflict and explicit neurosis in the life of the soul, there is always the possibility of these things, however, since the ego can enjoy peace and harmony only on the basis of adaptations, transpositions, and sublimations, all of which occur more or less unconsciously. Any given trauma is sufficient for "regression" occur; that is, the revival of the impulses and the complexes in their original forms, in their original ends, and in their original objects.[8]

Now we can proceed to some fundamental critical clarifications. First of all, Freud has been accused of "pansexualism" on account of the Freudian characterization of libido as the fundamental stem of the unconscious. He sometimes sought to exonerate himself from this charge. He writes, "We call by that name [libido] the energy (regarded as a quantitative magnitude, though not at present actually mensurable) of those instincts which have to do with all that may be comprised under the word 'love.'" He says that this includes even the love of the poets and attachment to concrete objects or abstract ideas. But he immediately adds: "psycho-analytic research has taught us that all these tendencies are an expression of the same instinctive activities (*Triebregungen*); in relations between the sexes these instincts force their way toward sexual union, but in other circumstances they are diverted from this aim or are prevented from reaching it, though always preserving enough of their original nature to keep their identity recognizable (as in such features as the longing for proximity, and self-sacrifice)."[9] This being the case, when Freud says that whoever happens to desire or prefer a less crude expression instead of libido can speak of eros in the generalized Platonic sense, it is clear that he is equivocating. And in reality everything he tells us

---

8. For example, the forms of tenderness are for Freudianism nothing but transpositions and dilutions of impulses, which, in a moment of a crisis, "regress" and take up the form of incestuous, homosexual, narcissistic-homicidal instincts, and so forth.
9. Sigmund Freud, *Group Psychology and the Analysis of the Ego,* trans. James Strachey (New York: Boni and Liveright, 1920), 37–38.

about the genesis of the fundamental complexes both in childhood and in that of savages and the "primal horde" remains baseless without the closest relationship between the libido and sexuality.[10]

In fact, psychoanalysis in its essential part resolves into a general interpretation of individual and collective existence in terms of sexuality, so much so that one suspects it could have emerged only in the mind of a person for whom sex constituted a true monomania. Freudianism reflects the pandemic of sex, or obsession with sex, which plays such a great a role in the contemporary era, and it is precisely to this that it owes much of its success, serving in turn as the corroborator and pseudoscientific framework for this pandemic. For "orthodox" psychoanalysts, sex is a true idée fixe, something that "impels" coercively like a Trieb or a complex of the id, impeding them from seeing anything else, in just the same way that they claim it is a function of the id to inhibit the consciousness of the neurotic, to prohibit him from seeing and recognizing whatever he does not want to. Precisely, this must be stated, and decisively, whenever the psychoanalysts go so far as to brazenly claim that any opposition to their doctrine means that it has hit the mark, since every objection betrays an internal resistance, which the anti-psychoanalyst is unable to conquer, so that before speaking of such things he himself should submit to psychoanalysis. Exactly the opposite is true.

Here it is not a question of challenging the great role that sex plays in human existence. Instead it is a question, in the first place, of limits, the disrespect of which transforms sexual interpretations into something absurd and contaminating. Secondly, it is a question of recognizing that Freud has focused attention on sex only in its lowest and darkest (and even "dirty") aspects, in its effectively subpersonal

---

10. Regarding the unveiled pansexualism of psychoanalytic circles, a disciple of Freud, Silberer, gave an ingenious variant of the first words of the Gospel of John as the motto of a book dedicated to the psychoanalytic interpretation of symbols and myths: not "In the beginning was the Word," but "Im Anfang war penis und vulva"; that is, "In the beginning were the male and female genital organs."

aspects, limited to a sort of demonic realm of sex and libido. Now, sex also has a different dimension besides the aspects of an elementary power of the psychic subsoil; it has the dimension of a possible transcendence, which can be identified through a truly in-depth analysis of various significant phenomena of the same erotic current. This has been recognized explicitly in manifold traditions, to such an extent that these traditions attributed sacral, mystico-ecstatic, and magical possibilities to sex, in terms totally different from those of the transpositions and the sublimations theorized by psychoanalysis, because the essence here was something truly elementary and specifically transcendent: transcendence of an almost metaphysical order and not the compulsive and blind force of the libido and of *eros,* which subjugates and carries away the individual. And a metaphysics of sex might even go so far as to recognize that the most murky, lower forms of sex are an involuntary degradation of that higher impulse.[11]

Thus it can be seen that, while on the one hand Freudianism goes too far when it gives itself over to a generalized sexual hermeneutics in the field of the human psyche, on the other hand it stops halfway by recognizing only a part of sex and confounding the remainder with this part, or reducing the remainder to it. A certain broadening of horizons was attempted by a former disciple of Freud, Wilhelm Reich, insofar as he in a certain way lifted sex out of the dregs of Freudian casuology and brought it back to an energy of an almost cosmic character, which he called orgone or orgastic energy (because he held that it was nakedly displayed in the orgasm). He applied the psychoanalytic theory of blockages, repressions, and pathogenic "armor" worn by the ego so as to protect it from this energy. But this broadening of perspective is more quantitative and intensive than it is qualitative: in essence, the "lower" quality of Freudian sexuality remains and the disauthorization of every higher power of the psyche is even accentuated.

---

11. On all of this, see our book *Eros and the Mysteries of Love: The Metaphysics of Sex* (Rochester, Vt.: Inner Traditions, 1991).

Two other points should be considered. If Freudianism gave the libido a generalized character, it could be an advantage over the more vague and spiritualistic conceptions—typical of other "unorthodox" tendencies in psychoanalysis—regarding the fundamental stem of prepersonal subterranean life, because it would then be possible to trace a fundamental traditional teaching back to the idea that "desire" or "yearning" is the root of all "natural" life. In this regard, however, it is necessary to again go back to a metaphysical plane. That profound alteration, that crisis and that irrational agitation by which the spirit ceases to "be" itself, becoming lost in the enjoyment of itself and in yearning identifications, was specifically considered by a prenatal and preconceptional metaphysics both in the Occident (for example, in the Neoplatonic exegeses of the myth of Narcissus) and in the Orient (especially in Buddhism), as the principal and primary force, or dynamis, that conducts one into the conditioned world, and, in particular, to birth as a mortal man. If, correspondingly, it was affirmed that "desire" is the substratum of mortal life in general, one did not stop at the subjective aspects of this desire; that is, neither at the special case of sexuality, nor at the other forms of the affective and passional domain. On the contrary, an elemental force, an id, was recognized, which acts in the very consciousness of things, in the very experience of the external world: *bhoga* (a Sanskrit term that signifies "to enjoy, to enjoy the object of a desire") constitutes the cloth on which human experience, in the most general sense, is formed. Every perception contains kāma (desire) and bhoga: it is an identification, through desire or "thirst," of the knower with the known, it is a turbid and thirsting mixture of the two that gives rise to the initial fall, as allegorized in the myth of Narcissus. For this reason, man does not know what pure consciousness might be, neither as consciousness of himself nor of things.[12]

---

12. Cf., for example, in Bhagavad-Gītā, III, 39–40: "This is the wise man's eternal foe; by this is wisdom overcast, whatever form it takes, a fire insatiable. Sense, mind, and soul . . . are the places where it lurks; through these it smothers wisdom, fooling the embodied" [The Bhagavad-Gītā, trans. R. C. Zaehner (Oxford: Oxford University Press, 1969)].

Moreover, in the Christian idea of the original sinfulness, or *cupiditas* [avarice] (not unrelated to sexuality)—which men since Adam carry within themselves and which would be the basis of all their "natural" works, until they are "reborn" and "redeemed"—in this Christian idea, even if in a moral-religious and not a metaphysical form, one might rediscover the traces of the same teaching.

It therefore appears that with "pansexualism," the theory of the id or sexualized libido, Freudianism once again takes the part for the whole and the derivative for the original. In the framework indicated, sexuality indeed constitutes nothing else but an episode with respect to something considerably vaster, and, if you will, considerably more dangerous. It is significant, moreover, that there has today been a presentiment of this truth only in the primitivistic terms of the Freudian theory of the libido.

There is another point that merits clarification in the sexological field. Against the accusation of pansexualism, it has also been proposed that Freud later recognized that, beyond the *Lustprinzip*, the impulse toward the pleasure of the libido, there acts also a *Todestrieb*, a death drive, which would reflect a general tendency of the organic to return to the stasis of the inorganic world. More generally, we are speaking of an impulse toward destruction.[13] The matter is not entirely clear, nor have the disciples of Freud developed it in a single direction. For the most part, Freud held that the two impulses are independent from one another but not to such a point that the second has no sexual value. Indeed, he used the death drive to explain the phenomena of sadism and masochism: if, in its manifestation as the destructive impulse, it is directed toward the subject himself, this gives place to masochistic tendencies; if it is directed instead toward others, to sadistic tendencies.

But some psychoanalysts have derived the second impulse from

---

13. Sigmund Freud, *Jenseits des Lustprinzips* (Leipzig, Vienna, and Zurich: Internationaler psychoanalystischer Verlag, 1920) [Beyond the Pleasure Principle, trans. James Strachey (London: Hogarth, 1961)].

the first: it would be the repression of the pleasure principle that neurotically gives rise to the destructive impulse, as in a certain kind of anger. The self-destructive introverse form would bring one also to the aforementioned "Nirvana principle." This continues, moreover, into broader generalizations, because aggressivity as such is referred to as "discharges" imposed by the pleasure principle (in Reich's theories, it is attributed to orgasmic energy), at those points when this principle is repressed and polarizes itself in the direction of the destructive impulse. There are many applications of this idea on the typological, sociological, and sociopolitical planes: the tendency toward authority, command, dominion, and despotism is related back to the sadistic manifestation of that impulse; the tendency to obey, follow, serve, and sacrifice oneself is related back to its masochistic manifestation. Thus, following Freud, the two complementary components that would constitute the existential base of every nondemocratic system have been interpreted in terms of repression and of sexual pathology. In the domain of sociopolitical applications, one can also observe that an author who has received a deal of recent publicity, Herbert Marcuse, after having deprecated and criticized the current system of the highly developed industrial and consumeristic society, sought to indicate (in his book *Eros and Civilization*) the foundations of the society that ought to replace it in the attempt to liberate man; and in this he kept himself strictly to the presuppositions of the most orthodox Freudianism, to the double impulse of pleasure and destruction, to their derivatives, and to the outlets offered on the one hand by sublimations and on the other by the loosening of the repressive system. Thus, one sees how far the distorting influence of the Freudian and para-Freudian idées fixes can go.

Returning to the psychological field, the admission of the second impulse—of the Todestrieb—might constitute a step forward toward a deeper erotology, if we do not separate it from the pleasure principle, indeed, if we it see it as acting in tandem to a varying degree with the latter, thus disregarding its alleged derivation from repressions.

It is a profound truth that every sexual *libido,* every yearning desire, is already in itself "ambivalent" insofar as it also contains an unconscious destructive and "mortal" charge. But this is to be understood in a different sense than the tendency toward destruction and toward a stasis analogous to that of the inorganic world. In every sufficiently intense voluptuousness there is a voluptuousness of self-destruction—and of destruction: an externalization of both hatred and love.[14] It is for this reason—as we have observed in our treatment of this whole phenomenology[15]—that in the ancient Roman world Venus as *Libitima* (from the same root as *libido*) counted, at one time, as the divinity of sexual love and of death; the same was true for Priapus; in Dionysism there is a well-known mixture of orgiastic voluptuousness and a destructive and self-destructive paroxysm; and, finally, in the East, Kāma, Māra, and Durgā are likewise divinities of both desire and death.

Once more, teachings of a higher order can therefore be indicated, which are only confusedly obfuscated by the psychoanalysts. Now, if one refers to this superior order of ideas regarding the libido and the rest, departing the domain of the purely human and indeed neuropathic assumptions about sex in which Freudianism has confined itself, one might admit that various apparently iconoclastic aspects of the Freudian critique of reality may even have some justification, if only they were to lose, if you will, their unconscious tendentiousness.

In fact, the first step toward a truly spiritual development is to become aware of the non-spirituality of many things that are held to be spiritual by men, to recognize specifically in these things the transpositions, sublimations, and surrogates that have very little to

---

14. In this context both the sadistic tendency and the masochistic tendency appear to be congenital elements of the sexual libido itself; they are not "derived" but rather form a part of its very essence. They have the character of derivations only when they are absolutized, conditioning the entire erotic process.

15. Cf. our book, which we have already cited, *Eros and the Mysteries of Love.*

do with the higher nature of being. This eminently applies to the framework of a civilization of an entirely "human" type, such as the modern one: in it there are indeed all too many "values" that can be explained on the basis of a deduction akin to the psychoanalytic one: surely these values take the guise of refuges and compensations for repressed forces, and above all for the impotence and fear that the individual has in the face of reality, and faced with himself. The restrictions imposed by social conventions and by all the hypocrisies of Western morality do the rest: and so necessity is transformed into a virtue, weakness takes the name of strength and of character, while on account the same state of division, contrast, and inadequacy with respect to the deep forces of life, today more than ever those subconscious processes are at work that generate neuroses, supercompensation and autistic hysterias, and psychic traumas.

To explode all these pseudo-spiritual superstructures so as to expose the subterranean force of our deepest and most subconscious life could therefore be a principle for whomever is firm in his absolute will to overcome. However, this is certainly not the case for psychoanalysis: just as with mediumship, once the door to the "lower realm" has been opened, psychoanalysis offers no means of defense, no method of effective control. Hence the danger that it constitutes for most.

Indeed, given the inconsistency of today's man, the possible paths are reduced to these two: either to return, albeit in a conscious form, to the compromise of transpositions, sublimations, and other evasionistic methods or compensatory dislocation—or else to accept the impulses of the libido and the id and making himself their agent, the conscious and rational instrument for the direct satisfaction of them.

Both of these paths represent an abdication. Psychoanalysis can counsel nothing else. The second path is asserted above all by the current of Adler, which desires that the ego, after having eliminated any inferiority complexes, should assume all responsibility and assert its will in the environment, to shape it accordingly. But, given the premises, what sense can "responsibility" and the "formative will" even have? Wherever the idea of personality as an autonomous principle, higher than the naturalistic order, is lacking, all these other concepts are devoid of any foundation. And indeed, at that point the "therapeutic" demand can give rise to the revolutionary social one. This is the direction which Reich and his followers have most recently followed in their polemics against Freud. Reich has observed, with undeniable consistency, that if the primary cause of the neurotic life (the life that is genuinely neurotic and which psychoanalysis in general attributes to multiple human behaviors) is a "repression" imposed by the "system," the environment, and the ideas of the environment, then it is not a matter of beating around the bush with half measures, with the palliative of individual adaptations, which allow the primary—objective and social—cause of the evil to subsist, but rather we should destroy this evil in its own place, blowing the structures and the orders of the ruling system sky high, despite Freud's recognition and timorous respect for them: hence the transition to open protest and revolution is indicated as the true radical and general therapy. And from the form already in progress of the so-called sexual revolution, of which Reich was the main apostle, it would be necessary to move on to further anarchoid unblockings, so that a "repressive" society can give way, more and more, to a "permissive" society. The problem of discrimination—and let no one proclaim here that "everything is permitted"—is not even touched upon; it seems that with an almost Rousseauian naïveté (detectable, moreover, also in classical anarchism) one believes that everything that can emerge from the human underground and from the unconscious when every dam is removed is only pleasant, beautiful, and healthy, in any case so as to let the possibility exist of some positive social order. In truth, Freud was more realistic in this connection: recognizing the turbid character of what prevails in the psychic subsoil of most, he also admitted the limits imposed by what he called the "reality principle."

But the most important point can be indicated with reference to a saying: to be "unchained" does not at all mean to be free. And it is shown in those situations where the inner counterpart to the protesting and revolutionary demands, indeed their evident premise, represents a capitulation—the identification with one's own subrational and instinctual being, returning to it deliberately and uninhibitedly as a solution to the crisis, cannot be called anything else. In the psychological and psychoanalytical domain, the current of C. G. Jung here enters into the question; Jung is considered the "spiritualist" among the psychoanalysts, because his morality—painted in spiritualistic hues and thus rendered acceptable to those for whom the views of Freud seem too crude—is that the ego must "come to terms" with the id, and man with his unconscious, both the individual and the archaic-collective unconscious, through a harmonization and a kind of narrowing of the limit between the one and the other. One cannot speak of overcoming this limit, because the presupposition is always that the "other" is an unconscious, not a subconscious. But we may let Jung speak here himself.

> In accordance with the old mystical saying, "Give up what thou hast, then shalt thou receive," they are called upon to abandon their dearest illusions in order to let something deeper, fairer, and more embracing grow up within them. For it is only through the mystery of self-sacrifice that a man may find himself anew. It is a right ancient wisdom that once more sees the light of day in psycho-analytical treatment; and it is especially curious that this form of education proves to be necessary at the moment when the culture of our time has reached its height. It is a kind of education which can be compared, in more than one respect, with the method of Socrates.[16]

---

[16]. C. G. Jung, "The Unconscious in the Normal and Pathological Mind," in *Two Essays on Analytical Psychology,* trans. H. G. and C. F. Baynes (London: Baillière, Tindall, and Cox, 1928), 22.

These are pretty words. However, let us see what their true meaning might be. As much as Jung shunned the radicalism of the Freudian libido and gave the collective unconscious the indeterminate characteristics of "Life," he could not change the situation: this life is understood as a reality in itself and as the primary element, and an ego must "integrate itself" in it or else it will be "uprooted," shifting the center of gravity toward "a virtual point between the conscious and the unconscious."[17] This is also the essence of what Jung calls the "process of individuation," which has as its key the *mysterium coniunctionis* [mystery of the conjunction]—an expression, for him, of a yet mythical thought that "scientifically" alludes to the wedding—the union—between the conscious and the unconscious. And it is also characteristic of his thought that even this union, or perfection, which is supposedly adumbrated in the ideal divine figures of the religions, has for Jung a coactive character, pressing toward itself the cogent, potentially vengeful force of an "archetype," of an id, since the conscious has a passive role even here, instead of being an exceptional and free vocation. This is the true sense of the psychoanalytic mystery of sacrifice, the renunciation of "the majority of one's most cherished illusions" that would allow one "to renew one's soul." And this would be the modern reevaluation of the "right ancient wisdom." If we were to describe a method for possession, we would choose words not very far off from these. It is the resolution to the discord that is obtained with the defeat, with the cessation of all moral tension. And the sense of liberation and satisfaction given to this détente, which comes by unburdening oneself of the weight of the ego and of the task

---

17. Cf. C. G. Jung, *Commentary to The Secret of the Golden Flower: A Chinese Book of Life*, trans. Cary F. Baynes (London: Kegan Paul, Trench, Trubner & Co., 1931), 106–27 [quote at 123]. For a deeper critique of the views of Jung, cf. the essay "Esotericism, the Unconscious, Psychoanalysis" in Julius Evola and the Ur Group, *Introduction to Magic*, vol. 3, trans. Joscelyn Godwin (Rochester, Vt.: Inner Traditions, 2021).

of spiritual form and autonomy, is exchanged with the sense of a "detached consciousness" and with the breath of a "deeper, fairer, and more embracing" existence.

We will have occasion to return to upheavals of this kind in later chapters. Here it is important to observe that in the psychoanalytic practice, the psychoanalyst—who more or less takes the role that the spiritual master once had before the disciple, and the confessor before the devotee—actively intervenes, helps the subject to realize this self-sacrifice, this *catharsis,* through the varieties of the technique of transference, to which we will refer later. René Guénon is therefore not mistaken in seeing something diabolical in this practice. In truth, whoever knows how to peer beyond the veils of the sensible shall hear, at the precise point when these subjects feel they have been liberated by virtue of a psychoanalytic catharsis, the same mocking laughter that he would perceive whenever the spiritists confuse mediumistic phenomena for revelations of a higher world, and larvae for the personality of the dead.

However, to return to the point from which we began, in considering the internal state of modern man, it is difficult for him to conceive of the possibility of avoiding either of the abdications mentioned above, once psychoanalysis has opened his eyes. On the whole, a crisis is exacerbated by this process, which in most cases can only have a negative solution. It is known that to awaken a somnambulist marching along a ravine is the best way of causing him to plummet into it. Ignorance, in some cases, is a strength: once it has been removed in the interests of overcoming some pathological form of the conflict between the ego and the subconscious, it cannot be reinstated in those other cases in which an illusion of personal autonomy would be salutary—cases in which this illusion can be pragmatically efficacious and, given certain premises, might even serve as a basis for a higher development. Moreover, the attention that psychoanalysis directs and concentrates onto the roots of the will to pleasure or to death, together with all the suggestions of a demonic-sexual order,[18] produces a true fascination, which multiplies the routes of entry into the already undermined recesses of the ego, thus favoring the emergence of the darkest and most contaminated influences lurking in the "subliminal." The pertinence of these observations increases all the more when psychoanalysis becomes a state of mind that—as has occurred in certain circles—has something collective about it, or when it even leads to sociological and ideological applications of the sort we have already mentioned.

Here, then, is the precise point of reference: apart from some very special cases of psychotherapy, psychoanalysis is dangerous insofar as it does not premise itself on a discipline dedicated to forming a spiritual unity, a true personality in place of that external and inconsistent one created by social conventions, upbringing, environment, and heredity—and also by the mediocre fragments of an assumed and domesticated desire and by hysteroid outbursts of the "autistic" type. In other words: psychoanalysis as "depth psychology" can have a positive value only when it is preceded by a kind of "asceticism"; and this in itself appears inconceivable and devoid of any point of support when, for a start, one rejects Freudian anthropology and the Freudian conception of man, which, as has been seen, is characterized by *the* denegation and disavowal of *the* reality and the possibility of the *I* as the central and autonomous principle. But then this would require a fundamental shift and broadening of perspective in the field of the psychoanalytic technique itself.

---

18. One can see, with this example, how far the theory of the "censor," which inhibits the conscious mind and the memory, might go: a psychoanalyst can ask you in all seriousness if you have ever experienced incestuous or homosexual feelings, even in images in dreams. If you respond that you have not, perhaps he will deem you a "serious case": for if nothing of the sort has reached your consciousness, this means that those impulses are so strong that they impose radical measures of censure, so much so that nothing of them reaches consciousness. Think how far a man who is easily open to suggestion might be led along such a path.

In fact, the technique of psychoanalysis proceeds more or less along the same lines as the practice of mediumship: it consists of removing the "censor," the unconscious and semiconscious inhibitions, and favoring states in which unconscious impulses and complexes betray themselves by means of spontaneous mental associations of memories, dreams, analogies, involuntary movements, and so forth. In regard to the subject, everything therefore reduces itself to the practice of a faculty of détente and "regression," which, once acquired, constitutes a condition exactly opposite to that of the integration of the personality. But there is more: the very technique of transference, and the part that the psychoanalyst has in these procedures, constitute a further movement against this integration. The ego not only opens the doors of its "underground," but it does so by abandoning itself to another person: this often leads it to equivocal and pathological situations in the rapport between the psychoanalyst and the psychoanalyzed.[19] So far as awareness of the unconscious goes, the identification of the various impulses is not made directly by the subject; it is essentially the psychoanalyst who carries it out through an inductive and hermeneutic procedure, which is to say, a procedure that is always hypothetical, based on material furnished to him by the subject in the states we have just mentioned; the subject can, at a later moment, "as if awakening," recognize the truth of what the psychoanalyst tells him, but here we must acknowledge the entire influence that the role of suggestion could potentially have in this process. In any case, one

---

19. An American psychoanalyst, Smith Ely Jelliffe, went so far as to propose, as a method of "affective transference," a three-way situation: the psychoanalyst is supposed to have a female psychoanalyst as an assistant so that the psychoanalyzed has at his disposal both the one sex and the other as the object on which, by transposition, his complexes can "discharge"—the male psychoanalyst participating if these impulses are homosexual, and the female if a surrogate is instead required for the incestuously hungered-after sister or mother. The fees for psychoanalytic treatment are almost always very steep. But one must grant that, in this case at least, one's "complexes" are being offered a proper service with every comfort!

cannot ever speak here of direct consciousness; this, as has been said, is already excluded a priori when one begins to consider the id as an unconsciousness.

The first step on the path of integration of the personality, as opposed to the path of "analysis," would be to have a sense of the "other" that the I carries in its own bosom; Jung, here, speaks with good reason of an anima, an irrational and demonic creature contrasted to the animus, which would be the properly personal principle. The question is first how to separate oneself from this "other." Later, one should dissolve, so far as is possible, the amalgams that desire has established between him who experiences and the material of his experience, both internal and external. As long as one is identified with the "other," one cannot have consciousness of that which acts: by detaching oneself, and freeing oneself from the obstructions established in the I, we find that I, so to speak, before us.

Then one could proceed into a field to which the psychoanalysts, to their credit, have brought attention (certain studies on hypnotism—for example, those of posthypnotic suggestion[20]—have also contributed to that attention). In fact, psychoanalytic investigation leads to an awareness of not one but of two kinds of unconscious. In addition to the unconscious and active dynamisms of the id, there is an unconscious that acts in a subtle and intelligent way within the fabric of waking consciousness itself. The various processes of censure, blockage, inhibition, repression, and even sublimation in defense of the ego are themselves carried out in the shadows, and it is only through the taxing psychoanalytic procedure that one comes to discover existence of this unconscious and reconstruct its modalities.[21] But the ongoing "influences" of such processes extend well beyond those having to do with the relationship between the

---

20. Here we are dealing with a subject who, put into a hypnotic state, is commanded to perform a certain act. He performs it and almost always finds reasons to persuade himself that he has done it of his own free will.
21. In Freudian terminology, this is the "preconscious" as distinct from the "unconscious."

ego and the libido. In some cases, they can even bring us back to a very general level that includes the hidden genesis of theories, suggestions, and "myths" that in the history of civilization are usually deemed "spontaneous," or else are explained with reference to two-dimensional, extrinsic factors. But in one way or another, this is an aspect according to which psychoanalysis can raise a healthy alarm; namely, it is important to challenge the existence of a "logic of the subsoil" acting between different forms of consciousness, a logic that is distinct from the genuine subconscious. Now, in contrast to the technique of psychoanalysis, in a discipline of true overcoming and consolidation of the personality, one tends toward a refinement of direct perception; this refinement, by almost creating new senses, allows one to catch unawares those subtle and infraconscious actions that determine certain processes, judgments, and resolutions of the waking consciousness. In a subsequent phase, it allows one to reach—through a direct vision—the extra-individual sources of such actions. By freeing oneself from the limitations of the fictitious I, the threshold of ordinary consciousness is removed. Beyond the emergent forms of external consciousness, one can therefore discover its roots, previously hidden in the deep and murky waters of the subliminal. Disciplines of this kind were known in traditional civilization in the form of a science. Psychoanalysis, which presumes "to penetrate more deeply into the depths" (Jung), is, on the contrary, only in its first steps.

At this point we must proceed to speak of the genuine subconscious and its exploration—or, better said, its destruction. In this regard we must limit ourselves to a brief comment, as we will return to this subject in a later chapter. Apart from being the agent in the "logic of the subsoil" we have just mentioned, the subconscious contains very distinct layers and "regions." To begin with, we must consider the zone of the subconscious whose principle is "desire" or cupiditas in the superindividual, metaphysical sense already indicated: it is the force that caused the fall from the state of "being" and which first led to the creation of bodies and of becoming in the world. Cosmologically, it is the region of the "demonic" in general, in its various forms. The stems of the souls of the races, not to speak of the roots of instincts and human passions, fall within this layer of the subconscious. When some psychoanalysts speak of the dramatizations of the collective and "phyletic" unconscious in the form of symbol-types—when Jung, in a kind of psychoanalytic-irrationalist reformulation of the Platonic doctrine of the Ideas, deals with the so-called archetypes—it is to this zone of the id that we are referred.

Now, this unconscious was always given the characteristics of a barrier. One should only make contact with it so as to cross it, conquer it, and overcome it. This has been symbolized in myth in a variety of ways. The "hero," who descends into the "lower world" or penetrates into the "cavern" and confronts the serpent, dragon, or bull, expresses in an allegory the conscious principle, integrated through the ascesis, that crosses the threshold and confronts the originating impulse. In myth, the victory of the "hero" over the symbolic wild creature, and his killing of it, always brings him to a rebirth, a vita nova [new life]; a resurrection, or the possession of the "water of life" or a "drink of immortality" follows the descent into the "lower world"; spikes of life [= ears of wheat] are born from the mortal wound inflicted upon the Mithraic bull; a "virgin" is liberated from the dragon; the fruit of immortality or some other equivalent symbolic object is attained (as in the myths of Heracles, Jason, etc.), and so forth. Here we are not dealing with sexuality, no matter what sort of extension one wishes to give to this concept; we are dealing, rather, with a transcendental action on the force that places and maintains consciousness under the condition of an animal body—an action aimed at reintegrating the person into that state of "being," with respect to which common human existence was traditionally compared to a fallen state, a state of torpor, drunkenness, or paralysis.

This state of "being" is the true supernatural, the "metaphysical" state. And the restored contact with it is the awakening. Then the way opens for the resolution and elimination of that which, as "unconscious," modern psychologists have erroneously conceived of as a principle in itself. In truth, in the still deeper depths, beyond the region of "desire," this unconscious exists alone, so to speak, as the task of a higher consciousness. Its layers or grades correspond exactly to powers or grades of the superconscious, the integration of the personality, and the "re-welding of the broken sword."

To proceed in these higher regions means above all recognizing that the surpassed world of the unconscious, however real it may be with respect to the world of men and of things, corresponds on the cosmological plane exclusively to the reign of sleep, dreams, hallucinations, and obsessive monoideisms in the individual. Metaphysically, it appears as the world of dreams and ghosts, to which already Homer opposed the realm of truthful vision. When it is the superconsciousness that takes itself into those depths, the nightmare is resolved, the mists clear, the ghosts disappear, and every residue is overcome to its furthest roots.[22] At the limit of what would otherwise be a dreamless deep sleep, the very knowledge of superreality (the ὑπερκοσμία of the ancients,[23] the "intelligible forms" of the real world) opens up to it, in its various degrees. The forms are what first determine, in general, the experience of a world—an experience that in the common

---

22. In the "experimental" field, one might, moreover, recall the interesting results of studies such as those of Oskar Kohnstamm (Medizinische und philosophische Ergebnisse aus der Methode der hypnotischen Selbstbesinnung [Munich: Reinhardt, 1918], cited by R. Rosel). In the midst of hypnosis, three states of the subconscious have been observed: the "subconscious orderer" (a notion that could take up the same "logic of the subsoil"), the "subconscious that experiences" (the emotive subconscious, which might extend itself to the "lower realm"), and, finally, the "deep subconscious." Subjects feel the latter, "fundamentally, as something that does not belong at all to their person," as "impersonal" and "superpersonal." It should be recognized that if, for the lack of a better term, one wants to call it an "ego," it is absolutely different from the I of ordinary waking consciousness. While the other two "unconsciouses" might be influenced by affects and complexes, the "deep subconscious" is "absolutely objective and truthful." In special states of hypnosis it is drawn from its latency; that is, it is made to become conscious. These are already significant adumbrations of the aforementioned "metaphysical descent into the depths."
23. [Greek *hyperkosmía*, "supramundane"]

man is formed without the intervention of his I and his will.²⁴ Then there is the passage of the cosmic mirage itself into the state of pure metaphysical meanings, something that corresponds, to a certain degree, to what has sometimes been called its realization *sub specie aeternitatis*.²⁵

It is hardly worth mentioning that all of these horizons are completely unknown to psychoanalysis. Not knowing the personality in the true sense, even less can it have any sense of the ideal of the superconscious personality (or else it conceives of it as an extreme hysterical-autistic exasperation of the ideal ego). As a method, its "depth psychology" goes no further than an uncertain touch that immediately deforms whatever it comes into contact with rather than developing itself into a transcendental psychology. As a morality, it is reduced, in the best of cases, to a mysticism of instinct and irrationalism; as a vision of life, to a mere naturalism. With regard to modern man, psychoanalysis raises an alarm, poses a problem. But it does nothing for the formation of the superconsciousness and superindividuality that can truly solve the problem and might eliminate those dangers (which, even on the material level, could well be serious²⁶) of the analysis—a superconsciousness and superindividuality that could lead to recognition in a direct

---

24. So-called Western critical-idealistic philosophy, through gnoseology (or the "theory of knowledge"), has reached the idea that the experience of the external world rests essentially on forms ("categories") and functions, which reside in the I. It is the merit of Eduard von Hartmann to have shown in a compelling way that such a view does not hold up if one no longer conceives of the place of such forms and functions as the unconscious. The traditional teaching, especially in its Hindu formulation, is analogous: an unconscious is recognized as the "internal organ" that determines the experience of the world.
25. [Latin: "under the sign of eternity," i.e., "from the perspective of eternity."]
26. The psychoanalysts admit that knowledge of the world of the id, apart from producing various forms of neurosis, might have the consequence of mental alienation and suicide, the slow compounding of causes that—even through seemingly random accidents—will lead to death. Added to this is the variety of aforementioned morbid relationships between subjects and psychoanalysts, especially where the subjects are women.

way of the nature and variety of the subterranean forces with which one is dealing. Wherever psychoanalysis expands its boundaries and thinks itself capable of throwing light on the primordial and the archaic; whenever it refuses to remain among the chimeras of the abnormal, hysterics, and neuropathics, galloping unbridled in that field along the tracks of the various complexes of the sexualized libido, which appear to it as the supreme explicative principle of the world of symbols and myths, as well as of every spiritual phenomenon—whenever it behaves in this way, it presents one of the most pitiful, or most alarming, spectacles amid the host of such spectacles of learned ignorance in our time.

As for the fact that orthodox psychoanalysis is the creation of a Jew and that, among psychoanalysts, the percentage of Jews is very high—let each person draw conclusions from this as he sees fit, depending on the point of view that he takes regarding the Jewish question in general.[27] It is certain, in any case, that if we were to psychoanalyze psychoanalysis as a general phenomenon, at its bottom we would find a Schadenfreude, a malicious pleasure in demoralizing and contaminating, applied not only to others and to the spiritual world but also, in the general vision of life, to oneself—almost as if one of those autosadistic complexes of which we have already spoken was acting here under the guise of "science." It could also be called the counterpart of the Darwinian myth: it manifests the same tendency, the same unconscious joy in being able to reduce the higher to the lower, the human to the animal and the primitive-savage, which manifests in the so-called theory of evolution. Thus—as has already been said—psychoanalysis as a general phenomenon is a symbol, a

---

27. However, Jung, whose views—albeit subtler and more spiritualistic—are no less dangerous than the others, is not Jewish; meanwhile, in the field of psychotherapy, one of the best critiques of psychoanalysis, written from the perspective of a methodology that, by contrast, respects the value of the personality, was written by a Jew (Viktor Franckl, *Aerztliche Seelsorge: Grundlagen der Logotherapie und Existenzanalyse* [Vienna: Deuticke, 1946]).

sign of the times. It is up to Western man—and his possibility of reintegration or his being definitively subjugated to a process of spiritual regression that has already been under way for centuries—as to whether this psychoanalyst myth will be proved true or false in the future.

IV
Critique of Theosophism

It is necessary to premise any examination of contemporary theosophy on the distinction between contemporary theosophy and ancient and traditional theosophy.

The latter, as the word itself suggests, proceeds from the exigency of an awareness—σοφία—of the "divine" (θέος). It therefore goes beyond the religious devotional position because it does not limit itself to "believing," to a mythology or a theology, but affirms the possibility of an effective experience and a knowledge of the "divine." Its superior dignity with respect to simple faith can be expressed by means of this correct observation by Schopenhauer: "[faith] is so by virtue of its containing what we cannot know. If we could know also this, then faith would appear as something quite useless and even ridiculous, just as if a dogma were set up over the themes of mathematics."[1]

In almost all the great currents of ancient spirituality, both those of the East and those of the West, "theosophy" has played a prominent role. One might even say that a tradition is truly complete only if it includes a theosophy in the sense just indicated. In original Christianity itself, the preeminence of theosophy was recognized

---

1. Arthur Schopenhauer, *Parerga and Paralipomena: Short Philosophical Essays,* trans. E. F. J. Payne (New York: Oxford University Press: 2000), vol. 1, 143.

when the Greek church fathers—especially Clement of Alexandria—counterposed the *gnosticos,* he who knows, to the *pistikos,* he who simply believes.

But it is not with traditional theosophy that we will occupy ourselves here. The theosophy we will consider is a new current, formed in 1875 in Anglo-Saxon territory, through the work of one Mrs. Helena Petrovna Blavatsky, as a strange mixture of Eastern and wisdom motifs on the one hand, and of Western prejudices on the other. This current developed under the sign of a reaction against the then dominant materialism (as indeed did spiritism), however displaying at the same time a polemical strain against the church, which it judged incapable of offering anything more than dogmas and confused hopes to the spiritual thirst of humanity.

Precisely on the pretext of offering something more, the movement under consideration appropriated the designation of "theosophy." But let us repeat it: we are dealing here with something very different from theosophy, and to clearly distinguish the two it is opportune to employ here the term *theosophism,* which was already adopted by Friedrich Schelling for similar currents, and more recently taken up again by René Guénon.

A critique of theosophism is not made any easier due to its mixed character. In any case, one must distinguish between the ideas and the personalities; between the ideas in themselves and the various deformations that the former have suffered in the overall mixture; and between certain exigencies and certain directives of spiritual development of the personality on the one hand, and the absence of their application on the other.

Our first reservation comes in regard to the origin "from the heights" that the theosophists love to attribute to their movement. "[In the face of the mental limitation of the moderns]," Annie Besant wrote, "the great Guardians of Humanity thought it wise that the old truth should be proclaimed in a new form suited to the mind and attitude of the man of the time."[2] According to this conception, certain mysterious beings—Mahātmās—that have sometimes even manifested as visible persons, transmitted the doctrine to the founders of the movement. We are of the opinion that this might even reflect a certain reality, but the theosophists here, in believing they were dealing exclusively with the "great Guardians of Humanity" (?), have betrayed an attitude that is not so very different from the passive, credulous, and naive one belonging to the spiritists and the mediums. The fact that something comes from behind the curtains—let us repeat it once more—does not simply mean that it should be taken exclusively as coin of a pure mint. Someone might have instilled certain "revelations" in the first theosophists, making use of them to create a specific collective psychic current: but who this "someone" was, and what his effective aims might have been, is a matter for discussion. And the discussion cannot do other than base itself on the intrinsic value of his communications.

Blavatsky has written, "Mediumship is the opposite of adeptship, one is controlled, the other controls."[3] This is exactly right: but the fact is that Blavatsky, for her part, falls more aptly into the first group than the second. It should also be recounted that, as in the case of many mediums, already from her childhood she had involuntarily provoked around herself certain paranormal phenomena, so that some even attributed this to the heredity of her ancestor Vseslav, who had had the reputation of being a kind of wizard. Many affirm that analogous phenomena were produced, too, when Blavatsky founded the Theosophical Society. She composed many parts of her bulky and chaotic works semiconsciously, almost in a state of "automatic

---

2. Annie Besant, *Popular Lectures on Theosophy* (Adyar: Theosophist Office, 1910) 3. [The bracketed insertion reflects the Italian translation that Evola originally quoted (*Le leggi fondamentali della Teosofia*, 1929) as no corresponding phrase appeared in the original English text.]
3. Katharine Hillard, ed., *An Abridgment of The Secret Doctrine, A Synthesis of Science, Religion and Philosophy by Helena Petrovna Blavatsky* (New York: Quarterly Book Department, 1907), 8.

writing"; in them many quotations were found from books she had never read. Thus, the origins of theosophism remain obscure. On the doctrinal side, we are often dealing with the surfacings of visions from "errant" mental complexes, in which one might discern a strong Eastern component, with manifest contributions from the dominant themes of the collective Western psyche of the time. Moreover, this raw material of original theosophism was engaged with and re-elaborated upon by various individuals, especially after the schism that occurred in the Theosophical Society in 1898. And some were able, both in Italy and abroad, to rise somewhat above its primitive level and to recognize theosophism merely as an incitement toward something better, something autonomous.[4]

The distinction between what is valid and what is negative in the theosophistic complex can generally be traced back, on the one hand, to a part that draws its inspiration from the great metaphysical visions of the past and of the East; and, on the other hand, to a part that is indebted to the Western mentality, to the influences of the epoch, and to the personal factor of the adherents, among whom there is a prevalence of females: this constitutes a symptomatic fact, as has already been mentioned. Also relevant is the part played by the infatuation with democracy and egalitarianism, since the aims of the Theosophical Society from the start included promoting the formation of a "universal brotherhood of humanity, without distinction of race, creed, sex, caste, or colour."

The first accusation to bring against theosophism is that it did not reach a true theosophy but instead an abnormal and syncretic complex of elements from various doctrines, without any sort of critical scrutiny, admixed with data that were derived from visions and personal experiences and that had the alleged character of higher truths. Concerning the latter, it is true that theosophism

---

4. As far as Italy is concerned, we can mention, in this regard, the group called the Lega teosofica indipendente [Independent Theosophical League] led by Decio Calvari, who also published a journal, *Ultra*.

sometimes points the way for others to rise in practice to the same certainties, supposedly of a very different type from what any theory is capable of giving. But—as has been mentioned in the case of Blavatsky, and can be repeated for a Charles Leadbeater, an Annie Besant, an Alice Bailey, and many others—even those who perchance point to ways of supernormal development that are in themselves straight, too often remained personally confined to the behaviors of mediumship and visionarism: behaviors in which there can be no criterion of true control, no principle of discrimination between the fallacious evidence of a hallucination (subjective, or induced by psychic influences external to their persons) and the real suprahuman, or *theo-sophic,* consciousness. As far as the vast majority of the other behaviors goes, they limit themselves to blindly accepting "revelations" and syncretistic complexes presented as the "secret doctrine," often on account of irrational and sentimental motivations. For these reasons theosophism, rather than carrying the individual, as would the true *theo-sophy,* beyond "beliefs," often substitutes one belief or religion for another, whenever it does not simply add on a dreadful and uncritical philosophy with resonances of the ideas of modern science.

This should not, however, impede our recognition that whatever in theosophism which relates, in spite of everything, to the exigency of a true theosophy, in principle has a positive value. And a method that seriously aimed for a direct spiritual experience, that obeyed the will to displace the usual level of consciousness, to transform oneself by strengthening self-consciousness so far as to make contact with the invisible reality, so as to bear witness to it at the same time through concrete forms of power—such a method would express the surpassing of the attitudes of both "psychic research" and of psychoanalysis. The words of a certain vulgarizer of theosophism, Georges Chévrier, are therefore entirely correct: "There is no true knowledge except where power attests it. All the rest is nothing but documentation via hearsay, without profundity and with no other benefit than satisfying a curiosity, which in the end will have to cease when it tires of being deluded."[5]

But to really adapt to such an exigency corresponds to another programmatic cornerstone of the early Theosophical Society; namely, that of promoting the "occult" development of man according to his latent possibilities. Given the inclination of the modern Westerners to bring everything back to abstract and inane speculations, theosophism should have adopted an entirely different style: one similar, for example, to that of early Buddhism, which said very little indeed regarding a description and "theory" of the occult and the transcendent. It limited itself to posing the problem of "awakening," furnishing at the same time and in every detail the technique apt to resolve it, and thus to make one directly experience the very thing about which it had kept silent and had encapsulated in a negative designation (*nir-vāna*).[6] Theosophism, rather than silence and practice, rather than the post *laborem scientia*[7] recalled even by the Western hermeticists, has instead preferred an aimless roving through invisible planes and bodies, "planetary journeys," intertwinings, evolutions, and involutions of entities of every sort, visions of the destinies of worlds, masters, races, subraces, cosmic ages, and so on, not to mention the sauces of humanitarianism, optimism, and progressivism. Unfortunately, this was what generally filled the heads and books of the theosophists above all.

As far as its doctrine goes, theosophism, as has been indicated, intended to bring the attention of the moderns back to the truths of a forgotten knowledge, whose sources have been sought above all

---

5. Georges Chévrier, *La Dottrina Occulta* (Milan: Monanni, 1928), 10.
6. Cf. Julius Evola, *The Doctrine of Awakening: The Attainment of Self-Mastery According to the Earliest Buddhist Texts,* trans. H. E. Musson (Rochester, Vt.: Inner Traditions, 1996).
7. [Latin: "knowledge after work," an expression used by the alchemists.]

in the East, and India in particular. Upon what teachings of real value might theosophism draw attention? And what misunderstandings and distortions have been superimposed onto these teachings through their adoption and vulgarization by theosophism?

Here we will limit ourselves to the examination of two notions that serve as cornerstones of the theosophistic conception: karma and reincarnation.

In the Hindu tradition, karma signifies "action." A fundamental viewpoint of this tradition is that "by action (karma) this world was created, by action it is sustained, and by action it will be dissolved." In particular: "According to what is done (karma), being arises. Heirs of the actions are the beings."

These sayings in themselves are clear. They allude to a general—and elementary—law of causality. We need only note that here the term *action*—karma—is not applied solely to action in the strict, material sense but instead embraces a much vaster conception. Every thought, every desire, and every acquired habit is likewise karma. Moreover, karma is extended to orders of influences that are elusive for the common man; it connects effects to remote causes from very diverse planes; it goes beyond the limits of the visible and of a single form of existence and, in contrast to the law of physical causality, it does not unfold in the dimension of time alone. Nevertheless, there remains in it the character, well visible in the laws of nature, of impersonal relationships following a necessary sequence. Thus, when one is dealing with man, the law of karma does not say whether one should do or should not do but simply enunciates the product of an effect, once a given cause has been created. It informs; it does not command. One is free, for example, to light or not to light the fire, but one cannot demand that the fire, once lit, will not burn. As regards karma, this notion should be extended to everything that exists in the manifested world—both as corporeal world and as psychic, moral, intellectual, and spiritual world; both in the ways of men and in those of the invisible forces and the "gods." According to the doctrine in question, everything forms itself, transforms itself, or passes over in this way, in the heights as in the depths: through pure relationships of cause and effect.

We find ourselves thus in the order of a universal determinism, which does not, however, exclude liberty; on the contrary, it presupposes it as a first cause and, moreover, as a principle capable of producing new causes, new series of tendencies, of actions and reactions, either solidaristic or else antagonistic with respect to those already enacted. Karma excludes the ideas of "chance," "destiny," and also of "providence" in the anthropomorphic sense of a principle of interventions or divine sanctions having a moral character.[8] Action and liberty therefore consume this vision of the world. Every being is that which has been made. Karma does nothing but draw consequences from created causes, and the I in the current of its life follows only the riverbed that it, knowingly or not, has dug for itself. Thus, there exists no fault—in the Western sense—at all, just as there exists no merit; there exists no sin and there exists no virtue. There are only certain "actions," be they material, psychic, or spiritual, that will necessarily bring certain conditions, be they material, psychic, or spiritual. A priori, all roads are open, both the high and the low. Having set oneself upon one of them, nothing is to be hoped for nor feared, save that which will proceed impersonally from the nature of this road. In the most absolute sense, all things and all beings are left to themselves.

This teaching brings a purification of one's gaze. It accustoms one to consider everything according to a clarity and a law of reality, analogous to the laws that are in force in the free world of things. It

---

[8]. As a conception, moreover, it is not exclusive to the Eastern teaching. In the classical traditions the notion of "providence" did not itself have a "moral" character, with relation to the care of a theistically conceived god, but it was thought to be a complex of conditioning and impersonal laws, like the warnings that the objective science of a doctor might furnish on what to do and what not to do—to use a Plotinian analogy (*Enneads,* III, 3, 5).

frees one from the phantasms of both fear and hope. It carries one back to oneself as to something simple and strong, something that rests on itself. And this is the premise of every higher realization.

Such is the sense of karma according to the tradition, to which the notion legitimately belongs. But what has become of it in theosophism?

First of all, karma shifts over from the framework of freedom to that typically modern context of a kind of evolutionistic determinism. The multiplicity of free paths—which from the point of view of the individual is the elementary truth, every further conception belonging to the metaphysical plane[9]—is substituted with the single direction of a mandatory "progress," and one's only alternative is to walk this path sooner or later.

In fact, according to the theosophistic views, the "gods" and the adepts are beings who have gone further ahead in their "evolution"; the animals, "our lesser brothers," are less "progressed." But it is only a matter of time: everyone will come to port, those who are further ahead "sacrificing themselves" for the others; and the varieties of karma serve only as an instrument for "universal progress." As is clear, all of this cannot be considered other than an errant and adulterated addition of the theosophists to the authentic notion of karma. However, it should be no wonder if this notion from the plane of a transcendental realism often changes to that of a more or less philistine moralism, becoming a kind of Sword of Damocles suspended

---

9. Indeed, the traditional teaching knows the idea of a superior order, to which the Far Eastern notion of the "Path of Heaven" (Tao) corresponds, as does the Hindu idea of ṛta and the Hellenic idea of κόσμος. But it is an idea that is only valid specifically in the metaphysical realm, and which therefore must not be confused with the human notion of "purpose." It is through images alone that an allusion to the relations between this superior order and the plane of freedom and of causality (karma) is given (if it is given at all); Joseph De Maistre gives an example of such an image when he states that the universe is comparable to a clockwork in which, although the wheels each turn on their own, it always shows the right time; or it is like the Chinese saying that order is the sum of all disorders. There is, therefore, no tangible interference.

over the head of whomever does not conform to the "law of evolution" and to the relative corollaries professed by the movement, be they altruistic, humanitarian, egalitarian, vegetarian, feminist, and so on. And so, too, the practical value, the liberating potentiality of this teaching, which we have lately mentioned, is completely lost.

In theosophism, karma stands in a specific connection with reincarnation. Theosophism boasts that it has brought the attention of the West back to this other "teaching of an ancient knowledge." In reality, given the limitation of the horizons of modern men, for whom this present existence is the beginning and the end of everything, and who see nothing before and after it apart from vague religious ideas of the beyond (which, in turn, no longer constitute anything living to these men)—given this limitation, it would certainly be worthy to arouse in these men the sense of their having come from far away, of having lived many other lives and many other deaths and of being able to proceed yet again, from world to world, beyond the demise of this body. The trouble is that everything in theosophism is reduced to a monotonous series of earthly existences, separated by intervals of a more or less attenuated corporality. Thus, the limitation of modern man is almost not removed at all. Theosophism here claims to rest on an ancient doctrine, but in reality it rests on nothing whatsoever and refers entirely to exoteric, popular forms of that doctrine—and yet, once again, lacks all sense of the order of things in which it should bear itself.

To resolve the problem of reincarnation, one must start by clarifying the problem of survival, with which theosophism does not concern itself in the least, so certain it is of its positive "spiritualistic" solution and the personal survival of every human soul. It is perhaps in Vedānta that one finds the idea of reincarnation nearest to that which the theosophists profess. But Vedānta provides a basis for this idea: it has the theory of the Self, of the immortal and eternal *ātmā*, identical to Brahman, the metaphysical principle of every thing. This theory refers to a spiritual state of man's consciousness, one that should no longer be sought, not only in the men of today, but already even in the humanity of the Buddhistic period. In Buddhism we indeed find the doctrine of the *anātmā;* that is, of the negation of the essentiality of the soul and of any kind of continuity for it whatsoever. Comparing Vedānta to Buddhism, we are not dealing with two philosophical opinions that stand in contrast to one another, but rather two theories that are different only because they refer to two different spiritual conditions. The soul (ātmā) that Buddism negates is not the same as what Vedānta affirms. The soul of Vedānta is nothing other than that which Buddhism considers, not as a reality present in every man, but rather as an end that may be reached only exceptionally, through ascesis. Here one might establish a relation with the esoteric sense of many traditional teachings and myths, some also of Western origin; for example, that of the "fall." It is a question of observing, at a given moment, the identification of the personality with a psychic form that is conditioned and determined essentially by the body: from here comes the birth of the I to which a modern person might refer—the I whose transience and unreality Buddhism forcibly asserts on the basis of reason, on the basis of a metaphysical realism.[10]

Now, reincarnation might have had a certain sense for that man in whom the I counted more or less directly as a universal principle, superior therefore to every particular individuation (ātmā = brahman, Vedānta); but this is not the same as the sense that the same doctrine might have if brought back to an ordinary human I, one closed in on

---

10. It is interesting to observe that the age of the birth of Buddhism (approximately 600 BC), which affirmed the doctrine of the anātmā, coincides with that of the rise of philosophical and naturalistic thought in the East and above all in the West (Greece)—that is, with the manifestations of logical consciousness connected to the brain—these take the place of anterior and superior forms of consciousness, which constituted the existential basis of such doctrines as the Vedāntic. It is of the utmost importance to realize that the great traditional doctrines are not mere human inventions and that their differences are not arbitrary but rather elative to the adaptation of their teaching to effectively diverse historico-spiritual states of affairs.

itself, such as the I in more recent times: for this latter kind of I the contacts have been severed, there is no longer anything that, like an unalterable silk thread, might pass through and connect an indefinite series of pearls representing individual existences. The sense of self is bound unequivocally to the support of a body and a brain, and the consequence might well be the definitive impairment of that continuity of individuated consciousnesses, which has been dealt a serious blow already at birth (an event that, in general, extinguishes the memory of all anterior experiences).[11] In facing this existence, the spirit as "personality" also faces a fundamental risk. And we are no longer dealing with reincarnation in the Vedāntic sense: we are instead dealing with the alternative between "salvation" and "perdition," which, to a certain extent, is decided here on this earth. Perhaps this is the sense and the concrete, historical raison d'être for the teaching regarding salvation and perdition that has succeeded in more recent traditions, such as, for example, in the Catholic and the Islamic ones.[12]

For the average Western man, this teaching is therefore true, while reincarnation in the Vedāntic sense is not. Thus, if one still wishes today to speak of reincarnation, one can no longer do so for the soul as a personality but only for other principles included in the human entity, and always in a sense that excludes, for most, a true continuity of personal consciousness. It might be said that what in the present conditions is perennial, and which is transmitted from being to being, is no longer the "immortal ātmā" (the superpersonality) but rather "life" as "desire" in the Buddhistic

---

11. One therefore comprehends why Catholicism, in relation to the period in which it was formed, declared the doctrine of the soul's preexistence with respect to the body to be a *heresy*. In reality, the soul, as a merely "human" soul (and today one cannot speak, in general, of any other kind), is born with the birth of the body.

12. The hardening of the alternative between salvation and perdition, which can be observed in Protestantism as opposed to Catholicism, is to be explained with the increasingly physical character that the I took on in the even more recent age of the Reformation, contemporaneous with the rise of so-called humanism.

sense of the term.[13] It is the deep and animal will to live, in terms of a kind of subpersonal entity, that creates ever new births and which is the matrix of every mortal I; and this will is, at the same time, the barrier to higher worlds. We are therefore brought back to a number of things that we have already discussed in our treatment of psychoanalysis. Hence, if we would like to continue to speak of reincarnation and karma, we must seek the vision conforming to reality in teachings like the Buddhist one, which specfically has in view the transcient soul, or the exceptional soul that is released from the state of nirvāna through ascesis.

According to Buddhism, the man who has not reached awakening and spiritual illumination nonetheless generates, through his thoughts, words, and actions (karma), another being or "daemon" (called *antarabhāva* or also *vijñana*), which is materialized through its unrelieved yearning for life; and this daemon receives its fundamental tendencies from that yearning. This being generally survives death. The fatal force of the inclinations that compose it and that after death are no longer held back by any will, brings it back to earth, toward a body and a life conforming to its nature; conjoining with physical and vital elements furnished by its parents, it constitutes the basis for the manifestation, among the species of man, of other entities, which, themselves adulterated by "desire," conjoin and assimilate with it according to the laws of affinity, foregoing other states of existence. In this way a new human consciousness is born, in the form of an entity much more complex than what is commonly believed, composed of various inheritances; an entity that has no true relationship of personal continuity with that of the dead. This is so, notwithstanding the fact that a law of cause and effect (karma) might on the one hand locate in a previous life the origin of that which, as a specific form, is due to the antarabhāva and on the other

---

13. As has already been mentioned, translated into moral terms, this notion corresponds in Catholicism to the theory of the heredity of "sin" that the flesh of man bears, from Adam, as *cupiditas* or *appetitus innatus* [innate appetite].

hand might also explain why the composite fatally attracts the new being that it incarnates.[14]

Apart from "spirits," the larvae and psychic fragments of which we have spoken in our critique of spiritism; apart from the antarabhāva, the blind creature protruding from the stem of desire—nothing else survives death, in terms of a personal continuity, for those who have not already attained a certain level of enlightenment in life. If, on the other hand, this level has been reached, it is only then that one can speak of a survival for the soul: the soul, maintaining its continuity of consciousness, can face even those experiences of the post-mortem, in relation to which we have already cited a Lamaist text, and the overall complex of which could be designated by the term *purgatory*—it can face them in such a way so as to be able to attain one or another state of existence beyond the human and subhuman world. On earth, in any case, nothing returns save that which belongs to the earth. The "soul" does not come from other bodies, but from other worlds—that is, from other conditions of existence—and it does not go into other bodies, but, if it cheats the "lower worlds" by conforming to its supernatural purpose, it goes to other of these "worlds." The repeated passage of the soul (and not of this or that psychic complex of which the soul is composed, as the soul of a mortal man) in the condition of a human body represents an absolutely exceptional case. For the soul there can therefore be transmigration: something entirely distinct from the reincarnation that might occur only with inferior elements, mainly collective and impersonal, of the human composite.

---

14. One might designate the irrational form, with which a soul identifies itself and which remains the basis of the various human psycho-vital functions, with the term *daemon,* used in the classical sense, and recall the Plotinian teaching that the soul "has chosen from the first its daemon and its life," in conformity to the nature of the tendencies that it has developed in itself (*Enneads,* III, 4, 5–6).

Antarabhāva literally means "that which exists between the two"; it alludes to that which takes the place of the I in the discontinuous interval between one and the other terrestrial (but, strictly speaking, not only terrestrial) existence. [On all of this, cf. Evola, *The Doctrine of Awakening.*]

Generally speaking, this is how matters stand for reincarnation with relation to present-day man. What echo is there of this in the doctrine asserted by theosophism? Every theory or superstition—let us repeat—is always, in some aspect, a barometric indicator of the times. It can be said that "reincarnation" is a correct idea if it is referred solely to that irrational entity which, having worn out the body in its uniform and inexhaustible thirst for life, passes to other bodies, never elevating itself to a higher plane.

Since in our present time, for the majority of men, the beginning and the end of life are played out in a similar mode of being, and the case of "liberation" appears ever more anomalous, it can therefore be said that for the humanity of the present period, reincarnation, in the sense of a perennial terrestrial repullulation, naturally has a certain degree of truth to it—apart from the optimism that has been added to this in the sense of "evolution" and "progress," and apart from the presumption, entirely gratuitous, of an "immortal self," in place of which instead there is an entirely "natural" and subpersonal being with its creatures, unconnected to one another in any true continuity, and with its appetitus innatus [innate appetite], the root of all becoming in temporality and in what in the East is termed *samsāra*.

Even in this connection one might indicate as a characteristic of theosophism the lack of any truly supernatural vista. From the point of view of the human state of existence, there can be nothing truly supernatural without a premise of dualism, such as was asserted by every superior civilization, and the "evolutionistic" conception of theosophism contrasts sharply with this premise. As in the Catholic tradition there is a clear line between the temporal order and the eternal order; thus, in the Eastern traditions there is a neat distinction between the limitless series of possibilities and of "rebirths" subordinated to becoming and to desire (possibilities that include both "divine" as well as human and "infernal" states) and true liberation. That sequence is portrayed as a perpetual circle (a concept that is to be found in the Hellenic tradition: ὁ κύκλος τῆς γενέως)[15] and here every "progress" is illusory; one's mode of being does not substantially change even when one reaches forms of existence far above the common level. Liberation instead corresponds to an exceptional path, a path that is "vertical" and "supernatural," equally distant and equally near with respect to any given point of being and of time. But theosophism, by contrast, abolishes this opposition: the two terms are placed on the same plane; the supreme aim is conceived of as the end of an "evolutionary" development through a limitless series of rebirths in the conditioned world. Thus, where it speaks of development, it cannot have the personal soul in view, but rather the natural and animal stock of "humanity"; and its "spiritualism," at bottom, is reduced to a mystical extension of collective social progress utopias with needs and concerns that, from a higher point of view, seem more deserving of being called zootehnics than ethics. As for the "immortal self" given to each person, one needs nothing more than this to fall into a slumber, to distract oneself from the alternative realities—the alternative between salvation or perdition that is to be resolved in this existence— therefore precluding oneself from the path to a true liberation.

This is not the only place in theosophism where such an antisupernaturalistic spirit is revealed. Among the principles held by the movement is that of the immanence of a "One Life" in every form and in every being; there is, at the same time, the principle of the task, on the part of each individual "self," to achieve an independent self-consciousness. With a strange application of the anti-aristocratic conceptions proper to certain new moralities, there has even been talk of a renunciation of the primitive divinity, which one "possessed without meriting it" and only to won back "deservedly" through struggle and the hard experiences of repeated immersions in "matter." This, in the reformed theosophism of Rudolf Steiner, corresponds to a plane

---

15. [Greek: "the cycle of births"]

all its own, onto which "Ahriman" and "Lucifer" have been duly conscripted. Thought through to the end, these views should have as their logical conclusion that the "One Life"—that is, the aspect of "oneness" in Life—represents the "least," the substrate, or *materia prima,* from which every being, in forming itself, should differentiate itself as a distinct principle, thereby positing, as a value, a law of difference and articulation. But no: the "One Life" becomes the aim, the perfection. Despite various appeals to the traditional paths of superhuman attainment, despite the whole occultist arsenal gathered from the most diverse sources, the idea of development in theosophism is colored with mystical tints and inclines toward the degenerative direction of a simple blending with the substrate of the undifferentiated "One Life," rejecting the "illusion of separation" and of the "self." Here, too, we are dealing with confusions that proceed from the misunderstanding of a barely glimpsed metaphysical teaching: for the purely metaphysical notion of the "supreme Identity" has nothing to do with that of the "One Life." It is a grave error to confuse the promiscuous pantheistic One—in which, to put it in Hegel's words, everything becomes equal like "the night in which all cows are black"—with the metaphysical One, which is the integrating apex of a well-articulated whole, differentiated and ordered with forms, of a κόσμος in the Greek sense (and moreover it is an error that is likewise committed by certain contemporary neo-Vedāntic currents, which are distinct from theosophism and refer directly to the indiscriminate teachings of certain contemporary *gurus,* the epigones of Hinduism). The possible effective point of reference in theosophism can be seen, moreover, in its consequences: in the corollary of democratic ideals of brotherhood, love, equality, universal solidarity, and the leveling of the sexes and of the classes. All of this replaces that virile law of hierarchy, of difference, and of caste, which the great traditions have always known when they took the right direction as their living axis: that of integration of the supernatural dignity of man in the supersensible. And this is one of the determining reasons why, even in an already external context, apart from its doctrinal confusion, the theosophistic current, together with various other "spiritualistic" currents that are akin to it, constitutes a factor in the crisis of contemporary civilization—a factor that joins a great many others, at work on multiple planes, precisely in the sense of a regression into the collective and the promiscuous.

There are various other things we ought to say with regard to theosophism. But these will perhaps come up again in our treatment of the remaining spiritualistic currents, and besides, it is not the details (which could perhaps have, in and of themselves, a certain value) that we are concerned with here, but with the general sense that holds sway over the new currents as a whole.

Theosophism ascribes to itself the merit of having reawakened interest in the West for the spiritual East. Indeed, through theosophism, many views of a universal tradition, which, however, have been conserved above all in the East in distinct forms, have been disseminated to numerous European and American circles. But precisely which views? Already in the brief overview we have made, we find nothing to convince us that true Eastern spirituality is known to a greater degree now than it was before. It is instead a counterfeit that has taken the place of, and has been confused with, the East—and moreover it is a counterfeit in which certain typically modern prejudices have had occasion to reaffirm themselves.

Since this is how matters stand, there arises a doubt that is certainly very serious: What is the true "invisible" origin of theosophism? What effective intention or plan has compelled its appearance in the modern world? Are we dealing with "influences" that truly want to vivify the West by bringing it into contact with a spirituality of a higher kind, like the spirituality of the traditional East, with respect to confronting the modern world? And are the falsifications here therefore only accountable to the failures of the single individuals who have served as its intermediaries? Or are we, in fact, dealing with influences of the opposite kind: *in*fluences that want to neutralize a danger, to preemptively close certain doors, to prejudice and prevent a healthy effect—such as the East might exercise—by diverting one of the highest aspirations?

The fact is that if today various persons, who are not devoid of culture, harbor certain prejudices against the East, this is due in part precisely to adulterating "spiritualistic" divulgations, but also to certain modern Easterners engaged in adaptations and vulgarizations—individuals who seem to understand very little of their own traditions but who, precisely by virtue of being Eastern, make an impression on the layman. For example, apart from the correctness of certain exigencies that are expressed in it, the book by Massis, from which we cited a few sentences at the outset, represents a typical example of the consequences that might result from confusions of this kind: Massis's curious ideas about a "defense of the West," wherever they are in good faith, can be explained only on the basis of the aforementioned counterfeits of an Eastern wisdom.[16] And furthermore it is a sinister thing, this inclination of certain militant Catholic circles to go fishing in murky waters, taking advantage of all this confusion for the monopolistic purposes of their own myopic apologetics. They do not realize that to discredit the tradition of others—in this case, those of the East—means condemning their own tradition to attack as well, sooner or later, the very tradition that they had intended to exalt by such a path.

But, to return to theosophism, it is too serious a matter for us to assume the responsibility of responding to the above-mentioned problem concerning the true objectives that this theosophism has obeyed. Let it suffice here to have posed it, in order that whoever is capable of such a thing might keep his eyes open, recalling that certain matters are much more serious than is generally believed, even when they are clothed in an eccentric appearance.

---

16. Cf. René Guénon, *Orient et Occident* (Paris: Payot, 1924).

V

Critique of Anthroposophy

Anthroposophy emerged in 1913 through the work of an Austrian, Dr. Rudolf Steiner, the then secretary of the Theosophical Society, as an attempt at a kind of reform of the original theosophistic movement. Anthroposophy gained ground especially in the German countries, from which it passed into France and Italy. In Dornach, Switzerland, he created a center where he held courses on various branches of knowledge considered from an anthroposophic point of view. Indeed, Steiner's activity was remarkable. There does not seem to be a single discipline—from medicine to theology, from art to natural science, from history to sociology, from biology to cosmology—of which he did not seek to speak. The number of lectures he gave is incredible. On the other hand, Steiner does not specifically exhibit the characteristics of a medium or of a lunatic. In certain respects, it might even be said that he errs in the opposite direction—that of a mind that must be scientific-systematic at any cost. Although many of his conceptions are no less fantastical that those of theosophy, still, in contrast to the latter, one can say, along with Shakespeare, that "there is method to his madness."

Various components must be distinguished in the Steiner phenomenon. The first—and predominant—component is one that shares a common origin with theosophism, from which multiple elements have been adopted. The second component is connected to

Christianity. There is then a final factor, which would seem to correspond to a positive element, the need for a "spiritual science." The intertwining of these components—forcibly bound in the chainmail of a system that, in terms of its ingenuity, is almost on par with the "nature philosophies" of the German Romantics—forms the characteristic of anthroposophy. As in so many specific points of anthroposophic teaching, and likewise in Steiner's own overall personality, one has the painful sensation of a straight and clear direction that has been broken by sudden and tyrannical visionary influxes, and by irruptions of collective complexes. Steiner's is a typical and highly instructive example of what might happen when one ventures alone in the world of the supersensible without a connection to a proper initiatic tradition and without a protective chrism, utilizing a variety of practices and cultivating, for example, "thought detached from the senses."

In anthroposophy as a conception of the world, we definitely see the first of the aforementioned components at work. Thus, we find the same misunderstandings regarding the law of karma and a transmigration reduced to "reincarnation," the same "evolutionalist" superstitions, the same "cruising" through planets reincarnated on other planets, through spirits, angels, races, and bodies both subtle and non-subtle, and so forth, that we have critiqued in theosophism. Indeed, the mesh of a historic-providential determinism draws together here even more tightly: the "evolution of the world" is a fateful, predetermined, and supreme law. Every occurrence, every formation, and every transformation finds its raison d'être and its naturalistic-rationalistic explanation within itself—the future and the past are displayed on the screen of history as in a film, which already exists in all its scenes and can be seen with "clairvoyance" before it has been projected. Just as Hegel developed a history of the world from the intrinsic necessity of the "Idea," so, too, does Steiner; however, in contrast to Hegel, Steiner does not attempt a logical deduction, but gives us a kind of natural science of the spirit, a description of mere facts that succeed one after the other—facts to which man supposedly owes his present physical and spiritual state, preordained, in its turn, by other "evolutionary" forms that await it in the future, and so forth. Thus, compared to theosophism, there are far fewer traces to be found here of any opposition between history and superhistory, between temporality and eternity, between natural order and supernatural order. The category of time despotically dominates everything. Steiner, more than the theosophists, strives to enclose every purpose for man in history, to exclude any truly transcendent possibility, to channel all natural and extranormal energies in the direction of man—indeed, not even of man, but of the human collective, of humanity. The substitution of the term anthroposophy for the term theosophy already expresses the clearer awareness of this intention: instead of other "surpassed" wisdoms, such as the teaching that the truth is given to us in knowledge (sophia) of the "divine" (theos), here it is instead the knowledge (sophia) of man (anthropos—hence "anthroposophy") that will be the focus, and the beginning and the end of the new wisdom announced by Steiner.

The demon of Western "humanism," therefore, also dominates the Steinerian "spiritualism" from the roots up. But what is unusual is that Christianism works as its accomplice. Has not the Christian revelation declared that "God became a man"? Today we have seen all too much of this truth, albeit neither in a Christian nor a Steinerian sense. In any case, we see how it is that Christ might be grafted onto anthroposophic evolutionism. In contrast to the Catholic teaching, Steiner holds that the descent of Christ was not an arbitrary determination of divine grace, such that even in some other historical moment the redemption of sinful humanity might have occurred. The descent of Christ instead occurred in an exact, predestined moment, and an entire evolution—which was not only human, but cosmico-planetary, mineral, vegetal, and animal—was oriented toward it and had been busy slowly elaborating a body (with its various "subtle" components) suitable for making the incarnation of that "Solar Logos" (that is, Christ) possible.¹ Now that this incarnation has occurred, the divine is no longer "outside" of man, but within man himself, and therefore anthroposophy is substituted for theosophy. Thus, with the coming of Christ, the spiritual man is supposedly born. Before this there would have only been an impersonal, dreamlike, and diffuse spirituality: man was like a *medium* and had his spirituality, indeed even his self, outside of himself, in deity. Today, he has it instead within himself, so that a self-initiation might take place, an autonomous, lucid, purely individual method of internal development. Hence the idea of a modern initiation—but also called "rosicrucian"²—that would be counterposed to everything which came before; and anthroposophy in its practical aspect seeks to steer one toward this initiation. For Steiner, the event at Golgotha split the very spiritual history of the world into two parts. Moreover, the passive submission to the influence of the ideas of the Christian creed is clear here, and in this respect anthroposophy finds itself down below theosophism, which had seen in Jesus simply one of the various "great initiates" or divine envoys. For Steiner, on the other hand, Christ (albeit demoted from the "son of God" to the "Solar Logos") is—exactly as in the Christian religion—an unrepeatable figure, and his appearance is a unique and decisive occurrence for the entirety of universal history.

---

1. Steinerian evolution does not even let rest in peace those real or mythical personalities who were so clearly oriented toward the supernatural, such as Buddha, Zarathustra, Hermes, and so forth and so on; Buddha, for example, was supposedly not at all liberated from the world into nirvāna—even he, an instrument of the "evolution of humanity," evidently contributed to the preparation of Christianity, and his mission was to produce certain forces that would be reincarnated in Jesus. In general, anthroposophy adheres, *mutatis mutandis,* to that conceit of Christianity whereby it is imagined that all the pre-Christian religions were but preparations and "prefigurations."
2. It is hardly worth noting that Steiner's reference to the Rosicrucians is as gratuitous and illegitimate as the one made by a certain degree of Scottish Rite Masonry and by various contemporary fraternities. The true Rosicrucians were one of those initiatic groups that already "withdrew" from the West before the French Revolution, having ascertained the situation of the age.

Judged in terms of reality, the anthroposophic speculations appear to be mental constructions, substantially similar to those that, starting with Hegel, the academic current of the "philosophy of history" has produced so as to attain the best brutalization of whomever follows it and swears by it. One may "believe" or not—everything remains as it was before, apart from the limitations pertaining to a conception, such as the historicist conception in general. But whoever is capable of carrying out a kind of purification of the aforementioned anthroposophic views of historical temporality might come upon something valid. We would then find, in the abstract, a scheme fit to three stages, which we already have used as the point of reference for our critical considerations: the stage of a prepersonal spirituality ("pre-Christic," as Steiner calls it), characterized by the lack of active and visionary-mediumistic self-knowledge; the stage of the ordinary personality, which, however, in feeling itself distinctly and in seeing clearly what surrounds it, already announces the principle of true spirit (this is, in Steiner, the gift of the "self" that the "Christ Jesus" supposedly made to men); finally, the stage of a superconsciousness and a superpersonality (the "conscious initiation" of the anthroposophists). Steiner's error, due to his succumbing to a mindset prevalent in his day, is to have "historicized" and collectivized these stages, to have materialized them, making of them "evolutive" stages of "humanity," rather than seeing in them the permanent possibility of every historical point and every single consciousness. From here, in his "philosophy of civilization," things arise that have no place in heaven or on earth: things that leave one speechless, a true wilderness of falsifications, deformations, aprioristic enormities— things even worse than those that Hegel perpetrated so as to fit everything into his preestablished dialectic of thesis, antithesis, and synthesis, *an sich, für sich, an sich und für sich* [in itself, for itself, in and of itself]. It is naturally the ancient pre-Christian world that suffers most from this, since it is not authorized—given the verdict of Steinerian clairvoyance—to possess any form of truly individual and active spirituality. Steiner effectively denied any true understanding to that world, and thus to the East as well, and if someone truly followed him in this, the result would be a much more serious and systematic disavowal of spiritual fonts than is the case in theosophism.

Is it possible to separate this inferior part from the rest of the anthroposophical doctrine? For of the majority of its adherents, this no easy task. They swear in *verba magistri* [allegiance to the master], and woe betide anyone who tampers with but a single detail of master's doctrine. On the other hand, it is all too natural that at a certain level it is more comfortable to settle for the vision of cosmic evolution and all the rest, than to dedicate oneself practically to the method of "individual initiation." But, doctrinally, the distinction can be made, in the sense that one can recognize that here or there Steiner has provided some practical teachings and valid criteria for discrimination (except that they are neither new, nor do they solely belong to the post-Christian West, as he supposes), which might be utilized fully independently from the rest of it: from "evolution"; from reincarnation; from Christ, who now operates in us after having acted magically on the "soul of the earth" through the blood he shed at Golgotha; from the ideals of mystical collectivity and the inevitable "love" that here becomes even the very purpose of the present cycle on Earth; and so forth, and so on.[3] It is also worth recognizing the fact that Steiner indicated methods based on a solid internal preparation: however, one must not entertain too many illusions as to the scope of these methods in the context of "individual initiation"; that is, self-initiation, a path by which the simple human forces of the individual would be sufficient unto themselves, and the connection

---

3. The works of Steiner that can be mentioned for this positive aspect are *Wie erlangt man Erkenntnisse über die höheren Welten?* [1904; English edition: *Knowledge of the Higher Worlds and Its Attainment,* trans. George Metaxa (New York: Anthroposophic Press, 1947)] and, in part, *Initiaten-Bewusstsein* [1927; English edition: *Initiate Consciousness: Truth and Error in Spiritual Research,* trans. Olin D. Wannamaker (New York: Anthroposophic Press, 1928)], also translated into Italian and published by Laterza under the title *L'Iniziazione e Coscienza di Iniziato.*

to a regular initiatic "chain" or organization would be superfluous.

Steiner comprehends the fundamental point and expresses it clearly: it is necessary above all that man fully realize the power of clear and distinct perception, logical thought, and objective vision. He recognizes the antithesis between initiatic spirituality and mediumship. The Steinerian ideal is an exact science of the supersensible: a vision of superreality as clear, distinct, and objective as that which the experimental natural sciences offer of sensible reality. An anthroposophical saying has it that religion must become "scientific" in this sense of clarity and consciousness, while science must become "religious"; that is, it must be capable of embracing and providing in real terms the same spiritual or "divine" order that usually is the sole object of devout sentiments, dogmatic formulae, and confused mystical or ecstatic experiences. Correct, too, is the requirement that mere intellectual work does not suffice for this, but a transformation of one's own attitudes, one's reactions, and one's general conduct of life is necessary. In this connection Steiner is even able to overcome moralism, recognizing that the value of certain almost universal moral precepts is, for the disciple, only instrumental: these are the means for objectively forming the interior man and the organs of a higher consciousness.

If, therefore, one might pay tribute in positive recognition to Steiner's "spiritual science" as an *idea*, in terms of its content and as a practical anthroposophic example, one must conclude that Steiner preaches well but practices rather badly. To swallow whole the aforementioned theosophistic panorama as a "spiritual science"—though that panorama finds absolutely no reflection in the great traditional views of the East and the West—this is something one cannot demand of even the strongest stomach. Moreover, as far as the formal side of the exposition goes, such as the contents of the book *Geheimwissenschaft* [An Outline of Occult Science], there is the aggravating element of an attitude that is germane not to spiritual science but to naturalistic science. As we have said, Steiner simply recounts. He gives a kind of chronicle of a fabulous and spirited cosmic tale, precisely as a physicist would relate the phases of the material evolution of the planets. To be sure, we are dealing with the replacement of "thinking" with "seeing": but the "seeing" of a true spiritual science is an intellectual seeing, thus a seeing that is simultaneously a comprehending, not a seeing as a mere observation of facts and phenomena that pass before us in the same way as those of the sensible world. This holds even when the whole is not reducible to a system of digressions, fantasies, and hallucinations. Steiner speaks continuously of the necessity to form new organs for oneself, new senses beyond the physical ones, and does not realize that this is, in and of itself, unimportant. Will we call a blind man less spiritual for the simple fact that he has one sense fewer than other men? It is less a matter of creating this or that clairvoyant or clairaudient faculty so as to perceive other orders of phenomena than of an internal transformation, for which one no longer only "sees" but understands; one no longer perceives "phenomena" but rather the meanings and symbols of spiritual essences.[4] It therefore must be said that in the anthroposophic "science-spiritual" complex, even in its attitude, we are dealing much more with science, in the externalist-natural sense, than spirit; and yet the correct idea that emerged is immediately neutralized, not to say discredited.

Moving on to practice, anthroposophy has re-elaborated certain theosophistic conceptions regarding the doctrine of the various "bodies" of man. The positive contribution of such views is to make one understand that man is considerably more complex a being than those men believe who make him appear simplistically as a soul-body dyad. No ancient tradition has ever taught anything of the sort. In one way or another, whether explicitly or by way of symbols, intermediate forms and energies that exist between pure spirituality and pure

---

[4]. This is the opposition that runs between what the scholastics called *intellectual intuition* and *clairvoyance,* which furnishes nothing more than mere "visions" and does not have, at bottom, any truly spiritual value.

corporality, between the immaterial and the material, have always been acknowledged.

Theosophism took up theories of this sort, but it immediately materialized them; it therefore spoke of various "bodies," not troubling itself that the term *body* would already lead to misunderstandings; it discoursed on them anyway, as one might talk about on the various substances of a compound. For the theosophists, the number of the "bodies" generally amounts to seven: the physical body; the etheric (or "vital") body; the astral (of the instincts, passions, and emotions) body; the mental (intellectual dynamisms) body; and then three other "bodies," designated roughly with Sanskrit expressions (manas, buddhi, and ātmā), corresponding to higher states. According to the theosophistic mode of seeing, these "bodies" supposedly exist all together in every being: the clairvoyant differentiates them into a hierarchy in ever subtler forms, which proceed from matter to the Divinity.

Anthroposophy takes up this theory and sometimes does not merely leave it in its materialistic-classificatory form but materializes it even more—as when it teaches that "higher bodies" exist objectively "outside" (?) of the physical body, that in sleep the astral and mental bodies "depart" (?) from the same, and so forth—treating these "bodies" precisely as bodies; that is, as things, whereas they are nothing but modalities of being. But at other times it is finally able to see things sub specie interioritatis,[5] so that something of the correct view comes out of it. As a point of reference, it posits the completed self of a normal modern man who has reached the point of consciously possessing and controlling all his mental processes ("mental body"). In contrast to this self, there are, like a zone that glides slowly into the subconscious, the three lower "bodies": first and foremost the passions, tendencies, and emotions that, however much they might be superficially illuminated by the consciousness,

---

5. [Latin: "under the sign of interiority," i.e., "from an interior point of view"]

largely escape the control of the self (astral body); then those already subconscious psychic-vital complexes, connected to the nervous and glandular system, which we have already mentioned (etheric body); and finally, the pure unconscious of the physical form, along with the forces that manifest themselves in it and prop it up. These are the concrete facts. The first rational development of the anthroposophic view is to be found in the relationship between these three inferior "bodies" (astral, etheric, and physical) with three states: dream, sleep, and apparent death. The second development is in the relationship of the superior "bodies" (those designated with the Sanskrit terms) with three tasks and spiritual conquests that the "occult disciple" can propose to himself in relation precisely to the three states of reduced consciousness, to which the three kinds of body are made to correspond. In other words, the "occult disciple" can propose to reach a self-consciousness and a direct dominion not just in the order of his thoughts (mental body) but also in his emotional and instinctive life, in the vital energies and the very potencies that are behind the biochemical and physical processes of his body. The three states of spiritual illumination and of superconsciousness that permit this are surely nothing other than the three superior "bodies," badly divulged in the doctrine of the theosophists. Such bodies would stand, however, in direct relation to that destruction of the unconscious of which we spoke in our critique of psychoanalysis.

Such a view as this has the merit of somewhat dematerializing things and of indicating at the same time a scheme, the objective stages of the path to transcendent realization. The distance that already separates these horizons, no matter how encumbered it might be with rubble, must be cleared of psychoanalysis and psychic research. And one can also specify the meaning and the scope of the problem proposed in the terms indicated above. We have said that the I of which the ordinary modern man concretely speaks, with reference to an immediate datum of consciousness, is not any longer the soul as the simple and incorporeal substance of the scholastic philosophers nor the incorruptible ātmā of Vedānta. It is rather the functional unit of a complex of mental processes, tendencies, habits, memories, and so forth, which is more or less at the mercy of other functions and forces; one may little act on these things, since ordinary consciousness and the "will" would not have any idea how to reach them. The body contains these forces, at the same time giving the soul a basis in the sense of its personal unity, which it thus conditions. Therefore, in considering this bodily conditioned personality, it might be said that the soul, in a certain sense, though not being solely the product of the body, is born and dies with the latter. We therefore admit the possibility of the process described above, which extends downward by degrees, toward the corporeal, self-consciousness, and possession. It is clear that with such a process the I would control the very physical and "vital" conditions of the personality. This is the same process as the exploration and dominion of the deep strata of being, of which we have spoken in reference to psychoanalysis, and which in hermetic symbolism corresponds to the formula *Visita interiora Terrae rectificando invenies occultum lapidem veram medicinam.*[6]

If anthroposophy on the one hand evokes these views of an ancient wisdom, on the other hand we see it almost repent of this, returning to its evolutionistic obsessions. Let this lone observation suffice: the three superior "bodies," rather than being understood as atemporal and superhistorical states to which one might aim only exceptionally, become three achievements that the whole of humanity, duly guided by archangels and other beings of the sort, will realize in time on three future planets, which follow the present one as the reincarnations of the "soul of the Earth"!

Nor is this all. At one point in his book *Knowledge of the Higher Worlds and Its Attainment,* Steiner declares that during the spiritual

---

6. [Latin: "Visit the interior of the Earth; by rectifying, you will find the hidden stone, the true medicine."]

development of the "occult disciple," he will find himself at a threshold. He will be presented; that is, with the possibility of putting his acquired faculties in the service of human evolution or of retiring to transcendent worlds. For Steiner, those who opt for the second alternative belong more or less to the "Black Lodge," and never will a "true" initiate have anything to do with them.⁷ This is, once again, a clear indicator of the intellectual level of such currents. Even indulging their predilection for "altruistic" concerns of this sort, it must be said they have not even the slightest clue that to roll up one's sleeves and to put oneself directly to work for humanity is not the only way of aiding it; that whoever truly realizes transcendent states and makes of them his stable residence, transforms himself by that fact alone into a mighty hearth of energies, much more efficacious than those of the imaginary anthroposophic and Rosicrucian initiates who "renounce," dedicating themselves to the service of humanity.

But yet again and speaking more generally, it is the evolutionist error here that constitutes the touchstone for metaphysical insensitivity, for the lack of a true sense of the supernatural and the eternal. Traditional teaching has never recognized anything of the sort. We do know well (because we have ourselves had the amusing experience of it) that there are disciples of Steiner who, when one fails to find any evidence for the whole system in traditional teaching, have the impudence to retort by asking what authorizes us to say that their master has not seen more deeply than all the "great initiates" that preceded him; just as another follower has presented his para-Steinerian ramblings as something that "goes beyond the yoga, beyond the Zen" of the tradition. The anthroposophic infatuation goes that far! But as to this particular issue: according to traditional teaching, over and above any "evolution," there stands a cycle—the Hindu theory

---

7. It is possible that the basis for this view is to be found in certain popular expositions, taken literally, of Mahāyāna Buddhism, in which the bhodisattva renounces nirvāna and gives himself to the aid of the world—almost as if nirvāna were a house that might enter or exit, rather than a state that, once achieved, is inalienable.

of the kalpas, the classical concept of the "cosmic years," or aeons. The cyclical conception is the nearest to the supreme conception because, as was emphasized by Plato, Plotinus, and Proclus, cyclical time makes itself into a kind of image and symbol of eternity; hence, in the hierarchy of the degrees of consciousness, this conception is the final limit that separates one from the destruction of the cosmic mirage, and from the realization of an absolutely supertemporal order. And it might be said that the individual is bound to the cyclical law materially as well, in a kind of "eternal return," which, however, has nothing to do with reincarnation, so long as he is not capable of this leap, which is identified with "awakening" and with the "Great Liberation"; a leap in a perpendicular direction—a vertical direction—with respect to the horizontal direction of every temporality and every becoming.

What are we to say, standing before horizons such as these, regarding the obsessions of "evolutionism" and of the "development of humanity"...

These points will suffice to form a comprehensive idea of the scope and nature of anthroposophy. Much more than the other currents we have already considered, there is an essential part in it that is merely the personal construction of its founder, who, as we have seen, has clearly been acted upon by patterns proper to the Western mentality: the Christian myth; an attitude that, despite everything, remains naturalistic, along the lines of a "science of nature"; evolutionism reelaborated into a philosophy of history; and a rationalistic system. Regarding the fantastical panoramas of reincarnation, anthropogenesis, and Steinerian cosmogenesis, these often recall theosophism, from which Steiner took a great deal, despite the fact that he makes an appeal to personal clairvoyance. Thus, we can clearly see the contagion of the same influences that constituted the occult background of theosophism. The demand for a science of the supersensible (if understood on the level of "gnosis") and a conscious method opposed to mysticism and mediumship is something we should judge positively, but, as we have seen, it has practically remained at the level of a demand. The ideal of an "active" initiation might be valid, within certain limits and under certain conditions, in particular by setting aside the fixation that, through a simple system of individual "exercises," without a higher influence and through a "self-initiation," one can attain something essential and serious, and that one is somehow sheltered from those dangers from which the "master" himself, Steiner, clearly did not escape—insofar as one can speak effectively of his "occult" experiences.[8]

The presence of these positive points in anthroposophy, alongside a formal systematic apparatus, might perhaps partly explain the unusual fact that anthroposophy has been entertained even by persons who—unlike the majority of the theosophists—are endowed with a certain, not insignificant, level of intellectual culture. We have said "partly explain," however, because it is incomprehensible how they have apparently considered the errors in Steinerianism to be nonexistent—errors that are so enormous one can touch them with one's hands; not to mention Steinerianism's foundation in fantasies that often have something delirious about them—all of which, being

---

8. Regarding "clairvoyance," those who claim to possess it are careful not to give any positive proof for this. Rather than wandering through the "Akashic Chronicle" and referring to all manner of cosmic sagas and faraway evolutionary stages, both past and future, they would do well, in the first place, to give accreditation to their claimed faculty through some banal but verifiable fact. It is said of Steiner, who sees into the cosmic aeons and the occult future of the universe and humanity with his clairvoyance, that he did not so much as notice that his center, the Goetheanum, was going up in flames. Whenever such persons have dared some verifiable prediction, things have gone badly—like when the anthoposophists predicted that if man were to leave the earth's atmosphere, he would be disintegrated, he would be annihilated by tremendous cosmic occult forces; meanwhile, for example, human voyages to the moon are by now taking on an almost touristic character. Regarding the fixation with "self-initiation," it would be difficult to nominate a single anthroposophist who owes one of his exceptional qualities to the corresponding "exercises" rather than possessing it already from the outset.

inseparable from the whole, ought to suffice to make one decidedly reject it despite everything. These adherents must therefore also be subject to particular suggestions that generate something like intellectual scotomata, those spots in the field of vision that pathologically obstruct a portion of one's perception.

VI

Neo-mysticism–Krishnamurti

In relation to the distinctions that occupy us here, it might be useful to briefly consider the "mystic" phenomenon, in its broadest sense. The term *mystic* originates from the world of the ancient Mysteries, but subsequently it was used to designate an orientation of religious man who seeks to have an inner experience of the object of his faith, the limit to this experience being constituted by what is called ecstasy. So far as the latter is concerned, one has proceeded to a generalization on the basis of which the "mystical" has become synonymous with a form of enthusiastic identification that is no longer restricted to the religious sphere in the proper and positive sense.

This is not the place to investigate the character of religious mysticism, which moreover includes many variants.[1] For our purposes it will suffice to return to the summary distinction of two attitudes in the face of the "spiritual" and to the two modalities of its experience. It might be said that "mysticism" is characterized by its pronounced subjective, irrational, and "ecstatic" element. The experience has worth essentially for its content of sensation and for the rapture that unites it. Thus, in general, every demand for lucid control, for clarity, is ruled out. The acting principle is more the "soul" than the "spirit."

---

[1]. On this, see our book *The Bow and the Club,* trans. Sergio Knipe (London: Arktos, 2018), and the essay "Esotericism and Christian Mysticism," in Evola and the Ur Group, *Introduction to Magic,* vol. 3.

One might indicate the state of "intellectual intuition" as being the opposite of the mystical state; the former is like a fire that consumes the "mystical" form of an experience, objectively gathering from it, through clarity and not as "revelation," its content of ineffable transcendence and submergence. It is, moreover, active, just as mystical experience is passive and "ecstatic."

It is generally a principle of the traditional wisdom that in order to know the essence of a thing, one must become that thing. "One knows only that with which one identifies" by removing the law of a duality that governs everyday experience. But precisely in this regard the aforementioned distinction must kept firmly in mind between a lucid mastery of experience leading up to a clear superrational perception, as opposed to the act of losing oneself within the experience. Therefore, one cannot identify a true "noetic" character for the mystical experience as such. What Schelling said in evaluating similar attitudes holds for this as well: what happens, happens to the mystic; he does not know how to firmly place his object before himself, he does not know how to make it reflect in himself as in a clear mirror. Seized by the "ineffable," rather than mastering the object, he himself becomes a "phenomenon"; that is, something which is in need of explanation.[2]

Having spoken of "ecstasy," it is necessary for our purposes to indicate phenomena that, although having no bearing on religious and transcendent horizons, repeat the character of "ecstasy" on other planes. In this connection, we might take up an order of ideas presented by Paul Tillich as a means of orienting ourselves.[3]

Tillich notes that in the physical world, every reality exists already

---

2. F. W. J. Schelling, *Zur Geschichte der neueren Philosophie* (ed. K. F. A. Schelling; *SW* [collected works edition of 1856–1861], sec. 1, vol. 10), 187–89. [English edition: *On the History of Modern Philosophy,* trans. Andrew Bowie (Cambridge: Cambridge University Press, 1994).]

3. Paul Tillich, *Das Dämonische: Ein Beitrag zur Sinndeutung der Geschichte* (Tübingen: Mohr, 1926).

with its own form and its own unity; form and unity are visibly etched into being and as being, the reality of things. This is not so in the interior world. That which in this world corresponds to the form and the unity presented by material things—the personality, the I—is an invisible principle that tends to be fulfilled, and which, insofar as it fulfills itself, to that extent counterposes itself to being, because it tends toward independence from being and toward freedom.

But the following can occur: that, as a stronger and swifter current bursting upon another weaker one might absorb it and transport it in its own path, so, in certain special conditions, a given or ideal object might provoke in man a kind of rupture in the direction of the principal tendency, which ceases to direct itself toward its natural end, concentrating itself instead onto this object. The object thus provides a center, and so the process of internal formation is interrupted. This is the "mystical" identification with an object: it provides a way for the personality to dissolve and to effectively depart from itself. It is therefore like a liberation and a destruction at the same time. That which transports also grants one a sense of liberation, awakening a higher and seductive sensation of the vital force, unbound from the form.

One then understands how there might be a mysticism of profane things. Fundamentally, any object whatsoever can produce a mystical identification and a correlating degree of "ecstatic" rapture—an enthusiasm that, moreover, can also be creative. The fundamental structure remains the same. The fact that the mystical object is no longer a divinity but an ideology, a political party, a given personality, or even a sport or one of the "profane religions" of our day, is not indifferent from the point of view of the nature of the influences to which the "mystical" state allows access, though from the objective point of view it does not constitute a disparity. There is always a spiritual destruction, the substitution of a form and unity which are not that of the subject, along with the subsequent sense of release, détente, and ecstatic animation.

A consideration of the mystical phenomenon extending into these areas would take us very far afield: once more to psychoanalysis and through to the psychology of the masses, to the varieties of the new collectivism and the techniques of subversion and demagogy. We will limit ourselves here to a few indications.

Psychoanalytic practice officially recognizes and desires the phenomenon of the so-called transference. In this, the psychoanalyst, as has been said, comes in a certain way to substitute himself for the subject, in the sense that he provides a point of reference to discharge and liberate the subject from the tensions that rend his personality, to help the subject "vomit up" everything that has accumulated and been repressed in his subconscious. Now, apart from any possible therapeutic results that might follow from this, the counterpart to it from the spiritual point of view might be precisely the abandonment and interruption of tension, leading toward a true integration of the personality, of which we have spoken. Indeed, it is interesting that such "identifications" can be accompanied by the phenomenon of ambivalence: love that intermingles with hatred, or inverts into hatred. This phenomenon is significant because here we perceive, in smaller dimensions, the sense of what often occurs in a magnified way in collective phenomena of transference and "ecstasy." Even these can lead to "ambivalence," because the subconscious sentiment of intimate violation might assert itself as hatred after the transportation and exhilarating rapture aroused by the liberating identification. Even recent history shows us characteristic examples of this.

The technique of demagoguery generally rests on a transference on a grand scale and on "ecstatic" liberation. The explanatory hypotheses of the psychoanalysts, which here draw upon a reviviscence of the experiences of savages (the supposed ancestors of the whole of humanity), in turn interpreted sexually, are nothing but rubbish. There remains, however, the framework of the transference and of the projection of one's own center outside of oneself, with the concomitant and here quite visible phenomenon of an enormous psychic-vital potential that passes to the free state. Wherever demagogic leaders, adopting their "charismatic" character, are able to produce a mystical identification, there arise sweeping mass movements that cannot be stopped and in which the individual believes he is living a higher life. Freed from his own I, happy to transfer to others even his capacity to think, judge, and command, he might effectively manifest gifts of courage, sacrifice, and heroism that go beyond those available to any normal person, and even to himself, when he is detached from the whole. In modern times—perhaps from the French Revolution onward—such phenomena have presented a sinister character, because those who determine and guide these collective currents for a certain period of time are frequently themselves more or less the instruments of dark forces.

One particular case of "mysticism" is constituted by the messianic phenomenon. After all, the Messiah-as-savior is nothing but an unconscious ideal presented to the individual as realized in another being, which "ecstatically" diverts the forces of the personality from the realization of their ends. Even in cases such as this the phenomenon of transference is produced, with a syncope of the process of formation and integration of the I, and with the subsequent aforementioned discharge or liberation (here, the atmosphere of liberation that is formed around the Messiah).

Naturally, one cannot exclude the case of superior personalities whose forces might graft themselves onto those who are extended out in "messianic" expectation—so as not to alter, but to complete, the process of internal formation, thus guiding these individuals toward themselves, toward the conquest of their form. This case is as real as that of an effective elevation of the individual "through participation," when he consciously forms part of a traditional hierarchy centered on genuine representatives of spiritual authority.

In a reduced form, the messianic phenomenon is all too common in our day: wherever one looks, the search is on for gurus or those who are presumed to be such. In the majority of spiritualistic currents, when it is not the strangeness and fascination of "occult" doctrines that attracts these souls, it is specifically a vague messianic desire, which is concentrated upon the leaders of sects and schools, and surrounds them with the miraculous halo of "master" and "adept." In theosophism, this phenomenon has assumed a conscious and systematic character. Convinced of the necessity for a new "World Teacher," theosophism dedicated itself to preparing for his advent, creating a global association to that end—the Order of the Star in the East—which, according to the oracle of Annie Besant, finally designated a young Hindu as suitable to incarnate the long-awaited entity.

We are referring to Jiddu Krishnamurti—the same Krishnamurti who, moreover, having come of age and having gained self-awareness, in an indisputable sign of character and in a totally unexpected turn of events, resolutely took a new direction, the ambiguity of which was itself characteristic of the new spiritualism. And thus it is worth our while to briefly examine it here.

In the campground of Ommen in Holland in 1929, Krishnamurti dissolved the Order of the Star in the East, declaring at the same time its unmitigated credo. Here are some of his words:

> I have only one purpose: to make man free, to urge him toward freedom, to help him to break away from all limitations, for that alone will give him eternal happiness, will give him the unconditioned realization of the self.
>
> . . .
>
> You are accustomed to authority, or to the atmosphere of authority, which you think will lead you to spirituality. You think and hope that another can, by his extraordinary powers—a miracle—transport you to this realm of eternal freedom which is Happiness.

> ...
>
> You want to have your own gods—new gods instead of the old, new religions instead of the old, new forms instead of the old—all equally valueless, all barriers, all limitations, all crutches. ... [Y]ou have been preparing for me for eighteen years, when I say all these things are unnecessary, when I say that you must put them all away and look within yourselves for the enlightenment, for the glory, for the purification, and for the incorruptibility of the self, not one of you is willing to do it. There may be a few, but very, very few. So why have an organization?
>
> ...
>
> I maintain that Truth is a pathless land, and you cannot approach it by any path whatsoever, by any religion, by any sect.
>
> ...
>
> But those who really desire to understand, who are looking to find that which is eternal, without beginning and without an end, will walk together with a greater intensity, will be a danger to everything that is unessential, to unrealities, to shadows.[4]

In and of itself, this would have been a salutary reaction, not only against theosophistic messianism but also, more generally, against the extroverted attitude about which we have recently spoken. However, two points must be emphasized.

The first is that, despite these declarations by Krishnamurti, things changed very little; as before, there were large-scale conventions and gatherings of his enthusiasts, who have had him as their focal point; a "Krishnamurti Foundation" was created, which also proposed the acquisition of a fund in England to establish, according to the wishes of Krishnamurti himself, a center for the diffusion of his ideas; books came out with titles like *L'instructeur du*

---

4. "The Dissolution of the Order of the Star in the East," speech given by J. Krishnamurti, Ommen, 1929.

monde: Krishnamurti (by L. Réhault), *Krishnamurti, le miroir des hommes* (by Y. Achard), *Krishnamurti: Psychologue de l'ère nouvelle* (by R. Linssen), and so forth. Thus, the "myth" was reconstituted; Krishnamurti continued to act as "master" in his capacity as the herald of a new vision of life. It might be objected that this is not quite accurate, since the new Krishnamurti does not claim to take the place of the individual but instead wishes to incite him to grasp a deeper consciousness of himself in an autonomous way, and thus presents himself as an example and acts only as a "spiritual catalyst" for whomever goes to listen to him. Now, something of the kind could be conceived in the case of small and select centers, like certain Hindu ashrams and some initiatic groups in which a superior personality can effectively create an almost magnetic atmosphere, without any preaching. It is rather difficult, however, to conceive of such a thing when one starts holding conferences in every part of the profane world and for a wide audience, even in theaters and universities, most recently having even excited the snobbish interest of a public standing between the intellectual and the mundane. The least that can be said is that Krishnamurti has lent himself to all this, fulfilling the usual role of a "master" even if he was the one to proclaim that there was no need to seek a master.

The second point to note is that, despite everything, Krishnamurti has presented a teaching, a doctrine, which has remained more or less the same from the beginning up until today, and which is characterized by very dangerous ambiguities.

To liberate Life from the self—this is basically what Krishnamurti proclaims. Truth for him signifies Life; and Life signifies Happiness, Purity, Eternity, and various other things, too, all given nearly as synonyms. Moreover, to liberate Life and to liberate the self are also almost synonymous, because Krishnamurti fundamentally insists on the distinction between a false personal self and an eternal self, the latter of which then becomes one with Life and, in it, with the principle of all things. Man has imposed upon this self, which is to say,

Neo-mysticism—Krishnamurti

upon Life, every kind of limitation: beliefs, preferences, atavistic habits of the heart and mind, attachments, conventions, religious scruples, fears, preconceptions, theories, constraints, and exclusivities of every sort. All these things are barriers that must be blown sky-high to find oneself, to realize what Krishnamurti calls the "individual uniqueness." But as for this "self"—given that it is equivalent to the "self of all," to a realization of "absolute union with all things which brings to an end the sense of separation,"[5] is it in any way distinct from something like the Bergsonian élan vital or the object of the very latest, more or less pantheistic or naturalistic religions of the irrational and of becoming? With what justification can one call it the "self"? And is what properly can be called the self in Krishnamurti perhaps not just a negative principle in the end, a superstructure created by prejudices, fears, and conventions, that suffocates the Life what alone is real: exactly as in psychoanalysis and irrationalism?

Krishnamurti says nothing to help us understand what sense his talk of a "self," of an "individual uniqueness," finally has, when perfection and the goal are conceived of as mere undifferentiated life, protean—similar, according to his own words, to running water that always going forward and never is still; to flame deprived of definite form, labile, mutable from moment to moment, and thus indescribable, not circumscribable by anything, indomitable.[6] To grant to Life, on this basis, the attribute of Happiness, of free and ecstatic joy after any conflict is overcome, when no limit, no dam constrains it any longer, so that it might manifest and expand itself effortlessly, as pure spontaneity[7]—all of this is certainly possible. It is not possible to speak at the same time of incorruptibility, eternity, and true

---

5. *Krishnamurti, Life in Freedom* (Ommen: Star, 1928), 22. [Wherever possible, citations have been revised to refer to the original English text. In cases where the corresponding English material could not be found, Evola's references to the Italian translation, *La Vita Liberata* (Trieste: Artim, 1931), have been retained.]
6. *Krishnamurti, Life in Freedom*, 126, 82.
7. *Krishnamurti, La Vita Liberata*, 17.

liberation from the law of time. One cannot desire simultaneously that which becomes and that which is; that which changes perennially and that which is eternal and invariable. Every wisdom teaching has always indicated two regions, two states: world and supra-world; life and supra-life; fluency and flight of forms (saṃsāra), and permanency of the center. Krishnamurti blends the two things into a strange mixture, a kind of translation of the Hindu teaching ātma = brahman into the terms of the Western irrationalism of becoming. And to think that if this was indeed his deepest urgency, then he could have found in one of the traditions of his own country, Mahāyāna Buddhism, exactly what is needed to foresee in what sense something may actually exist that is superior to that opposition.

Krishnamurti is right in saying that man must abolish the distance between himself and the goal, becoming himself the goal,[8] no longer letting what alone is real, and in which he alone might possess and awaken himself, escape like a shadow situated between past and future: the present moment, that moment from which one never exits. This could indeed be a healthy reaction against the already indicted evolutionist illusion, which rejects in a time yet to come that fulfillment, which indeed can only be reached superhistorically, beyond time. But could it not also be the ecstatic reduction to mere instantaneity, the intoxication of a self-identification that destroys every distinction and every spiritual substantiality?

Expressing the principle that one should not depend on anything beyond oneself is not saying enough. It is also necessary to explain in what relationship one stands with this "self"; it is necessary to establish whether, with respect to this self, one is capable of dominion and of conscious, free direction, or else if one is incapable of differentiating oneself from that which, moment to moment, through pure spontaneity, the "Life in freedom" desires, actuates, and creates in us by electing such a state even as an ideal. If one then refers to the task

---

8. *Krishnamurti, Life in Freedom*, 62.

of giving oneself a form and a law in a personal being, it may even happen that on a certain level it is the limit that attests to freedom.

Krishnamurti speaks, it is true, of a kind of revolt that is illusory, because it expresses a concealed self-indulgence and impatience.[9] He says that to understand what he means by life in freedom, it is even necessary to establish liberation from life as a goal.[10] He observes that, if true perfection has no laws, this is not to be interpreted as a state of chaos but instead as a superiority to both law and chaos, as a convergence toward the germ of everything, whence arises every transformation and on which all things depend.[11] Finally, he asserts that we must create a miracle of order in this age of disorder and superstition—on the basis, however, of an internal order of our own and not on that of an authority, a fear, or a tradition.[12] But these suggestions, which in general might indicate a proper spiritual direction, are unconvincing given the spirit of the whole, and they are aided by no concrete indication of method and discipline because, as we have seen, Krishnamurti is opposed to every preestablished way: he thinks that there exist no paths for the realization of the Truth—that is, of Life—he thinks that a desire and an aspiration to happiness, which is so intense as to eliminate every particular object one by one, a limitless disindividualized love, not for a life, but for life itself, not for a given being, but for any given being, suffice to lead one to the goal.

Beyond this, the only path he indicates is the suspension of the automatisms of the self and of its contents, the arrest of the mental flow in a kind of spiritual "resolution of continuity." When there are no more barriers, when there is nothing left in us that is determined by the past and by what is already known, nothing that tends toward

---

9. In the journal *Ananda* I, 5.
10. Krishnamurti, *Life in Freedom*, 49.
11. In the appendix to *I. de Manzialy and Carlos Suarès, Saggio su Krishnamurti* (Genoa: Lattes, 1929), 83.
12. *Krishnamurti, Life in Freedom*, 53.

something—in this moment one might have consciousness of the true self, the apparition of what Krishnamurti sometimes mystically calls "the Unknown," as a spontaneous fact and with a sudden character, not as the "result" of a discipline, a method, and an initiative of the self, because it would be absurd if that same self might "suspend" and "kill" itself; every one of its efforts would come to enclose it in itself. After this hypothetical awakening the self disappears; it is no longer the self, it "becomes Life."

Besides so-called Christian quietism (in which, however, the concept of grace plays an essential role), these views would seem to show similarities with those of Taoism and one of the two principal schools of Zen, about which Krishnamurti seems to know very little, however, given that in a recent declaration he included Zen (together with Hinduism, the Christian method, and "all systems") among the "nonsense," repeating that a mind which operates on the basis of any given system or method "is incapable of comprehending what is true." In fact, the aforementioned similarities are only relative; Taoism and Zen have a background and historico-existential implications that are very different. Perhaps, however, one must take into consideration the excess, partly explainable, of a reaction against the cumbersome theosophistic edifice and its relative baggage of beliefs, "initiations," "exercises," of planes and "bodies," and so forth.

With regard to the confusions indicated above, it is also possible that these words betray Krishnamurti's thought and that the very nature of his personal experience, together with the lack of a solid doctrinal preparation, prevented more adequate formulations. However, these expressive confusions could also reflect the ambiguity of his own experience, with the result that no true orientation is given.

In general, the fact remains that Krishnamurti is characterized by the absolute and indiscriminate rejection of every authority (which could also be explained psychoanalytically, since Krishnamurti had to suffer a crass paternal despotism in his family), the negation of every tradition—thus, an individualism and an anarchism in the spiritual field, and also, at the same time, a kind of fierce bitterness toward that which is "self"; he puts the construction of the self, "that illusion which is the self," on the same plane as the "original sin" of which the Christians speak. Now, on this point something must be understood. The correct reference might be given by the initiatic maxim: "Ask yourself if it's you who have the I, or the I that has you." Undoubtedly, one must liberate oneself from a certain I; *the via remotionis* [way of remotion], the destruction of the "old man" (who, however, from another point of view is none other than the more recent "new man"), is a condition that has always been recognized for spiritual reintegration. But at the same time, one must underline a fundamental continuity and not insist on rigid antitheses. It would therefore be appropriate to refer to the symbolism of alchemical Hermeticism, which contemplates rather a cleansing in a "water of Life" that destroys and dissolves, cautioning however that the substances one might wash in such a bath must contain a grain of indestructible gold (the symbol of gold refers to the I principle) destined to reaffirm itself over that which it has dissolved and to reemerge in a superior potency; without which, the perfection of the "Great Work" is not achieved and one is arrested at the so-called albedo stage, which is under the sign of woman, indeed that of the dominion of the feminine over the masculine.[13] This scheme is much more oriented toward developing what is intermixed with the ambiguous ideas of Krishnamurti, in the order of which the negation of the self would derive from the fact that the self is supposed to be a static factor, an "inert packet" that opposes itself to that continuous change and continuous transformation which is supposed to constitute the ever new and incoercible essence of the Real.

On a more contingent plane, Krishnamurti ought not to have

---

13. On this hermetic teaching, cf. our work *The Hermetic Tradition: Symbols and Teachings of the Royal Art,* trans. E. E. Rehmus (Rochester, Vt.: Inner Traditions, 1995).

forgotten a maxim from the tradition of his own land, which, together with every other, he would like to cast overboard: "Let the sage with his wisdom not unsettle the mind of those who do not know." To go around proposing such ideas—which, if anything, are valid at the level of a genuine "liberated one"—to those deviants who, as modern men, already have more than enough incentives toward chaos and bad anarchy, is certainly not wise. The fact that spiritual and wisdom traditions, symbols, and ritual and ascetic structures are now often no longer anything more than surviving hollow forms, should not impede one from recognizing the positive function that they might have had and which they might have once again in the context of a more normal civilization, and with reference to the few who still know how to understand, for whom alone it is worthwhile to speak, and who might also devise an authority that is not at all a principle of repression or alienation. Such action might explode the superstructures, the supports and the barriers (often intended only to uphold) of whomever already feels capable of standing. Krishnamurti seems not to bother himself with this: he democratically incites everyone to the great revolt, not those few alone for whom it can be salutary and truly liberating.

It is significant enough that after 1968 one can observe a certain receptivity for Krishnamurti's ideas among the circles of those students of a many great universities who have become involved in "protest" and the rejection of all traditional systems and values, in the name of a "free attainment of one's being."[14] On the other hand, we have also observed the phenomenon of the "mystic beat," the beatnik attracted to Zen on account of its irrational elements and the almost nihilistic and iconoclastic negation that this initiatic doctrine presents. This confirms the troubling and distorted sense in which certain ideas might act today, if the plane that conditions all their legitimate formulations is not understood.

---

14. Robert Linssen, *Krishnamurti, psychologue de l'ère nouvelle* (Paris: Courrier du livre, 1971), 41. Another book titled *Krishnamurti et la révolte* (Paris: Le Cercle du livre, 1953) has also been written by André Niel.

Neo-mysticism—Krishnamurti

This allusion to certain circles of young Westerners who have also recently been attracted to the ideas of Krishnamurti also leads us to note a more general phenomenon, which, although it does not fall within the scope of "spiritualism," is likewise something along the lines of the "ecstatic" openings of which we have spoken, and which we have also observed in the phenomena of collective exhilaration.

In its clearest form, it is an orientation of the beat and hippy milieus of the most recent days, in which the impulse to evasion pushes toward openings obtained through various techniques of chaotic but sometimes even savage ecstasy. Here the use of drugs—LSD, marijuana, and hashish—is associated with jazz music, which takes up and exaggerates obsessive rhythms analogous to those of the evocatory and ecstatic ceremonies of blacks, sometimes adding "psychedelic" spectacles and dances to them, which, once again, recall those employed by savages as ecstatic techniques. Moreover, the intermingling of blacks in these circles is significant; furthermore, in jazz and bop, the most sought-after performers or improvisers, those who elicit the most frenetic enthusiasm, are themselves often also drug addicts, and in these gatherings, in which thousands of youths of both sexes convene, not infrequently even driven almost compulsively to sexual couplings, an atmosphere of collective obsession is established, which acts in individuals as a "liberation," just as in the other phenomena that we have considered.

We are here interested in considering all of this from the particular point of view of possible involuntary evocations of "lower" forces, as in the other cases. In fact, with regard to group phenomena, one would be inclined to see a similarity with the macumba and the cadombé, ceremonies that have continued in Brazil especially, and that consciously aim at provoking phenomena of possession. What must be emphasized is precisely that in the beats, in the hippies, and in any other individual who follows those profane rituals, the whole of this might not reduce itself to a simple ecstatic or frenetic liberation of a psychic underground alone; equally possible is the incorporation in him, too, of extra-individual "lower" forces, to which, by these very paths, a door has been opened. Certain criminal and absurd actions perpetrated at the margins of that world should be explained with reference to these forces rather than being attributed to the individual and to the simple influences of an ideology that negates every notion of guilt and therefore leads toward the plane of a truly "liberated" life.

VII

An Excursus on Esoteric Catholicism and "Integral Traditionalism"

We have already observed that one of the causes that has brought about the diffusion of neo-spiritualism is to be sought in the very character of the religion that has come to predominate in the West: Christianity, and Catholicism in particular. By presenting itself essentially as a theological-ritual system on the one hand, and as a devotional and moralizing practice on the other, it seems to offer very little to the need for the supernatural, as has been sensed by many persons in recent times, who as a result have been attracted to other doctrines that seem to promise something more.

Naturally, in such cases it is a matter of the supernatural being viewed as an experience, because Catholicism is otherwise characterized by the claim of having, more than any other religion, its own true theology of the supernatural, with reference to the conception of a personal God detached from the whole natural world and above this world. But these individuals had not gone seeking just any theology, and the theistic Catholic conception of God as a person seemed to be inadequate already from the start, since in principle it admitted only a "dual" relation, between "I" and "You," between the creature and the Creator. It is true that a Christian mysticism exists, too, and that Catholicism has had its monastic orders, which intended to cultivate a life of pure contemplation. But apart from the fact that this involved extremely specific vocations and that, moreover, in its removal of the distance deriving from the conception of God as a person, orthodoxy sees a dangerous heresy in the mystic life itself (thus strictly limiting the concept of a *unio mystica* [mystical union] or a "unitary life"), Catholicism of modern times, practically speaking, has emphasized all of this to an increasingly lesser degree. The "pastoral care of souls" has become its main preoccupation—not to speak of certain recent post–Vatican II revolutions in the direction of "modernization" and an "opening to the left," which have brought to the foreground mere social and socializing claims intermixed with notable shabby humanitarian, pacifist, and democratic ingredients. Everything that might have been characterized by a true transcendence has thus been sidelined, or at least it has not been encouraged in the least. From this has come the emptiness that, along with the crises of the modern world, has pressed many to seek elsewhere, in some form or other of contemporary neo-spiritualism, thus exposing themselves to the danger that dark forces might pervert their highest aspirations.

But in an objective analysis, certain things must be recognized.

If we are referring to early Christianity, it presents itself as a typical religion of the *kali yuga,* of the "dark age," which in the Western formulation of the same teaching corresponds to the "iron age," in which Hesiod believed that the destiny of the many would be "to extinguish themselves without glory in Hades." Christian preaching, which was originally addressed mainly to the masses of the dispossessed and to those lacking the tradition of the Roman ecumene, took as its presupposition a human type quite different from that which traditions of a higher level had in mind: a type who, so far as access to the divine went, was in desperate straits. Thus, this Christianity took the form of a tragic doctrine of salvation. The myth of "original sin" was affirmed, and the alternative was given between eternal salvation or eternal perdition—an alternative that was to be decided once and for all for everyone on this earth, and which was intensified by startling depictions of the afterlife and apocalyptic visions. This was a way of arousing in certain natures an extreme tension, which, especially if it was associated to the myth of Jesus as "Redeemer," might also bear its fruit—if not in this life, at least at the brink of death or in the afterlife, whenever these indirect means, working on human emotionality, succeeded in profoundly modifying the basal force of the human being.

In addressing itself to the broadest masses, subsequent Catholicism concealed, to a certain degree, the extremist crudity of these views, preoccupying itself with providing support for the human personality, whose supernatural destination it has recognized, and exercising a subtle action on its deeper being by means of the power of rite and sacrament.

In this context, one might point out the possible pragmatic, practical raison d'être for several aspects of Catholicism. Already certain principles of Catholic-Christian morality, such as humility, caritas, and the renunciation of one's will, if understood in the right way and in the right place, might have been formulated as a corrective teaching, in light of the closure and the individualistic self-affirmation toward which Western man often inclined. In view of the same limitation on the intellectual plane, and of the corresponding "humanization" of any capacity of vision, it might have been desirable to present in the form of a dogma, and through an authority, that which is situated above the common intellect, but which, at a higher level and at least for an *élite,* might instead become knowledge, direct evidence, and gnosis. It is possible that for a similar reason it was thought desirable to speak of "revelation" and of "grace": to underline the character of relative transcendence of the true supernatural with respect to the possibilities of a more or less fallen human type that would demonstrate itself ever more prone to all sorts of rationalistic and humanistic prevarications. In the end we have already mentioned that the relationships of simple "faith" in a theistic context, with the distance that these allow, while they are certainly limiting (for in more complete traditions they have always been addressed to the inferior strata of a civilization), might be such as to guarantee the integrity of the person—that individual who, amid pantheistic mysticisms and forays into the supersensible, as has been said repeatedly, can no longer find any solid ground.

These are the limitations of the Catholic doctrine, which have potentially positive aspects, useful with respect to the great mass of men, in light—let us repeat—of the negative conditions of the latest epoch, the "dark age." At this level, ideas like those of a Catholic such as Henri Massis, and also Jacques-Albert Cuttat, might be justified as well: Catholicism represents a defense of Western man, whereas any form of spirituality that is not dualistic-theistic (and in this respect he often delights in referring to the East) may represent a danger for him. But when one no longer keeps to that level, the matter changes, and significantly so. If one aims at positive openings to the supernatural, and one has in sight as a goal what might be called the superpersonality, which is to say the integrated personality beyond common human conditionalities, then to turn to Catholicism (to say nothing of its present-day version) is no longer a limitation that protects and preserves but instead an ossifying factor that destroys itself through the reactions its intolerance and sectarianism can provoke and has provoked in those who aim toward that other realization of self and who have brought attention to non-Western and non-Christian traditions or doctrines in which the metaphysical or initiatic content is more visible than its religious, dogmatic, or ritualistic reduction in the form of a rigid theistic mythology.

It is difficult today to revive the potential of primitive Christianity as that "tragic doctrine of salvation" described above, except in rare cases and in dangerous existential crises. For those capable of it, the problem does not exist; and we would go so far as to say that if individuals who have known nothing besides the quite vain constructions of philosophy and the profane plebeian-university culture, or the contaminations of various contemporary individualisms, aestheticisms, and romanticisms, should "convert" to Catholicism and at least really live the faith, with total devotion and if possible a "sacrificial" purpose, this would not signify an abdication for them but rather an advancement.

However, here we must direct our attention to the special problem that we have noted for a different human type and a different vocation. Then we might ask: Are a conception and an adoption of Catholicism possible, which do not *compel* one to seek another path elsewhere?

There are spiritualist circles that have considered this possibility in the context of what is called Christian esotericism and the "integral tradition." Let us see how matters stand.

To begin with, it would be well to distinguish the concept of Christian esotericism from that of a Christian initiation, the first having a doctrinal character, the second an operative or experiential character. As to whether a Christian initiation ever existed, this is a controversial question that relates (if anything) to times other than our own and that in our opinion admits an essentially negative answer. If one is clear on what *initiation* means in the integral and authentic sense of the term, one cannot help but observe, to begin with, an opposition between Christianity as a doctrine centered on faith on the one hand and the initiatic path on the other. In Christianity's origins, there might have been intermingling that took place due to the interference of the ancient mystery traditions and their proximity; traces of the latter can thus be found among the Greek church fathers. When dealing with theosophism, we have pointed out, for example, the distinction made by Clement of Alexandria between the gnostikos, who has some traits of the initiate, and the pistikos, he who simply believes. But any precise retrospective assessment in this regard is difficult or even impossible, and everything that has been adduced by some observers in support of the existence of a hypothetical Christian initiation, referring above all to the Eastern Orthodox Church and not to Roman Catholicism, seems to have less of an initiatic character than one concerned with the simple imparting of "blessings." Even those who think otherwise have been led to believe that Christian rites originally having an initiatic character were later lost, and nothing of them was passed down save for a merely religious and symbolic reduction and transcription: such has been the case already from the Council of Nicaea onward. Aside from this, all that remains is the world of mysticism. Within the church, there is no trace at all of an initiatic transmission, which by its very nature should be strictly superordinate over that of the existing apostolic hierarchies.

As for claims of a Christian initiatory tradition outside the church and in our own day, these, whenever they are not merely mystifications, have as their basis spurious combinations in which Christianity is but one ingredient, without any true root of traditional transmission. This also applies to those who qualified themselves, even in our day, like the Rosicrucians.

However, leaving aside the issue of whether a verifiable Christian initiation can be attested even in the past, the question regarding "Christian esotericism" remains open; that is, the possibility of integrating what is present in Catholicism (and not in some vague Christianity) into a wider system, in reference to which the deeper meanings of structures, symbols, and rites might be indicated. Integration, as noted, has a primarily doctrinal character. Needless to say, the plane to which one must refer is not that of the "esoteric Christianity" of Annie Besant and Charles Leadbeater, let alone the exegeses of the Gospels that Rudolf Steiner carried out by heaping unbelievable absurdities one atop the other. Here the question is instead of what might supply the current of "integral traditionalism"—that "integral traditionalism," which was essentially founded by René Guénon. The basic idea is the notion of a unitary primordial metaphysical tradition that exists beyond any particular tradition or religion. Here the term *metaphysical* is not being used in the abstract sense it has in philosophy but rather with reference to a knowledge about what is not "physical" in the broadest sense, a reality that transcends the merely human world with all its constructions. Such a tradition has had, in its various particular historical traditions, many more or less complete manifestations, with adaptations to the various environmental, historical, and racial conditionalities, realized in ways that evade profane research. This presupposition would open the possibility of rediscovering constant or homologous elements in the teachings, symbols, and dogmas of these particular historical traditions in reference to a superior plane of objectivity and universality. Ideas of this kind also made an appearance in theosophism and in some milieus of Masonry, though in an inadequate form; it is precisely the Guénonian school that has succeeded in presenting them and developing them in a serious and rigorous way, with the corresponding thesis of a "transcendent unity of religions" (the expression is from F. J. Schuon and is also the title of one of his interesting books). It must be emphasized here that we are not dealing with a "syncretism" or even with those correspondences—sometimes actual, but always empirical and external—that might be observed in current history of religions. The presupposition is an opposite and deductive method, based on fundamental knowledge and principles, that—almost in the same way one can, from the definition of the triangle, deduce theorems that apply to individual cases—likewise provide a means of understanding how, under certain conditions and in relation to a variety of possible expressive forms, as well as in view of various exigencies, proceeding from certain meanings and symbols of the one tradition, one comes to one or the other corpus of teachings, beliefs, dogmas, mythologems, and even superstitions—these "constants" that persist in spite of every diversity and even every apparent contrast.

Now, the initial "esoteric" integration of Catholicism would consist precisely in the following: starting from the doctrines and symbols of the church, one must know how to perceive what within them—to be truly "catholic"; namely, universal (*katholikos* means "universal")—goes beyond Catholicism, gathering also illuminating connections of an "intertraditional" character, so to speak. This would not require an alteration of the Catholic doctrines but rather a valorization of their essential contents on a plane superior to that of simple religion, on a metaphysical plane and with realizational perspectives that might aid whomever aspires to the transcendent.[1] Yet one must be sure not to invert the procedure—as unfortunately has already happened—by taking Catholic doctrines as the primary element, in their specific limitations, and juxtaposing some "traditional" reference onto them. It is rather these traditional references that should constitute the primary element and point of departure.

Needless to say, it is solely from this "traditional" (or supertraditional) perspective that the axiom of the church may be true: "*Quod ubique, quod ab omnibus et quod semper*"[2]—not, of course, on the plane of the Catholic apologetics that one could easily call "modernistic," in that it has fanatically insisted upon the of novelty and uniqueness of Christianity from the very beginning, with the only reservation made for those anticipations and "prefigurations" in reference mainly to the Jewish people, the people chosen by God. The "novelty" may alone be conceivable with regard to a particular adaptation of the doctrine, which is only new because it refers to new existential and historical conditions (which, however, imposed an exposition of the

---

1. Vincenzo Gioberti spoke of a "transcendent Catholicism" (Della Riforma Cattolica [Turin: Botta, 1856], 317–18): "True universality is not found elsewhere than in transcendent Catholicism. Vulgar, practical Catholicism, being restricted to a specific place, time, and number of men, always has more or less the semblance and characteristics of a sect. Catholicism is therefore not truly catholic, except insofar as it is transcendent. And vulgar Catholicism cannot call itself catholic except insofar as it unites itself with the transcendent." However, Gioberti, who remained in a philosophical ideology of the Hegelian type steeped in politics, was surely the last person who could have an adequate idea of the essence of "transcendent Catholicism."
2. [Latin: lit. "what everywhere, what by everyone, and what always (has been believed)," a saying of the fifth-century Christian monk Saint Vincent of Lérins.]

An Excursus on Esoteric Catholicism and "Integral Traditionalism" 119

teaching in a form that is anything but superior). To be able to sensibly affirm the Catholic axiom cited above, one's attitude ought to be the opposite: rather than insisting on the "novelty" of the doctrines, almost as if this were a claim to merit, one should tend to bring to light its archaicity and its perennity, precisely by demonstrating the degree to which these doctrines might be traced back, in their essence, to an superordinate body of teachings and of symbols that is truly "catholic" (= universal); one should avoid being locked into any time or any particular formulation by proceeding to the bottom of each of these doctrines both in the pre-Christian and in the non-Christian worlds, Western and non-Western, both in extinct traditions and in those that have passed into involutionary and nocturnal forms, as is the case for those beliefs that often are conserved among savage populations. Catholicism admits the idea of a "primitive" or "patriarchal revelation" given to humankind before the coming of the flood and the dispersion of peoples.[3] But it has made no use of these ideas that would carry it beyond the aforementioned limitations. The single exception is perhaps the Catholic ethnologist, Father W. Schmidt, who, in his powerful work *The Idea of God,* has made use of it on the plane of ethnology. Catholicism thus remains characterized by a uniform closure and a sectarian exclusivity.

With respect to Catholicism's origins, a notion like that held by the theosophists, who see everywhere the personal action of "masters" and "great initiates," is too simplistic. By contrast, the contents of Catholicism show themselves as susceptible to a "traditional" derivation, and the peculiarity of many correspondences—in terms of mythologems, names, symbols, rites, festival institutions, and so

---

[3]. These events are not "mythic" except in the form they are presented in the Old Testament, which concerns, moreover, only a specific historical cycle. The tale of the "flood" should be considered as the echo of the memory of those catastrophes that destroyed the original centers—arctic and Nordic-Atlantic—of the prehistoric race that took as its heritage the one primordial tradition, leading therefore to a fracture and a dispersion. On this, see Evola, *Revolt Against the Modern World* (Rochester, Vt.: Inner Traditions, 1995), and also *Sintesi di dottrina della razza* (Milan: Hoepli, 1941).

on—with many other traditions that are diffused across time and space, suggests something more than mere chance, something more than what might be revealed through empirical and historical investigations. Instead, it is necessary to take into account an action that is not perceptible and not always linked to persons—a "subliminal" influence, which, without ever being suspected by the founders of the Catholic tradition, might have ensured that these men, who often believed they were doing something completely different or even thought they were being forced to act by external circumstances, became the instruments for the preservation of the tradition by transmitting certain elements of a primordial and universal wisdom, which—as Guénon says—can thus be found in a "latent state" in Catholicism, hidden by its religious, mythical, and theologico-dogmatic form. Moreover, such a view could be partly accepted by the Catholic orthodoxy, only if it meant in more concrete terms the action of the Holy Ghost, which throughout the history of the church supposedly developed the primitive "revelation" by being invisibly and inspirationally present in every council. In the formation of every great current of ideas, one must take into account how much of it may be due to influences of this kind (but in this case of another nature), more than the common man might imagine.

From the point of view of present-day Catholicism, the founder of the religion itself, Jesus Christ, presents a serious difficulty for the traditional integration of which we are speaking, because, as has been noted, the idea that his person, his mission, and his message of "salvation" have a unique and decisive character in universal history (which is precisely the basis for the exclusivist claims of Catholicism) cannot be accepted, whereas for Christianity in general it constitutes the first article of faith.

The same conception of Jesus Christ's function as the savior or redeemer, to the degree that it is presented in the terms of a "vicarious experience," an expiation on the part of an innocent for the sins committed by others (in this case, for "original sin" burdening the line of Adam), presents an intrinsic absurdity. Clearly, the presupposition here is a fundamentally materialistic and deterministic conception of the supersensible. Indeed, the theory that a sin cannot be erased unless someone expiates it, implies an acknowledgment of a kind of determinism or fatalism, a kind of karma: almost as if the sin had created a sort of charge that in any case must be discharged, if not on one individual then at least on another, so that the sacrifice of an innocent or a stranger might be worth as much, objectively, as the expiation in the guilty person. All of this falls within an order of ideas that stands very far from that religion of grace and supernatural freedom, which Christianity would like to be in contrast to the ancient Hebrew-Pharisaic religion of the Law. Already in the first centuries of the religion, the opponents of Christianity correctly observed that if God wished to redeem men, he would have been able to do it with a simple act of grace and power, without being forced to sacrifice, by way of a vicarious expiation, his son—giving to men, with this act, the occasion to commit a new horrendous crime; as if the remission were an almost physical iron law, against which God is helpless.[4] This shows the difficulties that arise for those who adhere, with respect to the story of Christ, to the exoteric-religious point of view and do not know how to separate, on the other hand, the internal and essential side of the doctrine from the motifs that originate in inferior conceptions, and which solely on the basis of sentimental exigencies (divine sacrifice for humanity, love, etc.) have been able to move into the foreground and become "articles of faith" in Catholicism itself.

The problem of the historical reality of the Gospels is fundamentally irrelevant. From the point of view under consideration here, it

---

4. The law of expiation, which represents a particular form of the law of causality, actually applies only to a certain plane of reality, in which it justifies various rites of ancient peoples who were not superstitious; however, that law can no longer apply, with characteristics of ineluctability, to the divine order if by this we mean an order that is truly supernatural.

would instead be important to establish the degree to which the life of Jesus—in the same way as various myths relating to the demigods or "heroes" of the pagan world—can also be interpreted as a series of symbols referring to phases, states, and acts of the development of being, in conformance with a given path. We have said "also" because in the case of certain events or figures in history, certain occult convergences can bring it about that reality is symbol and symbol is reality. Thus, the life of a real being can simultaneously have the value of a dramatization or sensibilizing of metaphysical teachings, almost like in the dramatic representations of the classical Mysteries, which were aimed at arousing deep emotions in the initiates and apt to start them on the way toward carrying out certain transformations of their being.

It is only the case that from esoteric point of view, what has the greatest value in these eventual encounters of symbol and reality, is not the aspect of reality—which, from this perspective, has an instrumental and contingent character—but the aspect of symbol, through which one might reach something universal, superhistorical, and illuminating.

Already in their own day the church fathers had conceived a symbolic interpretation of the material of the Gospels, and partly that of the Old Testament as well, but this went no further than the moral plane, or the mystico-devotional plane at best. This was also the case for the so-called Imitation of Christ, in which Jesus is presented, apart from historical facts, specifically as a model to emulate, as the indicator of the way. It should be noted, however, that it has been declared a heresy to attribute this meaning to Jesus; namely, to neglect his historical reality and the belief in his magical action of the redemption of humanity. Moreover, also with respect to the "Imitation of Christ" and of the utilization of this figure sub specie interioritatis, one must always keep in mind the distinction between the mystico-devotional plane and the plane of metaphysical realization, onto which one can also graft oneself according to the perspective of "integral traditionalism." But the fact remains that, in general, the highest Christian ideal is always the fundamentally moral and non-ontological ideal of the saint, of *sanctification* [sanctification], and not of the *divinificatio* [divinification] to which the Greek church fathers sometimes referred: it is the ideal of "salvation" and not of the "Great Liberation."

As far as the esoteric interpretation goes in the terms of a "spiritual science," it can be said to be nonexistent in Catholic orthodoxy, and this was already the case in early period; there, consideration is given almost exclusively to moral and allegorical meanings. The sense of the "Virgin," of the so-called immaculate conception[5] and the divine child,[6] the awaiting for the "Messiah," the curious correspondence between the name Bethlehem, the birthplace of Christ, and Bethel, the name given by Jacob to the place where he, sleeping under a stone, had the well-known vision and awareness of the "threshold of the heavens"; the "walking on the Waters" (not without relation to Saint Christopher, who helps the infant Jesus cross the "river"); the

---

5. Even the date of Christmas might be integrated into a larger whole with a cosmic backdrop, given that it corresponds approximately to that of the winter solstice, the point of the rekindling of light in the turning of the year—a turning that was already also the basis of a primordial sacred symbolism in Nordic-Atlantic prehistory. Outside of Christianity, it is known that "pagan" Rome, in a certain relation with Mithraism, likewise knew that date as the Natalis Domini = Natalis Solis Invicti ["Birthday of the Lord" = "Birthday of the Invincible Sun"].

6. The literal interpretation of this birth, which is an article of faith for the Christian community and which constitutes the basis for Mariolotry or the "Marian cult," betrays the absurdity of the most opaque exotericism. Apart from the accentuation of the sexual theme in relation to the exaltation of physical virginity, it is unclear why one should have recourse to the exaltation of an abnormal family in which a married woman remains a virgin; nor do the Gospels provide any exceptional proof of merit or excellence on account of which this "Virgin," Mary, should be preselected and, after having served as a sort of instrument for the incarnation, be elevated to a divine figure and the "Queen of the Heavens," with all the attributes that are found in the Catholic liturgy. The truth is that in Mary a mythologem that already existed in Mediterranean prehistory has again resurfaced (corresponding to the mother with divine child even in ancient Egyptian iconography) in a predominately "gynocratic" context.

changing of the water into wine; going into the "desert," ascending the "mount," and speaking from "mount"; later, yet, being dressed in the false regal robe and afterward being stripped of it; the crucifixion in the middle of a double cross; the blow of the lance to the heart, the issuance of water and red blood; the darkening of the "sky" and the opening of the "earth"; the "underworld," which Jesus descends to so as to visit, like Aeneas, the "dead"; the fact that no cadaver was found in the sepulcher, and the rising again and the ascension to the "heavens," followed by a descent of the Holy Spirit (Pentecost) and the gift of tongues; what the spiritual body and the "resurrection of the flesh" might mean, the water that slakes one's "thirst" forever, baptism, no longer by water but by "Fire" and "Spirit," and, finally, the "having no bones broken" and the "judgment of the living and the dead"; the question as to why there should be twelve disciples, three Magi (and what the true significance is of those figures), forty days and nights in the withdrawal to the desert, and—again—forty hours of resting in the sepulcher; and so forth. To give an explanation to all of this sub specie interioritatis by connecting it systematically to a body of esoteric doctrine is a task that one cannot carry out so long as one firmly adheres to the limitations of faith, devotion, and everything else that is proper to the simple religious consciousness.

Perhaps a brief clarification is in order regarding "miracles," also because, as has been mentioned, for modern spiritualism it is above all the "miraculous" that makes an impression. One does not go too far if one acknowledges the reality of miracles, starting with those of Jesus. It is known that the representatives of the ancient Roman tradition found no cause for scandal and astonishment in the miracles attributed to Christ: in ancient civilizations, certain extranormal possibilities were always admitted, and even considered a sui generis science (magic in the strict sense), for the production of certain "phenomena"; and it is only the "free thinker" of yesterday who would greatly question such things, just as it is only the masses who draw the reason for a faith from the "miracle." But Catholicism rightly does not content itself with this. It distinguishes between one miracle and another and does not posit the "phenomenon" as its criterion but rather the cause, which—as we have already observed with respect to spiritism—might be very different even for one and the same phenomenon. However, so far as Catholicism's criterion goes for making this distinction, its position remains weak. To say that "occult" phenomena are due to diabolical forces or latent forces—but still "natural" ones—in man and things, while the true miracle is due to "God," does not suffice to provide a sure and practical criterion: among other things, it would be necessary to begin by objectively specifying what limits "nature" has and to completely neglect what is said in the Gospels; namely, that the Antichrist will have the capacity to produce "signs" of equal potency to those of the "Son of Man." On the other hand, if the condition is upheld that the phenomenon of the miracle must serve for conversion or else for ethical purposes, one ends up at a rather low level. The only element needed to maintain a certain consistency here is the requirement of a significance, an illuminating force, that is tied to the phenomenon in an essential way and, moreover, its relation to a truly superior personality.[7]

This brings us to the criterion proper to the metaphysical point of view, according to which a phenomenon is truly "supernatural" when it simultaneously presents, as the indivisible parts of a whole, three aspects: a magical aspect, a symbolic aspect, and an aspect of internal transfiguration. One can explain this by means of an example. "Walking on the Waters" is not unique to Christianity; it is an esoteric symbol with a specific meaning, and for specific conditions of existence. Over the "waters" is equivalent to over the "torrent of forms," above the mode of being of those natures that are subject to becoming and are composed of a yearning that alters

---

7. On the distinction between psychic phenomena and miracles from the Catholic point of view, one might consider the book by the Jesuit Georg Bilchmair, *Okkultismus und Seelsorge* (Innsbruck: Tyrolia, 1926), in which some valid critiques of the various forms of modern spiritualism can be found.

life and deprives it of any stability. Now, it is possible to imagine that in specific circumstances the integral realization of that symbol's meaning on the part of a personality might be accompanied by the realization of a magical power, which imbues one with the effective possibility of walking on waters without sinking, such that the symbol transmutes into a fact, which, in its turn, is a symbol as serves as the signal and witness to a reality and a law of a superior order. The example we have chosen corresponds, of course, to one of the wonders of the Gospels. Other examples of the same kind might be found both in those texts as well as in the texts of other traditions.[8] It is the capacity to understand things from such a point of view that might elevate whomever wishes to discover the metaphysical content latent in the "sacred history" taught by Catholicism and to reach the sense in it that is truly "supernatural" and not phenomenalistic. He might then learn to read this content not only in the Gospels and in the Bible but also in many dogmas and Catholic theological doctrines: he might understand that, as Guénon has observed, much of what is said theologically concerning angels holds true metaphysically for transcendent states of consciousness—states of reawakening and inner rebirth that can be reached through ascesis; while the "demons" symbolize forces and states below the human level.

In an examination of Catholicism one must further account for everything in it, beyond its doctrinal part, which, to have sense and an objective scope, refers us back to magic in the strict sense. Magic is based on the existence of subtle forces, of a psychic and vital character, and on the possibility of a technique that might act on them and through them, with the same characteristic of necessity and impersonality, and with the same independence from moral qualities in the object and the subject, that the technique

---

8. Compare Evola, *The Doctrine of Awakening,* in which other examples are indicated in our discussion of Buddhism, with the distinction between "Arya" (noble, holy) miracles and "non-Arya."

An Excursus on Esoteric Catholicism and "Integral Traditionalism"   127

of material forces presents. Now, such characteristics are visible in everything that is ascribed by orthodoxy to the rites and sacraments of Catholicism, in which truly nothing is "arbitrary" and "formal." Consider the rite of baptism, which is held to be capable of inducing a principle of supernatural life in those who undergo it, regardless of any intention or merit; also, the quality established by the ordination of the priest, which is not destroyed even when the priest sullies himself with moral indignities; finally, the power of absolution, both ordinary and in extremis [i.e., when one is "at the point of death"], which is, fundamentally, the power to dominate and suspend the law called, in the Hindu tradition, that of karma. These are only a few cases in which Catholicism would refer us back to a plane of spiritual objectivity, superior to the unreality of sentimentality and human morality: to the plane, indeed, of magic. Without a reference point of this kind, the defense of Catholicism is bound to be weak against those who, with the profane and rationalistic mentality of the moderns, indict the superstitious and even "immoral" side of this sacramentalist aspect.

But it is difficult for a Catholic to adopt such a point of view. Instead, it is to be assumed that everything which is rite and sacrament, even if it may have once had a true "magical" potentiality, has lost the latter and in Catholicism remains on the level of religious facsimiles that only formally repeat the structure of magical or initiatic rites.

It is precisely within this context that the Catholic doctrine of the so-called effects *ex opere operato* [from the work performed] should be examined. Strictly speaking, this doctrine, if rightly understood, establishes the aforementioned objective character of the forces that act in the rite; and these forces, once the required conditions have been created, act by themselves, creating a necessary effect, independent of the operator (not *ex opere operantis* [from the work of him who performs]), almost as in the case of a natural phenomenon. However, just as with the production of natural phenomena, so here, too, certain premises must be present. In themselves, the structures of the rite are as inefficacious as the articulations and mechanisms of a motor into which no electrical energy is conducted. To act—that is, to create certain conscious or infraconscious psychic effects—the rite must be vitalized; that is, there must exist a state of rapport with that supersensible plane that simultaneously provides the consciousness with primordial and nonhuman symbols and the magical force that specifically gives efficacy to ritual operations: and, in one aspect, the notion of the "Holy Spirit" is really nothing other than this, especially if it is brought back to its origins, when it was not yet theologized. Without this, the ritual and sacred corpus is simply superstructure—and at that point, one might as well bring religion, "faith," and morality into the foreground, as Protestantism has consistently done by dismissing all the rest.

The relationship with the metaphysical plane can come about in an irregular and sporadic way through states of exaltation, of "holy enthusiasm" of the soul, so long as an adequate orientation is maintained, such as to preserve one from the conjuring of invisible forces of an inferior character. Generally speaking, when one is dealing with a tradition, a figure is needed who acts as a stable and conscious bridge between the visible and the invisible, between the natural and the supernatural, between man and the divine. According to the etymology of the word itself, this was the pontifex (= maker of bridges). The pontifex constituted precisely the point of contact that rendered the manifestation of efficacious and real influences from on high possible in the world of men. And the chain of the pontiffs—which in the higher and most original forms of traditional civilization was strictly identical to the chain of representatives of the "divine regality"—guaranteed the continuity and the perennity of this contact, constituting the axis of the tradition in a literal sense, thus of the transmission of a "presence" and a vivifying and illuminating sacred force,[9] which, through participation, might benefit a regularly ordered sacral body—a force without which, as has been said, every rite is inoperative and lapses into mere ceremony or symbol.

The pontificate, an institution that already existed in ancient Rome, is nominally a part of Catholicism and stands at the vertex of its hierarchy. But one ought to ask what elements subsist in it of its original function and of the overall tradition. The prophetic hope of Joachim of Fiore for the advent of an "angelic pope" with traits almost like those of an initiate and who inaugurates a new "Kingdom"—that of the living, active, and vivifying Holy Spirit—has unfortunately remained a utopia. And if we want to take our bearings amid the contingencies of the most recent times and especially from the figures of the last two pontiffs, John XXIII and Paul VI, the climate of "bringing Catholicism up to date" and modernization, along with the growing aversion to Catholic "integralism" and so-called medievalistic residues, seem to have put the seal definitively on a disastrous outcome.

Thus, the conditions under which a positive response could be given to the question that we formulated at the outset—the question of whether Catholicism is likely to provide what many have sought elsewhere, and which has often driven them into the confusions and errors of neo-spiritualism—appear to be nonexistent, at least when the problem is considered in a broader context. After what has been said, it is problematic that the church, "the mystical body of Christ," is nevertheless the bearer and administrator of a true supernatural power, objectively acting through rites and sacraments, which might

---

9. The "Holy Spirit" in Christianity, dwelling in the church, is the shekinah of the Kabbala (*kabbala,* moreover, in fact literally means "transmission"), the prāna or brahman borne by the Brahmānic caste, the "glory"—*hvarenô*—donned like a "celestial flame" of "victory" by the Persian kings, and so forth. Given the nature of the present work, we must forego a consideration of the relationships between spirituality and the regal tradition, and spirituality and the priestly tradition. On this, see Evola, *Revolt Against the Modern World,* trans. Guido Stucco (Rochester, Vt.: Inner Traditions, 1995). Considerations of this sort cannot fail to highlight the very negative function that Christianity and Catholicism had in the Western world as historical forces.

benefit whomever becomes a member if they nevertheless aspire to experiences beyond those of denominational religion and do not see so-called holiness as the supreme end.

However, it has been recognized that Catholicism contains, in spite of everything, traces of a wisdom that might serve as the basis for an "esoteric" adoption of various contents by one or another personality in the aforementioned context of "integral traditionalism"; in that case, the following statement by one of the exponents of this current might serve as a watchword: "The fact that the representatives of the Catholic Church understand so little of their own doctrines must not bring us to demonstrate the same misunderstanding ourselves." Otherwise, there arise all the impediments and all the limitations that we have considered above and which are only removed with difficulty. Leaving aside secular Catholicism, one might refer to the Catholic ascetic primarily in the context of ancient monastic traditions, with reference to what concerns, if not an initiation, at least an interior discipline that concerns a start toward transcendence, an approach to the supernatural. But here, too, an exhaustive labor of purification and essentialization would be required, given the copresence of devotional elements and specifically Christian complexes, so perhaps it is difficult to gather together valid instruments for inner action, without also having knowledge of what other traditions offer.

A Catholicism elevated to the level of a truly universal, *unanimous,* and perennial tradition, in which faith might be integrated into metaphysical realization; the symbol into the path of awakening; rite and sacrament into an action of power; dogma into an expression of a consciousness that is absolute and infallible because it is nonhuman, and living as such in beings who have dissolved the terrestrial bond through an ascesis; a tradition in which the pontificate once more might assume *its* original mediating function—such a Catholicism as this could supplant any present or future "spiritualism."

But, considering the present reality, is this anything other than a dream?

VIII

Primitivism–The Possessed–The "Superman"

The argument of this chapter might not seem to have any direct bearing on the question of "spiritualism." In fact, as our point of departure we will consider an attitude that, apparently, constitutes the opposite of spiritualism: that is, the naturalistic revolution of a large part of Western humanity. Afterward, we will deal with ideas that seem to fall more within the philosophical domain. Here, however, we are speaking of experiences whose extreme consequences, as will be seen, lead back to a domain in which dangers analogous to those of spiritualist evocations present themselves. Moreover, some of the considerations we will undertake here will also serve to further clarify various points that have already been mentioned, while forming a natural segue to the material treated in the next chapter.

At the outset we must note the singular ease with which Western man has become inured to an increasingly degraded conception of himself. First, he has willingly accepted the idea of being a simple "creature," separated as such by an insurmountable distance from his creator and from the principle of every reality. Second, with the Renaissance and Humanism, he has become ever more accustomed to the idea of belonging to this earth alone, albeit as a being equipped with a superior consciousness and with every kind of creative faculty in the field of thought and of the arts. Finally, several decades of scientism, Darwinism, and evolutionism have sufficed to lead Western man, in a great majority of cases, to seriously believe that he is nothing more than the specimen of a given biological species, at the forefront, if you will, of natural selection but lacking any other substantial difference with respect to the various other animal species.

This reduction, however, is not something that could go on indefinitely or occur without producing more or less serious internal crises and upheavals. In various cases it has become clear that one has headed down a closed street, and that its closure is indeed one of the sort that produces short circuits.

All of this has been stated as a general premise. And now, as an initial phenomenon, let us consider the return to nature. The return to nature, as it has occurred in the most recent period, essentially represents a form of escapism and goes back to commonplace notions and sinister influences. All of this began on the eve of the French Revolution, with the Enlightenment and Encyclopedism. In that period, there was a widespread myth of nature conceived of as the normal, healthy, and wise order to which man belongs in fact and by right; an order, moreover, in the face of which civilization, with all its laws and its positive forms of political organization, supposedly represents something artificial and deleterious. It is here that the concept of the "noble savage" emerged for the first time with the relative glorification of peoples still living in direct contact with "nature."

As with all the myths of the Enlightenment, this one, too, obeyed a suggestion that was widely in circulation at the time and that had precise practical goals in view. This "naturalistic" theory, which had as one of its integral parts the revival of the theory of so-called natural law, in fact removed its mask almost immediately, revealing itself as an instrument of subversion, which then took the field to undermine and root out all those residual forms of traditional authority and organization that still sustained Western man as personality. We are speaking, then, of a corrosive influence, in league with various others of a different sort that we have already had occasion to mention. All of this can be clarified with a brief glance at the concept of natural law, which more or less served as the basis for the notorious Jacobin declaration of "the rights of man and of the citizen." The reclamation and affirmation of such a law constitutes a phenomenon of regression and primitivism. The classical formulation given to natural law by Ulpian, and the identical use that the Catholic Church has made of it, do not hinder the expert eye from recognizing its illegitimate origin. It is the merit of a brilliant scholar of the world of the origins, J. J. Bachofen, to have brought into strong relief the fact that the conception of a naturalistic equality of all human beings, with its respective juridical and sociological corollaries, actually refers us to a "truth" proper only to matriarchal civilization, for which the idea of a true supernatural realm was alien. This matriarchal civilization constituted a kind of substrate, against which civilizations of a Uranic and virile type took shape through the work of other races. These civilizations knew and affirmed a very different idea of the law with respect to their well-differentiated forms of social organization, announcing at the same time the true, heroic, and anti-naturalistic ideal of personality.[1] From this it can be seen where the shrewdly suggested reclamation of "natural right" may lead when taken as the universal and original right belonging to "every being with a human semblance," whereas it had been evident only within a certain lower humanity.

This concerns one side of the naturalistic revolution. For the other side, we must however observe that things are exactly the opposite to the manner in which the aforementioned Enlightenment mythology presents them; namely, the very "nature" that was glorified and to which man wanted to return in order to become healthy and

---

1. See J. J. Bachofen, *Das Mutterrecht* (Basel: Krais and Hoffmann, 1861) [Partial English edition: *Myth, Religion, and Mother Right: Selected Writings of J. J. Bachofen*, trans. Ralph Manheim (Princeton: Princeton University Press, 1967)], and also our own essay, "Ist das 'römische Recht' römische?" *Europäische Revue*, no. 3, 1942.

normal once again, is really something artificial and abstract. It is, in fact, neither nature as cosmos, as a living entity shot through with meanings and supersensible energies, as the ancient traditional man could still perceive it and conceive it, nor is it that particular dimension of the whole, about which we have spoken in the first chapter. It is essentially a rationalistic construction. For the normal modern man, this nature is, and can only be, an aggregate of disanimate forms and physical forces, something external and detached from the whole; something, therefore, in which one might feel at home only if one is operating internally with an analogous separation and disintegration of the spiritual unity of the personality, and the sense of self is concentrated specifically on the physical aspect of one's own being. Thus, even when the rationalistic myth of "nature" exhausted its original subversive task, the modern forms of its revival in an atavistic, "health-conscious," and even sports-related sense likewise show a process of regression; they have as an innermost presupposition the need to relieve oneself of the burden of intolerable, or at least disturbing, spiritual tensions. The idea that this return of modern man to nature, which in some cases leads to a kind of infatuation, might be accompanied by a relaxation, a reinvigoration, and almost to a biological galvanization—that therefore this revolution might appear as positive and desirable on the large scale to those for whom a type of zootechnics serves as the entire essence of human development—all of this is comprehensible, but it does not touch upon the core of the matter at all. Here illusions may arise only if one agrees to consider man not on the basis of the values of the personality but instead on the basis of his "nerves" and his physical organism, both of which are more or less ruined in modern city life and in need of reintegration and biological compensations. In many cases, however, this is only the most external aspect of a process that has also its internal, subtle counterpart, in relation to which all of what we have just said holds true. And this becomes very apparent when we consider the human type that takes form in the modern naturalistic-sporting direction: it is an indisputably primitivistic and regressed type, as virile and athletic in body as it is emasculated and empty in spirit.[2]

If the Enlightenment reclamation of "natural law," according to what has already been said, represents a primitivism, the Encyclopedist myth of the "noble savage" was the precursor of another kind of primitivism, which developed at a point in time when one no longer relied on vague nations of these savages but began to study them closely. The new myth that arose is that savage peoples are "primitive" peoples; that is, the subsisting remnants of humanity as it originally was. They would therefore be our ancestors, remaining, thanks to special circumstances, in an almost pure state.

As a matter of fact, the progressivist myth often intervened here: the civilized humanity of today has supposedly "evolved" from that primitive state. But this is not always the accepted way of thinking, especially since it has been found, thanks to the magisterial works of Émile Durkheim and Lucien Lévi-Bruhl, that "primitive" mentality and modern, or "civilized," mentality do not represent two "evolutionary degrees" but are two essentially heterogeneous mentalities, the one irreducible to the other.

However, the truth of the matter does not correspond to either point of view and, again, after Joseph De Maistre, it is Rene Guénon who has contributed to shedding some real light on the question. Both as a biological race and as a civilization, the savages, in most cases, are crepuscular vestiges of cycles of a humanity so ancient that even its name and the memory of it have been lost. Thus, they do not represent the beginning, but the end of a cycle; not youth, but extreme senility. They are the last degenerative offshoots, and therefore the very opposite of "primitives" in the sense of original peoples.

As for the relationship between the true humanity of the origins

---

2. It is interesting to compare the modern concept of sport with what it represented in antiquity, the "games" and the variety of actions in the certamina, the *ludi sacrali* [sacred games]. On this, see Evola, *Revolt Against the Modern World*, pt. 1, chap. 10, trans. Guido Stucco (Rochester, Vt.: Inner Traditions, 1995).

and the not yet "evolved" but normal humanity, these show a much higher degree of continuity than one might believe. Here, by "normal humanity" we mean the humanity corresponding to the great traditional civilizations, which until historical times, both in their sensibility and in their conception of the world and of institutions, preserved the legacy of the vanished world of the origins.

This being the case, anyone can see the consequences that result from referring to supposed primitives as the ancestors of a humanity that we will not call superior but simply normal. Here we will leave aside what derives from primitivism in the context of a certain type of modern art, which in some cases, especially in music and dance, has even had vast collective repercussions; we will also leave aside certain consequences of a sociopolitical order (in the United States, there are some who seriously think that the influence of blacks has a revitalizing effect on the race and civilization of that continent, to such an extent that they have fought for so-called integrationism and against the "racism" of the whites).[3] Instead we will focus our attention on certain contemporary currents and schools, highlighting, for example, that without these primitivistic superstitions the ground itself would have be lacking for such aberrant interpretations as those undertaken by Freud in his book *Totem and Taboo,* or even in *Group Psychology and Analysis of the Ego.* Indeed, one knows what the sense is of such interpretations: first there is Darwin's idea that the so-called primal horde represents the original form of human association; then there is the conviction that certain forms of savage life, themselves deformed by way of a sexualized psychoanalytic interpretation, represent the pri-

---

3. In this particular case one can nevertheless speak of elective affinities. Another of the errors of our time is to consider the North Americans as a "young people," referring to them be as the latest offshoot, and almost a revival, of the ancient European races. But whoever looks closely here will not see youth so much as infantilism, in the sense of regressions that occur in senility, in multiple aspects of the American soul. It is therefore no wonder that the two extremes of a cycle meet.

mary heritage that every person supposedly carries within himself, and that this alone provides the explanatory principle for collective groups.[4]

The so-called sociological and ethnological interpretations of religions proceed along an similar line, albeit not so base, and likewise result in a myopic reduction of the superior to the inferior, making broad use of material that is every bit as spurious and degraded. This has extended itself to the domain of mythology and symbology. It is painful to see the contemporary researchers in this domain, who wish to move away from the earlier trivial naturalistic interpretations (in which myths and symbols were seen as mere allegories for natural phenomena), but who do not know how to handle the so-called ethnological material, which is for the most part comprised of represented residues of the traditions of the savages and of folklore, if need be associating it, for example, with the theory of the "collective unconscious" (as occurs in Jung), which itself sends one back to primitivistic and "vital" layers of the human being.

An example will serve to clarify where such errors might lead. In one of its polemics, German neopaganism accused the Catholic Church of being reducible, in its essence, to a community superstitiously centered on the figure of an omnipotent "medicine man," which is to say, a sorcerer of the savages. This was intended to suggest that the pontifical idea and the doctrine of the rite in Catholicism should be explained specifically as the surviving traces or transpositions of the magical superstitions of savages. This is exactly the opposite of the right approach. In fact, the right approach would have consisted in: grasping the meaning that given ideas preserve in certain higher traditions, considering this meaning as their primary element, and, starting from it, explaining which involutive processes

---

4. One "masterpiece" along these lines is the book by Fedor Vergin, *Das unbewußte Europa: Psychoanalyse der europäischen Politik* (Vienna and Leipzig: Heß, 1931), in which the various European political ideas are interpreted as the result of a reemergence of "complexes" of the infantile psyche and the psyche of savages.

have led to the superstitions and the tenebrous psychism of the savages and their medicine men.

Since we have mentioned the neopaganism of the recent German past, it may be useful for to us to point out a second case of primitivistic deviation, the scope of which unfortunately did not remain limited to the theoretical field. A certain current has been led to see as the original Germanic tradition a set of views and a climate that were, apart from gratuitous additions, characteristic only to a phase of the decline of the primordial Nordic tradition and, in this respect, they likewise had the significance of remnants. They are essentially the pathos of the "twilight of the gods" and the so-called heroic fatalism, observable above all in the epic of the Nibelungs and in some passages of the *Edda,* if these are taken in isolation. It is almost like a heroic will that knows of its defeat but nevertheless goes to face it, feeling it as a destiny that must be assumed and realized. Now, it would be interesting to see by what paths these benighted views, after the phase of their diffusion through Wagnerism and emergence out of the field of Germanistic exercises, passed into the collective subconscious of Germany and were not unrelated to its catastrophe. Indeed, there is no one with a refined sensibility who did not sense, as a dark omen of a fatal direction, this atmosphere of a "twilight of heroes" and a tragic "last-stand heroism" in many mass manifestations of National Socialism—manifestations that took place under the sign of an alleged revival of the Nordic-Germanic idea and in which, besides, "ecstatic" processes played a leading role. Even in its doctrinal sketches, that current of "paganism" was only able to take up and affirm spurious and degraded elements, which were already a precious incentive for the sectarian polemic of Christian apologetics against the ancient traditional world. This has been pointed out in another work of ours.[5] In the latter work we even showed how this consequence was a mixture of naturalism and rationalism that calls

---

5. *Sintesi di dottrina della razza.*

to mind in no small way the Enlightenment myth of "Nature." These same hybrid characteristics, moreover, have been evinced by a certain racism associated with neopaganism, in which the qualitative and aristocratic concept of race has been degraded to something oscillating between modern scientific biology and a collectivist nationalistic myth. But this is not the place to linger on this topic, which we have already treated elsewhere.

Thus far we have considered some developments of the naturalistic myth that have resulted, from the point of view of personality values, in a regressive disintegration. Now we shall consider and follow another possibility; namely, the case of those who, once they have adopted the naturalistic myth as their own, hold fast to it, affirm the personality, and take this affirmation to its extreme conclusions.

Dmitry Merezhkovsky has observed that the Western affirmation of Christianity in its renunciatory aspects, monastic and inimical to life, has ultimately brought about, as a reaction, the development of an immanentist, humanistic, and naturalistic tendency that is equally one-sided. In the West man has increasingly become the focus of attention and exaltation, the center and the criterion of every value has been shifted to him, and "life" and the here and now have been glorified. Opposed to Christ, the Antichrist has thus arisen; the epoch of the God-man has been supplanted by that of the Man-god, which culminates in the doctrine of the Superman. With regard this doctrine, Merezhkovsky refers above all to Friedrich Nietzsche and Fyodor Dostoevsky.[6]

This analysis is precise, and the reference to these two authors is also appropriate. Above all, Nietzsche should not be considered as an isolated thinker but as a symbolic figure; in the various stages of his thought or, better put, his experience, one might recognize the very

---

6. Merezhkovsky, *Tolstoy and Dostoyevsky*.

stages of the path trodden by modern Western man, as well as the ultimate meaning of this path, which is not clearly perceived by the many.[7] As far as Dostoevsky goes, the ideas that he, a tragic and torn figure, projects onto the most significant characters of his novels are particularly related to that ultimate meaning and to the cutoff point of the path of immanence.

Here we will only highlight certain points of Nietzsche's doctrine that have direct bearing upon the issue with which we are dealing. For a wider critique, we refer our reader to another of our works.[8]

Nietzsche presents himself as a typically modern figure; that is, he presents himself as a strongly defined personality but one completely deprived of the sense that the personality itself is only the contingent expression of a superior principle. Thus, a kind of closed circuit was created in him, in which power accumulates, differentiates itself, exasperates itself, and desperately seeks liberation. Nietzsche had virtually no understanding of the great spiritual traditions of the past. We are not referring here to his violent anti-Christian polemic, partly justified, which is explicable in terms of the reaction that has already been mentioned. But even the deeper, metaphysical side of the classical traditions, for which he had so much interest, eluded him, and he was largely quiet about some of his appreciations, such as Buddhism. Nietzsche therefore embodies the type of those who wish to be "free" as human individuals and are basically left to pursue their vocation. After he has spoken to the hermit saint, the Nietzschean Zarathustra,

---

7. Cf. Robert Reininger, *Friedrich Nietzsches Kampf um den Sinn des Lebens: Der Ertrag seiner Philosophie für die Ethik* (Vienna and Leipzig: Braumüller, 1925), 37: "The figure [of Nietzsche] is at the same time a cause. It is the cause of modern man, for whom here we fight, of this man who, uprooted from the sacred ground of tradition . . . seeks himself; that is, wishes to reconquer a satisfying sense of his existence, which has been by now entirely lost to itself." The work of Reininger was also published in Italian translation with our introduction, under the title *Nietzsche e il senso della vita* (Rome: Volpe, 1971).

8. See *Ride the Tiger: A Survival Manual for Aristocrats of the Soul*, trans. Joscelyn Godwin and Constance Fontana (Rochester, Vt.: Inner Traditions, 2003).

now alone with himself, says, "Could it be possible! This old saint has not yet heard in his forest that God is dead!"[9] The starting point could not be indicated in a more suggestive way.

The Birth of Tragedy is one of Nietzsche's earliest works, and yet it already contains the essence of all the successive developments of his experience. Nietzsche at that point took as his basis the Schopenhauerian conception of the world. Schopenhauer had asserted that the deepest substance in the world is "will," der Wille. In truth, he should have spoken of "desire," because the force in question is a blind, yearning, insatiable will, having necessity as its law. This yearning has nothing outside of itself, and therefore has only itself as its proper object; it feeds on itself, so to speak, and thus is affected by a fundamental rending and contradiction. Here one can recognize quite clearly a philosophical transcription of traditional notions we have already mentioned, especially those of samsāra and the appetitus primigenius [original appetite]. Except this is not conceived of as a law valid only for one mode of being, one state, or one "region" of the world but rather as a universal principle. However, as is well known, Schopenhauer contradicts himself the moment that he conceives for this yearning the possibility of negating, of overcoming itself. Moreover, it is only at this point—that is, with reference to this possibility—that we can speak of "will" in the proper sense, as a faculty of the human personality. But then, to be consistent, the Schopenhauerian *Wille* should not be placed as the beginning, but instead a principle that is one and twofold at the same time, as for instance "nature that takes pleasure in itself and nature that dominates itself," to use the formula of an ancient hermetic papyrus.

In Nietzsche, the problem presents itself as follows: on one hand there is the clear, unmitigated vision of the world as "will" in the Schopenhauerian sense, thus as something fundamentally irrational,

---

9. [Friedrich Nietzsche, *Thus Spoke Zarathustra,* trans. R. J. Hollingdale (London: Penguin, 1969), prologue, §2.]

tragic, and contradictory. On the other hand, there is man as "will" now, in the proper sense, that is, as a force that might posit values and choose a way. But what are the ways that might be chosen? There are only two: to love and will the world in spite of everything, or else to escape, discharging an intolerable tension by becoming a "pure eye," enclosing oneself in a world of forms and aesthetic contemplation, almost as in a mirage and in a hypnosis that distracts from oneself and makes one forget the tragic and irrational world.

Already in *The Birth of Tragedy* the description of the two ways, derived from the ancient Hellenic world, betrays a misunderstanding and the limit of the entire Nietzschean conception. The first way, that of identifying oneself with the irrational, and even willing it up to its most extreme forms, "tragically," is called the way of Dionysus. It is the essence of that which Nietzsche will later call "remaining true to the earth."[10] The second way, that of contemplative evasion in the world of pure forms, is called the way of Apollo.[11] This constitutes a total disregard of the essence of ancient Apollinism and, in part, also that of ancient Dionysism. In fact, as far as Dionysism is concerned, it also knew something more than the drunken and paroxysmal identification with the naked forces of life; it also knew the solutions of liberation, of the critical points in which, to use the terminology of Georg Simmel, the "Mehr-Leben" [more-living], living "Dionysically," changes polarity and leads to something more than mere life, to a "Mehr-als-Leben" [more than living] and therefore to something supernatural and incorruptible. As far as Apollo goes, apart from the aestheticizing assumptions proper above all to the figurative arts, his original

---

10. [See Nietzsche, *Thus Spoke Zarathustra*, prologue, §3.]
11. In *The Birth of Tragedy,* Nietzsche rightly sought an intermediate solution and believed he had found it in the type of the Dionysian artist, who, as creator, remains united with the irrational substrate of reality but, as artist, liberates himself at the same time and participates in a contemplative catharsis. But this equivocal conception was soon overcome by Nietzsche, who asserted ever more sharply, in various forms, the opposition between the two directions.

cult refers us to the opposite of everything that is evasion: Apollo is the Hyperborean god of immutable light, spiritual virility, and of a "solar" force, central and without twilight. And if Nietzsche had had any suspicion of what the Hyperborean tradition was, the scales would have fallen from his eyes and he would have also seen what should truly be understood as "Superman."

Returning to the views of Nietzsche, the Dionysian man does not lose himself in identification. And in Nietzsche's later works it can clearly be seen that the focus shifts increasingly from "will" in the Schopenhauerian sense to will as an autonomous power that manifests itself as pure determination, as a "will to value" and, finally, as a "will to power."

It is here that the net slowly begins to tighten around Nietzsche. We have a twofold development. On the one hand there is the systematic destruction of the world of evasion, understood now not only as that of "Apollinism" but, in general, as that of any "idol," especially moralistic idols; of "good" and "evil"; and of rationalistic and spiritualistic myths, going so far as to include even the world of faith and of religion. In short, there is the demolition of everything that can serve, or could have served, as an external support to the will and to the personality, which could have kept it standing by reference to something else and to values or laws presumed absolute. Here, in Nietzsche, almost as in an ontogenetic recapitulation of phylogeny, we find the essential stages of Western "critical thought," up until its extreme conclusion, complete nihilism. And the original tragic conception is reconfirmed, in the sense that the final result is the vision of the world as a set of forces that fundamentally have no object, but rotate around themselves, so to speak, without a purpose or meaning.

The other side of this development is the aforementioned motif of a *sui generis ascesis* of the will, which is increasing understood by Nietzsche as a force that can, indeed *must,* resist itself, must say "no" to itself and, precisely in doing so, feel and realize its highest power. The two points, then, intersect in a certain way, because the capacity to take on the aforementioned nihilistic truth without batting an eye, to resist and to keep oneself standing upright in a world deprived of meaning, no longer veiled by the unreality of ends and values; and not only this, but the capacity to say "yes" to this world, to affirm "It is precisely this that I want"—this constitutes the extreme proof of pure will.

But this is also a turning point. The concept of "value" as meaning, as a taste of life, remains despite everything at the center of the Nietzschean experience. And if all these objective values vanish and show themselves to be fallacious, there is only one solution: to conceive of one's own pure will as legislator, as the creator of values and giver of meaning to life. With reason it has been noted that, despite all appearances, Nietzsche the "immoralist" does none other than conduct the current of the so-called absolute, or formal, or autonomous morality into the depths. The sole anchor that remains is the principle of Kant's "categorical imperative" itself, detached from every affective and sensible element, from every "heteronomous" and "eudaimonistic" motif; except that in Nietzsche this principle is truly "pure," it avoids that deception through which Kant, at the point of formulating a concrete norm, allowed the humanitarian views of the current morality slip in unseen.[12] To the contrary, Nietzsche created

---

12. In the West, perhaps the only person to go further than Nietzsche is Max Stirner with his theory of the "Unique One," which, however, has only a quasi-social purview. In any case, it is certain that the exponents of another current, about which a great deal of senseless clamor has recently been made—namely, existentialism—did not go further than him. This, too, starts out from the idea of the world's irrationality, but from the subjective point of view; that is, from the incapacity of the powers of human reason to see it otherwise (Kierkegaard). This irrationality is assumed as pure fact, as an "existential reality." Faced with it, man is entrusted solely to himself, to his pure "responsibility" (Jaspers). But a way of discharging oneself is found through a reference, likewise irrational, to the unknown and unattainable God. Even Sartre, who unlike the other existentialists is an atheist and who instead of "responsibility" speaks of man's "not having an excuse," remains at a level of intensity far below the Nietzschean one. On existentialism, cf. our already cited work, *Ride the Tiger*, pt. 3, chap. 12 and 13.

a whole series of theories and points of view for overcoming these moralities, one after the other, and thus for confirming the sovereignty and unconditionality of the will.

But this constant going forward, burning one's bridges and ships behind oneself, one after the other, finds its limits in the following problem: How, in fact, can a new "table of values" be defined? What form is the purely legislative will to take, in order to make a *cosmos* out of *chaos*? This is where, in the later Nietzsche, we find the false biological turn. In searching for an anchor, he submits to the myth of "nature" and precisely according to those biological-evolutionary and selectionist undertones typical of his epoch. "Remaining true to the earth" and "not evading" propitiated this deviation: Nietzsche believed that in the world deserted by values and gods, the single real thing that does not lie is life as biology. Hence the new valuation: everything that affirms, confirms, and exalts life is good, beautiful, and just; everything that humiliates and negates it is evil, is decadence. The supreme manifestation of life is the will to power. The embodiment of the highest will to power is the Superman. The Superman in *Zarathustra* was presented as an end goal, as the end of an evolution, an end that will justify humanity and give meaning to it and to the world. After the awareness that "God is dead," the epoch of the affirmation of the world and of life begins, which gravitates toward the coming of the Superman. And present-day humanity is justified only in what the Gospel affirms, "Man is something that should be overcome," and it prepares the way for the coming of the Superman.[13]

And here the circle closes. What this Superman might be, positively speaking, remains quite confused in Nietzsche. In his middle period he had taken as his paradigm this or that despotic and dominating figure of the past, especially from the time of the Renaissance. But these are secondary and contingent references. The "biological"

---

13. [Nietzsche, *Thus Spoke Zarathustra,* trans. Hollingdale, prologue, §3.]

myth itself should not be taken too seriously; it is a superstructure, and nothing can lead one further into delusion than the unfortunate reference to the "magnificent beasts of prey." For Nietzsche, the way of the Superman is, after all, the opposite of any naturalistic immediacy. Let us repeat, it is the way of a continual, inexorable overcoming of the self; a commanding of the self; a disdaining, not only for pleasure but for happiness itself; a knowing how to say no even when an enormous force in us would like to say yes. The Superman might do anything, open himself to every kind of passion; but the passions in him are no longer "passions," they are like mighty chained beasts that leap up and are affirmed only when he wishes. The intimate essence of the Superman might rather be defined as an ascesis for ascesis's sake; as an extreme, quintessential accumulation of the will to power understood as a value and an end in itself. But whenever this direction is inflexibly maintained and, on the other hand, "remains true to the earth"—which is to say, whenever the conditionalities proper to the human person remain firm—this saturation might result in a short circuit, because the potential charge that the "children of the earth" can bear is a limited. Merezhkovsky, in this connection, has offered a felicitous image: if those beings who, leap after leap, having reached a peak, wish to carry themselves beyond it without knowing how to fly, as they advance further they will plummet into the chasm that gapes beyond.

A great deal of nonsense has been uttered about the illness and the demise of Nietzsche. It has even been supposed that his pathological state underlies his experiences and his conceptions, whereas, if anything, the opposite is true.[14] One must not forget that for

---

14. In reality, based on the psychiatric reports that have been unearthed, it appears that Nietzsche's case had "atypical" traits, in all probability "psychogenic" ones. Dostoevsky's epilepsy is beyond doubt; however, it remains to be seen up to what point it *conditioned* and to what point it had *determined* certain of his spiritual experiences. Some illnesses have the function at times of producing gaping holes in a dividing wall, without which, for the persons in question, the vision of what lies beyond it might not have been possible.

Nietzsche the doctrine was life, and if Nietzsche's exterior existence shows nothing of the deployments of a theatrical Superman, his inner life was entirely composed of overcomings; of continual, quintessential affirmation; and of pure will. In reality, Nietzsche's demise should be compared with the demise or tragedy of various others—some known to the public, such as Otto Weininger, Carlo Michelstaedter, and perhaps also Friedrich Hölderlin, and others more or less unknown—who have trodden a similar path. For all of these men one might use the expression of damned saints. They are the Western exponents precisely of an "ascesis for ascesis's sake," which the traditional teaching considered to be a great spiritual danger—a way that produces neither Free men nor Freed men, but often only chained titans and "the possessed."

The Possessed is actually the title of a novel by Dostoevsky, wherein ideas are to be found that serve as counterparts to the Nietzschean ones. In Dostoevsky, however, there is a more visible element, one which in Nietzsche is revealed almost only in terms of its effects; thus, in Dostoevsky one sees more clearly that the will to absorb something supernatural into man is what produces the crisis. But the intimate force that makes possible Nietzsche's "integral nihilism" and "ascesis for ascesis's sake" should not be understood any differently: it is the effort to insert something that is, after all, "not of this earth."

The views of Dostoevsky that interest us here are contained in the creed of Kirillov, one of the principal characters in *The Possessed*. The starting point, which confirms what we have just said, is Kirillov's assertion that "man cannot exist without God." We would say, a "God" must exist. But Kirillov adheres to the conviction that God does not exist and cannot exist. So, to be able to keep himself on his feet, there remains only a single way: man must discover that he himself is God. The history of humanity is thus divided into two epochs. The first includes a humanity that—as Nietzsche would say—does not yet realize that "God is dead" and that acts, thinks, creates, and fights only to numb itself, to stifle the presentiment of this awareness and to continue living. In Nietzschean terms, this would be the pre-nihilistic world wherein live the "idols," "good" and "evil," and the various mirages of Apollinism. The second epoch commences with the awareness of the nonexistence of God and with the assumption of divinity on the part of man, in a development through which he must become another being, spiritually and physically. These are the very horizons of the "Superman."

Man does not yet dare to recognize that he is God. For this reason he is unhappy. He is afraid of assuming the inheritance of the "murdered God." And he is not God only because he is afraid. Fear, and pain along with it, is what condemns him to misery and unhappiness. When he overcomes fear and pain, all roads will open to him. The starting point is to demonstrate to oneself the supreme attribute of divinity: free will. Man can do this when his "yes" and his "no" do not concern a particular sector of life, but life taken in its totality. By saying "no" to all of life, killing himself, he can demonstrate to himself "his terrible new freedom," he can demonstrate that God does not exist and that he himself is God. Kirillov performs this type of metaphysical suicide to seal his doctrine and open the way to the new man, the Man-God.

This action of a fictional character has, of course, only symbolic significance. However, one cannot fail to see in it an extreme, logical consequence of the life of "ascesis for ascesis's sake," the final self-overcoming of man as the quintessential will to power; and one can establish an intimate relationship between this symbol and the tragedy, or the collapse, of all those whom we have called "damned saints."

In Dostoevsky, one might say that the door is already ajar, but no more than ajar. He caught only glimpses of a higher truth, which was immediately clouded by his "humanistic" assumption. This is the point at which we must return to our main argument.

The doctrine of the Superman, formulated essentially on a cerebral plane, has not been translated into a "spiritualistic" practice. Nonetheless, one must bear in mind that it indicates, as has been said, a fatal direction of development for the Western man who "does not evade" nor set off down the path of regressions. Thus, we must remain aware of it, in all its dangers. The "Superman" constitutes a limit, something like walking on the razor's edge. At the highest vertex of an "ascesis for ascesis' sake," it takes almost nothing at all to transform the "Superman" into one of the possessed, at which point a superior human type becomes a dangerous instrument of obscure forces. This danger is greatest at that point where man, made of pure but untransfigured will, comes out of a kind of paralysis and acts. And this action, practically and technically, is for him a kind of necessity; in the world of the "Superman," certain discharges are necessary in the form of actions "beyond good and evil" and experiences of an extreme intensity, both of which might give rise to as many evocations. To analyze this order of things would lead us rather afar—in part, we will return to it in the next chapter when we speak of the danger of certain forms of magic. Contacts with the supersensible and the "spiritual" might be established on the path of the "Superman," even without wishing it and without realizing it, because one proceeds along the borderline that separates what is individual and human from what is no longer so. Unlike the cases that we will mention and also unlike what occurs in certain special methods of development,[15] here there is the exacerbating circumstance that the "Superman" knows nothing hypothetically of the supersensible, and therefore has no real defense in facing it; he is left to himself, "with no excuses" as Sartre would say, so he is truly "living dangerously."

Merezhkovsky, developing the aforementioned schema in a quasi-Hegelian sense, sees the solution of the problem in the synthesis and reciprocal integration of the symbols of the two epochs; that is, in

---

15. We are alluding to those methods that have their most typical expression on the so-called tantric Left-hand Path. Cf. Evola, *The Yoga of Power.*

an encounter of the Man-God with the God-Man. It is certain that there is only a single way out: to open a path up to transcendence, to recognize that the supernatural order alone is the one in which the true ideal of the Superman can be realized. This is the only way to advance while continuing the ascent, instead of falling over the precipice, breaking up or collapsing, after having reached the farthest peak solely on the strength of the human personality. And then the "Superman" will not be the outermost limit and the furthest empowering of the "human" species but will be of another nature, a different species, one that is "no longer man." The point of separation is not Kirillov's suicide but what the traditional teaching has conceived of as "initiatory death." There is only one solution for the tragedy of the titan, for overcoming possession, for the true realization of the precept that "man is something that must be overcome"—and this is the path of traditional initiations. Then, too, certain positions proper to "Supermanism" will lose their blasphemous tinge, be rectified, and they will bring one back to universal teachings of a higher wisdom.[16]

In addition, we will make several observations of a practical order. It might be said that within the current of the "Superman" the doctrine of will and of ascesis serves as a hindrance and counterweight to the evasionistic, mediumistic, and mystical direction of much of contemporary spiritualism. However, those who, having journeyed roads analogous to that of the "Superman," aspire to make the leap beyond the profane order, must realize that, in predisposition, they are almost always at a disadvantage with respect to any effective realization of the supernatural. They have cultivated an exaggerated, closed sense of their own personality. Moreover, whoever has worked the catharsis

---

16. For example, when Kirillov says that man must realize that he himself is God, and when the Nietzschean Zarathustra marvels about him who does not yet know that "God is dead," they are doing nothing other than re-presenting in a twisted form the Upanishadic teaching of the "destruction of ignorance" and the truth announced in the evangelical saying: "Is it not written in your law, I said, Ye are gods?" [John 10:34].

entailed by the destructive critique of every "idol" up to the point of integral nihilism is basically an intellectual who has his center in abstract thought; this almost always has as its consequence an atrophy or neutralization of the more subtle faculties that are required for starting off toward the supersensible. The faculty of thinking not in concepts or words, but by forming and animating plastic images, is particularly stricken. And this, too, is a serious disadvantage.

In the course of our critique of anthroposophy we said that one must not harbor any illusions about "individual initiation." Unless there is a special, favored disposition due to the existence of a sensitivity and a memory that are not completely obstructed by the human limit, the individual cannot, solely by means of his own strength, go beyond a certain point on the initiatic path. Thus, while some disciplines indicated by anthroposophy and similar groups can have a positive side where they aim to reinforce the personality and self-consciousness, and to limit any determination on the part of the external world and instinctivity, they, too, present the dangers of an "ascesis for ascesis's sake" when they are exaggerated and it is not possible to "break through." Here the danger reappears that relates to circuits bereft of transformers, in which too high of a potential accumulates. The contradictory ease with which, through the aforementioned disciplines, many "occult disciples" fall prey to hallucinations and suggestions, and transform into fanatics of this or that "spiritualism," devoid of any critical discernment, is to be explained on this basis and refers to the same situation whereby, on a different plane, the Superman may give rise to the possessed.

At a certain stage of the disciplines and development practiced solely with the individual's own energies, influences of a different order need to intervene. Only then does there arise a resolution to the tensions, and it is then that the current will proceed in the truly ascendent direction. The circumstances under which such a enlivening, integrating, and "anagogic" intervention can occur are quite varied. The most regular case would be to enter into contact with qualified representatives of an authentic initiatic tradition. But today this is not easy, given that most of the spiritual centers have "withdrawn" to let Western man go whither he will, without any tether. In this regard, as the theosophists would say, the man of today has to come to terms with a kind of collective karma.

Finally, since we have spoken of an "ascetics of evil," those who are familiar with the "family feuds" that go on among the various lodges and spiritualistic sects, and those who are aware of how often these groups accuse each other of "black magic," might well ask: Is such magic perhaps an extension of "Supermanism"? A "Supermanism" extended into the supersensible realm?

Here we must not lapse into equivocations. With respect to "spiritualism," especially of the theosophistic sort, there is a clearly visible tendency to stigmatize as "black magic" any attitude that diverges from an image of altruism and humanitarianism, and we have seen how Steiner goes so far as to label as the "black path" that of any initiate who does not renounce nirvāna so as to put himself at the service of the "evolution of the world and of humanity." These are, of course, nothing but fantasies and it must be emphasized in general that everything which belongs to the initiatic order, by definition—and this is because this order is defined by what lies beyond the individual and the human—knows neither "egoism" nor "altruism," neither "good" nor "evil" in the current sense.

Can one therefore speak of an "ascetics of evil"? One can, but not in a moralistic sense. The kingdom of "evil" corresponds, metaphysically, to that which Guénon has called counter-initiation. On the lower plane, there are certain influences that we have already referred to as "lower"—influences that, by way of their very nature, act destructively on all that is form and personality. But, higher up, there are intelligent forces, whose goal is to deviate, pervert, or invert every tendency of man to reconnect himself with the true supernatural. This is an order that can be called "diabolic" and, in the extreme case, satanic. Nor should it be conceived abstractly, but rather in relation to real beings, and sometimes even to certain centers and to a kind of occult front. Even this is a plane that is not simply human; and the concept of the "ascetics of evil" is defined precisely with respect to it, in certain cases. However, this is an order of things that is too "special" to be spoken of here, beyond the mention we have just made of it.[17]

---

17. One may see René Guénon, *The Reign of Quantity and the Signs of the Times*, trans. Lord Northbourne (London: Luzac, 1953), toward the end, chap. 38 and 39, where he also mentions the Islamic notion of the "Saints of Satan" (*awliyâ esh-Shaytân*), who are in a certain way the opposite of true saints (*awliyâ er-Rahman*).

IX

Satanism

Bringing our attention back to material that is more in keeping with the subject of this book, we may now descend a step and examine the satanism, which represents, so to speak, the extreme point of the modern tendencies toward the supernatural. Here there are also possible convergences with the involuntary evocations of which we have spoken at the end of chapter 6. It can be said that Satan and satanism are today in fashion, exercising a singular fascination. They have furnished the material for various articles, novels, films, and even a particular genre of "comic books." On the other hand, there are groups that openly profess themselves as "satanic" and claim to practice black magic: this is a special case in the teeming circles of those who go seeking for the sensational and the occult, finding in the "satanic" a more exciting ingredient for their experiences. After having just provided sufficient reference points for what concerns a specialized domain, that of counter-initiation, we may see how to orient ourselves with respect to this modern "satanism," which is diffused, peripheral, and often ephemeral in character.

In the interests of rigor, we should begin by defining the very concept of the "satanic." In our cultural area, Satan has had in the first place the significance of "adversary" (a sense that is however better rendered, etymologically, by the word diabolus) and "principle of Evil" (the Evil One). But the genealogy of Satan, if we may call it thus, is complex. The concept of Satan and of the principle of evil finds a place only in a religion that has as its vertex a "moralized" God, that is, a God defined solely by all that is commonly considered by men to be good, luminous, creative, and providential. Then whatever does not have this character (and to which, however, one must also refer when considering various aspects of reality and nature) can come together, and materialize and personalize itself in an anti-God, specifically the devil. However, in a metaphysical conception of the principle, this dualism (which has had its clearest expression in the ancient Persian religion, Mazdaism, with Ahriman opposed to Ahura Mazda) does not represent the extreme case. The supreme principle dominates the "moralized" god, it also embraces "the other half," both poles, manifesting itself both in the luminous and the tenebrous, the creative and the destructive, so the Western and Christian concept of Satan gives rise to that of another face of God. If, by referring to such a broader conception or theology, Satan is defined only as a destructive force, he would lose his tenebrous character, returning to a "dialectic of the divine."[1] As an example one might adduce the Hindu conception of the Trimurti, the triple face of divinity, from which is derived a cult of God as a creator and conservator of the universe (Brahma and Vishnu) as well as a destroyer (Shiva). Therefore, it is only with specific reservations that one might limit the characterization of the satanic or the diabolical solely in terms of a destructive force. It is necessary to add "wickedness."

At the margins of the Islamic and Persian world there has existed a sect of "devil worshippers," the sect of the Yezidi. Here we find a different view, one clearly affected by the theology of some currents of ancient Christian Gnosticism. The antithesis gives rise to a hierarchical stratification: "God" is recognized, but relegated to an absolute transcendence. It is Satan who governs this world, a god of a lower

---

1. In this connection, see Mircea Eliade, *Mephistopheles and the Androgyne,* trans. J. M. Cohen (London: Sheed and Ward, 1965), where he speaks of various mythologems in which the opposites find themselves reunited in the divine.

order; and whoever lives in the world and pursues worldly ends, whoever desires mundane success and happiness, must turn, not to that detached divinity, but to the "competent authority," precisely to the devil, *princeps huius mundi* [prince of this world], who does not have particularly negative connotations. The Yezidi have a cult and rites about which little is known since they have been kept secret, and naturally, a shadowy character has been attributed to them. We will notice certain correspondences of this view of the Yezidi with some fanciful forms of Satanism in our day.

The true characterization of satanism is obtained not by referring to the idea of "evil"—this being a generic term, with variable content due to its sociological and historical conditionality—but rather to a pleasure in perversion as such, to the impulse, not so much to destroy as to contaminate with blasphemy and sacrilegious outrage. Thus, so-called black magic and sorcery are not necessarily "satanic"; they might be practices for the achievement of ends that are adjudged morally wicked by a given society, and the incidence of "satanism" can only concern the forces activated for this purpose.

Now, what interests us is not the operative plane, but that of evocations and lived experience. It seems that there still exist, especially in Scotland, witches; that is, women dedicated to magic and to enchantments, who moreover do not correspond to the repellent image of the old medieval witches, since they might also be young and attractive. One might recognize an authenticity regarding what is attributed to them, their practices being connected to traditions and consecrations transmitted down the generations. The situation is otherwise for those persons today who take up certain rituals extemporaneously in an approximate way, without any kind of regular transmission and with the "satanic" only as a spicy addition. Thus, in the northern part of New York State there once existed a group called "WITCH," although here the letters served as the acronym for nothing less than the Women's International Terrorist Conspiracy from Hell. Other scattered groups are known to perform animal sacrifices for magical purposes, particularly making use of the blood of the victims. Now, despite the spurious and often grotesque character of all this, it cannot be ruled out that sometimes these practitioners achieve experiences that allow the introduction of "lower" and "diabolical" forces. One is led to think, for example, of a case that has aroused much uproar at the time of this writing; namely, the murder of the actress Sharon Tate and other persons at the hands of the "family" of Charles Manson. This Manson claimed sometimes to be "god," at other times "the devil." Sex and drugs appear to have played a role in the religion of his "family," and the authors of that crime (among whom were three young women who also apparently called themselves "Satan's slaves") were unable to give any kind of sensible justification for their actions (the sociological motivation, in which such acts are a "protest" against the system of a society that judges and controls, appears to be quite insignificant) and seem to have attributed them with a ritual character. All of this effectively moves one to suspect an underlying background of possession, owing to those involuntary evocations of which we have already spoken.

In a similar vein historically are events such as those that found their greatest expression in Marshal Gilles de Rais. Gilles de Rais had already fought alongside Joan of Arc without having ever given any sign of abnormality; all at once he transformed into an unparalleled monster, who enjoyed shadowy and savage ecstasies, connected, by his own admission, with supernatural apparitions, in the sadistic contamination and slaughtering of countless innocent children. The phenomenon of an abrupt demonic invasion in him seems to be confirmed by his contrition, a sort of transformation of the very semblance of Gilles de Rais before his execution—almost as if the forces that had taken possession of him had abandoned him.

If, as we have said, the character of blasphemy, sacrilege, and contamination—and not "evil" in general, or destruction—is essential to what is satanic, then the so-called black masses certainly fall in line with this, to the degree that they consist of a blasphemous parody of the Catholic ritual, with upside-down crosses, black candles, prayers spoken in reverse, desecrated Hosts, consecrations to the "devil," and so forth—but not insofar as they might consist, instead, of a distorted and grotesque revival of certain pre-Christian ceremonies. There is much talk even today about these black masses, predominantly with sex as a key ingredient, since it is supposedly a tradition that in these ceremonies a young woman, completely nude, serves as the officiant, altar, or host.

While it is doubtlessly true that in many cases the diabolic and even mystical apparatus serves only as a pretext for sexuality, there are two further points that should be considered. The first is the role that sex and the orgasm can play in processes of evocation, even involuntary ones; sex is the "greatest magical force in nature" that man has at his disposal, beyond any profane and libertine use of it. The second point regards a particular historical conjuncture. Speaking of the genesis of the Western concept of Satan, we have said that this concept condensed everything that was rejected by the conception of the moralized God. Now, in this conception of Christianity there was a strong component of "sexophobia"; sex was stigmatized as something sinful, as the enemy of the spirit and of the sacred; so it passed automatically into the "other half" and was associated with the diabolical, the "enemy," the "Great Tempter." It was natural, therefore, that both in the Sabbath and in other real ceremonies or ceremonies with the character of "psychodramas," the orgiastic unleashing of sex should accompany satanism. But in the present climate of sexual freedom and the "sexual revolution," with this conjuncture being by now to a large extent nonexistent, there is the danger that satanism too often acts merely as a bit of piquancy for those who essentially have sex in mind and, if anything, seek an ingredient for the enjoyment of more intense sensations.

The distances to which contemporary satanism might go is indicated by the case of the Church of Satan, founded in California by Anton Szandor LaVey on the last night of April 1966, which is the famous Walpurgisnacht, sacred to the ancient ceremonies of the Sabbat.[2] There is something amusing in the fact that in the United States, this church, which has its baptisms, its marriages, and its funerals, all celebrated under the sign of "Satan," has been recognized by the authorities; that its grand priest, LaVey, has had himself photographed together with his faithful wife, not a demonic consort in the least, and his dear offspring, just like a good bourgeois family; and that the press was allowed to attend the rites(!) in which, apart from various fervent recitations and a certain ceremonial, the only scandalous point (which is however, quite bizarre in a time when stripteases have become almost mainstream fare) is a naked woman on the "satanic" altar, the "focal point towards which all attention is focused during a ceremony" (however, "not in an immodest position," as a journalist has reported) because the woman is supposedly "the natural passive receptor, and represents the earth mother"[3]—all of which is vaguely reminiscent of the ancient "Women's Mysteries," where there was very little that was specifically satanic.

As for the rest, one can partly find in this "satanism" the aforementioned conception of the Yezidi of the devil as the competent power for things of this world, associated however with a sort of rather banal paganism. Satan is the "adversary," not in the cosmic realm (as the enemy of God, or the anti-God) but simply in the moral realm: he is the god of a religion of the flesh and of Life, opposed "to all religions which serve to frustrate and condemn man for his natural instincts." Satanism reduces itself therefore to affirming and consecrating everything that such religions consider as sin: its gospel is to "make the most of life—here and now! There is no heaven of glory bright, and no hell where sinners roast. . . . Say unto thine own heart, 'I am my own redeemer.'" Added to this is a Darwinism or a Nietzscheanism of the worst sort: "Blessed are the strong, for they

---

2. See Anton Szandor LaVey, *The Satanic Bible* (New York: Avon, 1969).
3. LaVey, *The Satanic Bible*, 135.

shall possess the earth. Cursed are the weak, for they shall inherit the yoke!"[4] One reads in *The Satanic Bible:* "I am a Satanist! Bow down, for I am the highest embodiment of human life!" And here is a sample of its invocations: "In the name of Satan, the Ruler of the earth, the King of the world, I command the forces of Darkness to bestow their Infernal power upon me! Open wide the gates of Hell and come forth from the abyss to greet me as your brother (sister) and friend!"[5]

There is the danger, however, that all of this is reduced to words alone; for if one seeks a doctrine that limits itself to exalting the "natural human instincts" and encouraging their satisfaction, a religion of Life and of the flesh, of strength and immanence without anything specifically perverse and blasphemous (apart from the negation of the Christian morality), it would suffice to refer to the worst elements of Nietzsche and his anti-Christian polemic, or even to the ideas of D. H. Lawrence, without bothering with "Satan" at all and without this whole Satanic theatricality; it would suffice to proclaim an atheism and a "paganism" (in the most profane sense of this word). It is not satanism, but specifically neopaganism, without any backdrop of transcendence and of transfiguration, that is the right and honest name for this Gospel of LaVey.

The suggestion that Satan is "a dark and hidden force which operates in processes for which science and religion do not give an explanation," is not developed here in the least. There is no talk of experiences, except in the sense of obscure ecstasies. We are in the same popular vein as those tales of characters who turn to the "devil" and make pacts with him to obtain the satisfaction of their desires or to destroy their enemies. Regarding the operative rites employed in the Church of Satan (which also include formulas of a hypothetical "Enochian language" transmitted by "an unknown hand"), we should be very circumspect before asserting that they might have some effec-

---

4. LaVey, *The Satanic Bible,* 33–34.
5. LaVey, *The Satanic Bible,* 144.

tive evocatory power. It must not be ruled out, however, that, in spite of it all, something "is moved" when strong emotional and suggestive charges are activated.

Finally, an orientation can be offered for this general scheme. Every tradition corresponds to a process, by way of which a form is impressed upon something formless. This material subsists within the form and beneath the form. It is possible to activate it, to liberate it, to make it emerge, and to reaffirm it by destroying the order of traditional forms. This is the essence of demonic evocations, whether voluntary or involuntary. There is, however, an alternative: that offered by a superordinate use of the substrate and of its liberation, whereby what is beneath the form can be used to attain what is above the form; that is, a true transcendence. But this possibility falls within the initiatic sphere; it also forms part of the tantric *vāmācāra,* the so-called Left-hand Path, with regard to which, however, it is easy to perceive the hazard it poses for anyone who lacks an exceptional qualification, an unequivocal inner orientation, and—as some maintain—even a "protective chrism."

To conclude this summary review of "satanism," we will include a word on Aleister Crowley, also as a way to segue into the material that we will treat in the next chapter. Crowley was a man whose personality certainly towers over that of the figures we have considered thus far. If we associate him with the vein of satanism, it is because he himself invites us to do so. Indeed, he gave himself the title of "the Great Beast 666," which is the Antichrist of the Apocalypse, while he referred to the women that he elected over time with the title of the "Scarlet Woman"—the name of the figure who, also in the Johannine Apocalypse, is the "Great Whore" associated with the "Beast." The epithet of the "wickedest man in Britain," bestowed upon him by London judge in relation to a certain court case, must have pleased him immensely, such was his taste for scandalizing others—and to this end he did not shun masks and mystifications of any sort.

Invocations used in ceremonies presided over by Crowley of the following kind

> Thou spiritual Sun! Satan, Thou eye, Thou lust! Cry aloud! Cry aloud! Whirl the Wheel, O my Father, O Satan, O Sun!

would seem to confirm his Satanism without a doubt, though not without other admixtures (consider the reference to the "spiritual Sun"). However, there is reason to believe that Crowley did not put Satan in the place of God, given the high consideration he held for traditions—such as the Kabbala—that venerate a divinity, albeit one metaphysically and not religiously conceived. Ultimately, as in the other cases considered, Crowley's ostentatious Satanism is defined only in terms of an antithesis to Christianity as a doctrine that condemns the senses and the integral affirmation of man—but in Crowley's case there is no naturalistic substrate but rather an initiatic and "magical" one. If dangerous forces were evoked, it seems that in Crowley's particular case the aforementioned conditions for dealing with such experiences were present, first of all because he had an exceptional personality and was naturally predisposed toward contact with the supersensible (in addition to his possessing a particular "magnetism") and secondly on account of his connections with quite serious organizations of an initiatic character. Primarily, we are referring to the Hermetic Order of the Golden Dawn, of which Crowley was a member, even if he later broke away to establish the Ordo Templi Orientis (the O.T.O., with its name reminiscent of the Templars, and even reviving the Templar's Baphomet). However, this order used many of the magical rituals of the Golden Dawn, which were thought to communicate with the so-called secret chiefs and with specific entities or "intelligences." Crowley, too, aimed at this, so much so that he would ascribe the genesis of the *Liber Legis* [Book of the Law], a compendium of his doctrines, to an entity that he evoked in Cairo—Aiwass, supposedly a manifestation of the

Egyptian Hoor-paar-kraat, the "Lord of Silence." There is reason to believe that, on the whole, this cannot entirely be reduced to fantasies; certain contacts between Crowley and a mysterious supersensible world were evidently real.

This is not the place to dwell on the life of Crowley, which was extremely eventful and prestigious, because, in addition to cultivating magic (as he put it, "I swore to rehabilitate magick, to identify it with my own career"),[6] he was a poet, painter, mountaineer (who attempted, among other things, the highest peaks of the Himalayas, K2 and Kanchenjunga), and an experimenter with drugs (he even wrote a *Diary of a Drug Fiend,* published in 1922).[7] Here we will limit ourselves to briefly indicating his doctrines and techniques. In the *Liber Legis,* we can disregard the anti-Christian and paganistic polemic, which is de rigueur in books of this tendency. Here one reads, among other things (II, 22): "Be strong, o man! lust, enjoy all things of sense and rapture: fear not that any God shall deny thee for this." But, concretely speaking, a doctrine is indicated for the individual that can be summarized in three principles. The first is: "Do what thou wilt shall be the whole of the Law." But one must not stop at the letter of this law, as if it prescribed that one may doing anything that one likes (as in Rabelais' *Fay ce que vouldras*), because Crowley refers to the True Will, which must be discovered within oneself and then realized. This discovery and this realization would be the essence of the Work (the disciple had to swear an oath before

---

6. [The Master Therion (Aleister Crowley), *Magick in Theory and Practice* (Paris: Lecram, 1929-1930), xii.]
7. For the biographical side of Crowley, cf. John Symonds, *The Great Beast: The Life of Aleister Crowley* (London: Rider, 1951); for some details on his doctrines, see also, by the same author, *The Magic of Aleister Crowley* (London: Muller, 1958) and the essay "The Mind and Mask of Aleister Crowley," *Enquiry,* vol. 2, no. 4 (Oct./Nov. 1949), 28–34. In the meantime, many other works on Crowley have been published, which attests to the interest that he has aroused even after his death. It seems that, at least in part, Somerset Maugham's novel *The Magician* was inspired by Crowley.

the "Great Beast 666" to dedicate himself to it), since—as Crowley asserted—only those who attain to such are truly men and lords, all others being "slaves" (presumably and above all from the inner perspective). Furthermore, Crowley also spoke of a self-discipline, at least in his own case, of "a morality more rigorous than any other, despite the absolute liberty with respect to every conventional code of conduct." The corollary that "the word of sin is Restriction," a restriction evidently meant with respect to the will, is to be understood from the same point of view.

The second principle is that "Every man and every woman is a star," in the sense they manifest or embody a principle that is in a certain sense transcendent, which generally leads beyond a mere "pagan" naturalism. One might resort here to the theory of the "Self" as distinct from the simple I. Therefore, a connection with the special concept of the will that we have just mentioned also seems evident here. Among other things, Crowley takes up again the ancient theory of the "two demons"; he speaks of a way of living understood as evoking the "good demon," not giving in to the temptations that would instead put him at the mercy of the other demon and lead to ruin and damnation, whereas by the first demon he would be inspired regarding the correct use of magical techniques. In a dramatized form, it would seem we are dealing here again with the profound principle postulated in the conception of the human being as "a star" (or as a "god"), whose presence constitutes the prerequisite for confronting the risky experiences of this path.

Finally, the third principle is "Love is the law, love under will," with love here being understood essentially as sexual love. This takes us from the doctrinal sphere to that of techniques, where the aspects of Crowleyism arise that might most alarm the layman, conferring his system with a problematic orgiastic hue (even if here we still cannot speak of something "satanic" in the proper sense).

On the path announced and traveled by Crowley, the use of sex, along with that of drugs, plays a leading role. However, one must recognize that, at least in its intentions, we are dealing with a "sacred" and magical use of sex and drugs, one which was also employed in various ancient traditions. The aim, consciously pursued, is to obtain experiences of the supersensible and contacts with certain "entities." In this respect, things present themselves in a very different manner from what goes on at the margins of the contemporary world and has the simple character of evasions, sensations, and "artificial paradises." "There exists a drug," says Crowley, "whose use will open the gates of the World behind the Veil of Matter."[8] But this formulation is imperfect, because in principle one should not speak of drugs *sic et simpliciter* [plain and simple]—whatever drugs these might be—but rather of a very special use of them, connected to precise and not easily achievable conditionalities.

The same is true for sex as a technique, beyond the generalities of the "orgiastic religion" announced by the *Liber Legis,* with a reference even to the "great god Pan." For Crowley, the sexual act had the significance of a sacrament, a sacred and magical operation; in intercourse one aimed, at the limit, for a kind of "breakthrough of level," by which one found oneself "face to face with the gods"; that is, openings to the supersensible occurred. It is important that, in this and in other contexts, Crowley spoke of things "which are to thee poisonous, and that in the highest Degree," being "transmuted into nourishment," and that, to explain the deleterious outcome caused in some of his disciples by the path he indicated, he referred to "doses of poison too high to be transformed into food." Once again, the condition constituted by an exceptional personality here intervenes; it is said, referring to drugs, that they are a food only for the "kingly man." As for sex magic, the technique often prescribed was that of excess: in orgasm and intoxication one should reach such a state of exhaustion, taken to the furthest limit, that "the person so exhausted

---

8. [The quote is actually attributed to Crowley's Golden Dawn mentor, Allan Bennett; cf. Symonds, *The Great Beast,* 28.]

is hovering on the brink of death."[9] Even in the field of evocatory ceremonies, the "magic dagger" that was employed—along with all the traditional equipment of signs, formulae, accoutrements, pentacles, and so on—was deemed as a symbol of "the determination to sacrifice all."[10] In the secret ritual of the Crowleyan Ordo Templi Orientis called De arte magica, in §XV one reads of a "death during orgasm" called mors justi [death of the righteous one].[11] The farthest limit of orgiastic exhaustion and intoxication was indicated also as the moment of a possible magical lucidity, the clairvoyant trance reached by the man or woman. Thus, at one place in Crowley's magical diaries there is talk of ardent and wild young women who all at once, "without any warning, passed into a state of profound calm indistinguishable with prophetic trance, in which they began to describe what they saw."[12]

As is to be expected, it is impossible to establish what issued from experiences of this kind, or with what invisible planes contact might have been made. It is certain that in Crowleyism there was a specific application of special magico-initiatic pursuits; one moves from the plane of chaotic, disorientated, and reckless experiences with wild sex, and with the drugs proper to youth cultures at the margins of the contemporary world, to something more serious—but, precisely for this reason, there is something more dangerous here as well. Crowley had certain disciples who, albeit entirely within the context announced by the "Law of Thelema," were subjected to trials and disciplines of every kind (in 1920, he even founded a "Magical Abbey" in Cefalù, Sicily; with the advent of Fascism, however, he was immediately expelled from Italy, on account of the rumors surrounding what supposedly went on in this abbey). But they do not seem

---

9. Symonds, *The Magic of Aleister Crowley*, 48, 130–31.
10. [Aleister Crowley, *Book 4* (Dallas: Sangreal, 1972), 66.]
11. Symonds, *The Magic of Aleister Crowley*, 131.
12. For other remarks on sexual magic, cf. our book *Eros and the Mysteries of Love*, chap. 6 (with references also to Crowley).

to have all shared the same fate. Those who were strong enough to hold fast, to not deviate, claimed that they had been renewed and integrated by these experiences with the Great Beast 666; however, there is also talk of other persons, especially women, who fell apart and even ended up in sanitoria; it even seems that there were suicides. In these cases Crowley said that they had not been able to perform the magical transmutation of the evoked forces that had been given free reign (or that the doses of poison were too high to be transformed into food); for this reason, they had been torn apart. As for Crowley himself, he was able to keep himself on his feet to the end, concluding his life in 1947 at seventy-two years of age, with all of his faculties lucid and intact. Aside from his disciples there were various personalities, even some of a certain rank (for example, the well-known General J. F. C. Fuller of the British army), who kept in contact with him; and given the general climate of our time, it is natural that his figure should continue to exert a strong fascination and that his ideas should often be cited.

The Crowleyan horizons may seem troubling and dark to many, but even objectively speaking, the properly "satanic" element, despite everything that the Great Beast 666 flaunted so theatrically, does not seem to us to be very significant. In Crowley the coloring that corresponds to satanism does not have as much prominence as that which, fundamentally, presents a magical, and partly initiatic, character.

For this, as we have said, our present discussion of Crowley can serve as a segue into the consideration of modern currents in which that magical and initiatic elements stand unambiguously in the foreground, without the admixtures identified in this chapter.

X

Initiatic Currents and "High Magic"

In the modern world, apart from theosophistic, anthroposophic, or neo-mystical types of "spiritualism" and similar trends, the tendency toward the supernatural has manifested in certain currents with a character that one might call initiatic and magical. In this field, too, there are notable deviations, especially when the "occultist" attitude is attached to them, which is to say the taste for obscure language, in pronouncing *ex cathedra* and *ex tripode*[1] with an ostentatious tone of mystery and authority, saying things halfway so as to imply that one "knows," while in most of these cases one does not know anything and one aims only at creating, in the eyes of the naive, the aura of "masters," possessors of who-knows-what tremendous arcane knowledge. While admittedly it is preferable not to go blurting out certain teachings in the presence of those who do not have the capacity to understand them but only to misrepresent them, this necessary and healthy reserve (moreover, one that was already adopted by similar schools in the past) has little to do with the aforementioned "occultist" style—a style that certain circles of French Hermeticists are unfortunately not immune from adopting.

---

1. [Latin: "from the (papal) chair" and "from the oracle," respectively.]

It is good to respond to the objection that "secretiveness" is necessary given the perilousness of certain teachings regarding practice. Well then, it must be said that in such cases there is almost always a "self-protection" in the sense that whoever lacks a certain qualification will achieve nothing through such practices, while whoever has such a qualification and is well directed will find himself already capable of dealing with eventual dangers.

In the overview that follows, the combination of magical tendencies and initiatic ones might seem arbitrary if we do not clarify the special concept of "magic."

"Magic" may take on two aspects. There exists a magic that is an operative experimental science sui generis, and there exists a magic—"high magic"—as a special attitude within the initiatic domain.

We have already touched up magic in the first sense. It is the art of consciously activating and directing certain subtle energies, whose place and field of action is the domain that exist behind "form"—that which has form both in the psychic field and in an external reality governed by the laws of nature. This magic, if authentic, goes beyond both mediumship and modern "metapsychics"; it is a forcing of the doors of the invisible by knowing its laws, and the way of attracting or rejecting, choosing, and creating causes and effects in the two aforementioned domains—internal and external—of what lies behind form. In antiquity, and still today in certain areas, magic in this strict sense was practiced even as a "profession" (here we cannot digress to show in objective—rather than moralistic—terms what composes the distinction between white magic and black magic or sorcery).

It is important to note that the appearance of magic in popular superstitions or among exotic and savage populations should not lead one to one-sided judgments. In point of fact, every rite that is not intended as a mere symbolic ceremony has a "magical" component. Hence we indicated earlier that, without the presuppositions of magic, the Catholic ritual-sacramental doctrine itself would appear empty and foundationless. But in discussing this doctrine we have also indicated what the presupposition is for a magically operative rite; this presupposition should be remembered in the case of those modern circles that have set out to cultivate what is called "ceremonial" magic; namely, a magic in which an essential aspect consists of formulae, signs, evocatory structures, and so on. We said, therefore, that just as a motor does not run if there is no motive power, so the entire magical apparatus does not operate on its own, but requires a real power of its operator, whether it is innate to him or transmitted to him. Magic is not improvised by exhuming it extemporaneously after getting ahold of ancient rituals found in books or libraries.

Moving on to the second possible sense of magic, we have said that it is essentially defined as an attitude of the spirit. It expresses a form of supernormal integration of the personality, in which the virile and active element comes to the foreground, whereby, fundamentally, it underlines particularly that which in general initiatic realization opposes every ecstatic, pantheistic, and vaguely spiritualistic form: the removal of that I which bars the access to deeper forces of being, by provoking not a descending, but an ascending transcendence. There is a relationship between magic understood in this sense and the regal tradition and initiation, as distinct from the priestly. Hence, this "high magic" brings one back to the discipline that in the hermetic tradition was called the *Ars Regia* [Royal Art], and it also has a certain relationship to the ancient *teurgia* [theurgy] and with that magic which in previous centuries was understood specifically as "divine magic" as opposed to "natural" and also "celestial" magic.

So much for a general orientation. Magic can be freed from various preconceived ideas, from the "occultist" aspect and from miraculist and superstitious notions, from the association with lodges and shadowy personages, and brought back to these essential meanings.

It remains for us to examine certain teachings of a magico-initiatic type that have been formulated in the modern epoch by several personalities. Having already mentioned the "magical" component that was present, despite everything, in the ideas and practices of Aleister Crowley, we will now say a few words on the views of George Ivanovich Gurdjieff and Giuliano Kremmerz (pseudonym of Ciro Formisano) and about what emerges from the writings of Gustav Meyrink, gathering moreover certain elements from an author of the past century, Éliphas Lévi—in whom, however, what is valid and what most interests us is intermixed with a fair amount of "occultist" dross.[2]

Proceeding by stages, we will first of all speak about Gurdjieff. He is part of the gallery of rather enigmatic personalities who have appeared in recent times. Originally from the Russian provinces of the Caucasus, Gurdjieff made his first appearance in St. Petersburg in 1913, having been in contact before that, it would seem, with Eastern masters, repositories of an ancient initiatic wisdom. Later, he carried out his activity in Western countries, transmitting his teachings to his disciples, founding his own center in the Château Le Prieuré near Paris, instituting "work groups" that transplanted themselves also to other nations. He died in 1949.

Of the teachings of Gurdjieff nothing is known save by indirect routes, and almost exclusively from two books by P. D. Ouspensky, who had been one of his disciples.[3] Gurdjieff's single large volume,

---

2. The principal works of Kremmerz were not available commercially at first. We might mention *Avviamento alla Scienza dei Magi* (Bari: n.p., 1917; rpt. Milan, 1938); *La Porta Ermetica* (Milan: Luce o ombra, 1910; rpt. Rome, 1928); and *I Dialoghi sull'Ermetismo* (Spoleto: Panetto & Petrelli, 1929). The best-known works of Éliphas Lévi are *Dogme et Rituel de la Haute Magie* (1854–1856; English edition: *Transcendental Magic, Its Doctrine and Ritual,* trans. A. E. Waite [London: Redway, 1896]) and *La clef des grands mystères* (Paris: Baillière, 1861). For Meyrink, see the novels *Der Golem* (1915), *Das grüne Gesicht* (1916), *Walpurgisnacht* (1917), and *Der weiße Dominikaner* (1921) [English editions, all translated by Mike Mitchell and published by Dedalus in London, are *The Golem* (2000), *The Green Face* (2004), *Walpurgisnacht* (1994), and *The White Dominican* (1994)]. From this group of works we will draw the main elements in what follows.
3. P. D. Ouspensky, *In Search of the Miraculous: Fragments of an Unknown Teaching* (London: Routledge, 1947); *The Psychology of Man's Possible Evolution* (London: Hodder & Stoughton, 1951). See also Louis Pauwels, *Monsieur Gurdjieff: Documents, témoignages, textes et commentaires sur une societé initaitique contemporaine* (Paris: Éditions du Seuil, 1954).

All and Everything, published in English in 1950, is nothing but a mass of divagations, sometimes even fabulous ones, a confused conglomeration from which it is very difficult to extract any valid element (this did not prevent an American from paying a large sum to have a glance at a part of the corresponding manuscript). As in the case of other personalities, anyone who tried to make an accurate assessment of them based on their writings would be at a loss; it is what they have communicated directly, and the influence they exert, which is essential.

Gurdjieff's teaching is not so much about contact with the supersensible as about a possible inner development of the human being. There is a reminiscence here of the Buddhist theory of the anātmā, that is, the negation of a true, substantial I in the common man. Gurdjieff specifically taught that man is nothing but a "machine," a complex of automatisms, and that the first step is to realize this fact. Everything that man does, his thoughts, his feelings, his habits, are the effect of influences and external impressions. He passes his entire existence in a kind of "waking sleep." Passivity is the constant note, despite every appearance to the contrary. One is not present to oneself; one identifies with the experiences one has, one loses oneself in them. Thus, Gurdjieff says, one is continuously "vampirized": by the landscape that I gaze upon, by the cigar that I smoke, by the pleasure that I take from a woman or by suffering itself, by the attitudes in which I indulge, and so forth. There is no true "being" behind it all. So the fact that "I do not exist," in the broadest sense, is the point that Gurdjieff's disciple had to begin to recognize, not theoretically but in a direct personal experience. Beyond this, the path indicated is that of "freeing oneself from identification" and "memory"—the memory of oneself, as a new dimension to insert into the course and contingencies of one's entire existence. Here, too, there is something reminiscent of Buddhism, insofar as in Buddhist ascesis the term satipatthāna indicates precisely the constant active and lucid presence of the self to itself. And while Buddhism speaks of "awakening," evidently this expression fittingly indicates the opposite condition to that of "waking sleep" associated, by Gurdjieff, with the common existence of those who, according to him, are not men but only sketches of men ("the true man is the awakened man").

Gurdjieff's teaching takes us a step further when it considers the duality of "personality" and "essence." In each individual the "personality" corresponds to the ephemeral being defined in relation to the external world and the environment, to what he has learned and constructed for himself, to what one might call his mask and that, according to Gurdjieff, is a lie. The "essence," on the other hand, is what would be truly be his own, the dimension existing in the depths of his being. In general, there is a discontinuity between the two principles, so that there may be men whose "personality" is highly developed and cultivated, while the "essence" is atrophied, the development of the "personality" being able to lead to suffocation and sadness of "essence." Gurdjieff claimed to know procedures of an ancient and secret art, of which the hypnosis known in the West was but a fragment, to experientially produce the momentary separation of "personality" from "essence" in a given individual, so as to permit the appearance of the state of both one and the other. And he asserted that there are men in whom the essence is dead, that he specifically recognized beings in the streets who, while living, were already dead in that sense. One can understand how Gurdjieff, in demanding from his disciples that all of this was not simply to be thought of but realized, could provoke also very serious crises with disastrous results. This was all the more so as Gurdjieff's manners and his language were often brutal; he did not refrain from insulting and pronouncing destructive judgments (the intent of which—or the excuse for which—was to provoke certain indicative reactions in such a manner). He recognized that to ascertain this "not being" could make one go mad and that to be able to face this vision with impunity it was necessary to already be, in a certain way, on the "path."

Therefore, the transfer of the center of one's being from the "personality" to the "essence," and the development of the "essence," appear to be the key for the realization advocated by Gurdjieff. For him this was also the condition for surviving and overcoming death. Thus we find here the theory of "conditioned immortality," about which we have already spoken and which we will see also professed by the other authors whose teachings we will shortly consider. He sometimes spoke of a kind of astral body, not in the theosophistic sense: a body that does not already exist, but is to be created through an almost alchemical work of fusion, unification, and crystallization of the elements of one's own being, which otherwise in common existence unite, separate, and re-associate in various labile combinations, like detached particles enclosed in a container subject to continual shaking, without forming anything permanent. The development of that entity, in all probability as a germination from the soil of its "essence," would be the condition for not dying in dying. But, for Gurdjieff, one must not fall into any illusions: "exceedingly few are the immortal I's."

Not much is known of the concrete practices proposed by Gurdjieff on a case by case basis. He considered an ardent desire for liberation to be a general condition, a desire such as to make one ready to sacrifice everything, risk everything. "A sacrifice is necessary; if nothing is sacrificed, nothing can be gained" (in particular, this would mean the renouncing of "identifications," the principal obstacle to "self-remembering"). The interior work and struggle can be "terribly hard"; states might even arise in which one is led to put an end to one's existence (as we have recently pointed out). He emphasizes that only extraordinary efforts count; but he doubted that these could have any continuity without the control of another person "who has no mercy and who possesses a method." Most likely this refers back to the so-called work groups and to the supervision by those who impart the teaching.

It should be observed that just Gurdjieff as seems not to have had any interest in an extranormal phenomenology, the work he envisaged toward a visibly initiatic orientation likewise did not focus on an absolute and exclusive transcendence. Thus, he would also speak of a "harmonious development of the man" and a work of personal integration, which addressed the question of the coordination of the three fundamental "centers" of the individual—the intellectual center, the emotional center, and moving center—and the removal of automatisms established in one's own being. Toward this specific and non-transcendent end, Gurdjieff also used exercises having the character of a kind of "sacred pantomime" and having a hidden significance that escapes the profane (Gurdjieff claimed that these were very ancient traditions of the East). In these exercises every movement was strictly defined and had to be developed to the limits of one's strength. As far as the background music goes, some had the rather profane impression of it being a sort of "very forced jazz." However, a key moment consisted of freezing in the position in which one found oneself when "Stop!" was exclaimed by the master. This was probably a matter of grasping and fixing a certain inner state.

These summary comments on the teachings of Gurdjieff will suffice. Like Crowley, Gurdjieff had contact with various personalities, also some of a certain rank. Despite the lack of direct systematic and clear expositions on Gurdjieff's part, he continues to be a subject for discussion and, as usually happens in such cases, there has been a certain "mythification" of this mysterious figure. As mentioned, we are almost exclusively relied on what Ouspensky reported about Gurdjieff's doctrines—including cosmological conceps and a "secret natural science," like as the strange theory of multiple "hydrogens,"which are of a rather rambling character.

Moving on to the group of other authors mentioned above—Meyrink, Kremmerz, and Lévi—with regard to their method, these men affirmed the principles of a realism and an experimentalism in confronting the problem of the "spiritual."

"Do not believe," says Kremmerz. "Distance yourselves from mysticism and the act of faith. It is better to know that one does not know, than to believe." He adds, "Spiritualism is poetry—ours is a pure experimental method." The criterion: "Either something is, or it is not." Meyrink says likewise: "They believe in a good and an evil—we know that good and evil do not exist and that there is only a true and a false"; he then teaches that we are not dealing with "ecstasy," but of a "brightening of the spirit, a going toward the light, until the point of vision."

The doctrine is based on the relation between magical integration and the conquest of immortality. The premise is the same as positivism (Kremmerz), and through positivism there come arguments that convince one of the impossibility of the survival of every personal consciousness. The authors in question admit that part or fundamental elements of the human composite survive and even "reincarnate" in the sense we have already elucidated. But posing the problem not for what is impersonal and derivative but instead for the soul as true and proper personality, they think this death—as Kremmerz says—might effectively be an "expiring"; that is, a returning of the spirit to a homogeneous mass in which it is destined to dissolve almost like air in air. The fact is, like Gurdjieff, they believe that, as far as the great mass of men is concerned, such a personality does not even exist among the living; the living are already like the dead. The "magical" analysis of human nature has anticipated and far exceeded psychoanalysis, leading to much broader horizons. The result of this analysis is that when one speaks vulgarly of personality, in reality one is alluding to none other than the historical individual (Kremmerz), an aggregate of tendencies, impressions, memories, habits, and so forth, most of which belong neither to our consciousness nor to our responsibility. Retracing the components of such an individual, one arrives partly at the prenatal life (the subconscious individual in the proper sense), but one is partly led into the collective, intertwining moreover with residues, sympathies, and habits drawn from others or from other modes of existence. Meyrink speaks of a kind of "coral rock," which is our body, the work of habits passed down by instinct for entire epochs, and of "thoughts" that are behind our own thoughts. In one way or another, a state of affairs is therefore recognized, since amid all this talk of a "personality," one is actually speaking of nothing other than a mirage and a ghost: from which Meyrink draws the logical consequence that the "souls" of the dead would be sought in vain in the hereafter, and if "the spiritists knew who it really is that obeys their call, they would perhaps die of fright." Éliphas Lévi, for his part, speaks of a kind of abyssal current, carried by a blind and eternal impulse, to which souls return and from which they arise anew, in a series that has no end until the supreme form of the awakened man is produced, the mage. These are ideas—as anyone might see—that bring us back to what we have already said when speaking of Life as "yearning" and *appetitus innatus*, of the doctrine of cycles and other kindred notions of the traditional teaching.

These premises might seem to be of a pure materialism. But precisely a materialism is necessary as a premise if one wishes to adequately understand a "supernatural" task, such as that which magic proposes. What is a man—what might a man be—beyond the "historical individual"? This is the question. The problem of the "hereafter" exists already in the here and now. "Those who do not learn to see here, certainly will not learn there" (Meyrink). Immortality is awakening, awakening is "inner growth beyond the threshold of death"; that is, in states independent of external impressions and the multiple internal heredities. The "Awakened" are the "Living," the only ones, both in this and in other worlds, who are not ghosts. Meyrink: "In the afterlife there are none of those who left this world blind."

The "magical" character of such views lies in the fact that beyond the historical individual there is not—as is usual—the universal, the Whole, "God," but instead the proper place for the realization of the true personality. This order of ideas is no different from that which we have already seen in Gurdjieff. The magical discipline is supposed to free an independent personal principle from the slag of the collective, and to give it a form. This concept of the spiritual form remains the fundamental point for the esoteric problem of immortality. Kremmerz says that the initiate, at his death, instead of a formless "spirit," emits a "spirit" in which, so to speak, he has sculpted another self, an immaterial, eternal, and indestructible man, endowed with certain powers, which constitute the integration of those that make germinal appearance in mortal man. The same author observes that the spiritists, straying from the point, "think that this miracle is occurs naturally, that all men dying exit into a new life with this subtler body that the hermetic philosophers and the mages in their philosophy glimpse as being creatable only exceptionally." And Meyrink: "Truly immortal is the man who is completely awake. The stars and the gods slip away; only he remains and can do whatever he wants. Above him there is no god. What the religious man calls God is only a state. This very existence itself is but a state. His incurable blindness leaves him in front of a barrier that he does not dare to climb over. He creates an image in order to adore it, rather that transforming himself into it."

The magical ascesis consists in progressively and actively stripping away from oneself the elements and aggregates of the historical I, "so that every detachment counts as an inner formation, as a growth beyond the ground of that I." The first step toward this task would be what Kremmerz calls "conscious neutrality": a state of serene, intact, and balanced consciousness, inaccessible to instinctive reactions, to good and evil, separated from feelings and inclinations and ready to judge them without any interest, as they are and not as they are filtered by worries, by impressions, by habits and memories, and, finally, by the entire ancestral and organic inheritance. Éliphas Lévi spoke in a similar way of isolating oneself from the currents of the "soul of the Earth" and emphasized the aspect of "trials"; that is, of resisting tendencies reported in manifestations of the very elemental forces of things (these are the trials of the Four Elements, known also in the classical Mysteries), of emancipating oneself internally from every need, exercising oneself to use everything and to abstain from everything at will, since—he said—the task and the key of every power are in the formation of an "extra-natural agent." In essence, these are the same rules that are found in every ascetic-initiatic tradition and which particularly in the texts of early Buddhism are given in purified and methodical form, free from any anticipation of the end, and from any moralistic or religious justifications. Here it is interesting only to observe the relation between the degrees of this denudation and the degrees of an active regression; that is, of an elimination of successive psychic layers until they are rid of entirely, emptying the consciousness of all human dross. Having reached the threshold of preconceptional and pre-uterine life, crossing it, one is released from the bond of human individuality: it is the "vision," the awakening—what in the Greek traditions was called "memory." Starting from this point, the center of gravity of being falls into another sphere, where like a sun it will radiate the incorruptible core of the personality in the absolute sense, or superpersonality. Here another form might come into play, drawn from the corporeal, which itself no longer belongs to nature, on the basis of the transformation that in certain circumstances "awakening" can induce in the forces of nature acting in the body.

At that point, magical possibilities in the strict sense might be determined as an application. Meyrink speaks of the "magical realm of thought." In fact, it is less a matter of thought than of what appears to the consciousness, thus renewed, as the secret source of thought. We start from the idea that the brain is not a generator of thought, but only a more or less sensitive receiving apparatus for influences, which, transforming themselves, take the form of thoughts. With the direct perception of these influences, one achieves the integration of common thought in "inner discourse" and visions of "divine" images.[4] Regarding the first point, Meyrink writes, "As the common

---

4. However, it is not always "divine." In Meyrink's novel *Walpurgisnacht* there are very suggestive pages regarding the forms of invasion that occur, especially in thought moved by passion, without the common man realizing it.

man thinks by unconsciously whispering words to his brain, thus the spiritually reborn man speaks a mysterious language of new words that do not give rise to conjectures and errors. And his thought is entirely new, it is a magical instrument and no longer a poor means of expression; and it brings him to know, no longer by means of concepts, but simply by seeing." And Kremmerz: "Coelum comes from coelare, to hide, to conceal as with a veil. The gods are all in the 'sky,' at that point of the horizon where our memories fall silent and there opens before us the surprising mine of the unknown within this moment, which was once our life and our breath." To free the consciousness from the sediments of the historical I is to expose deep and hidden forces (coelum) that act in the organic human unconscious but at the same time in nature: the "gods." Now, no longer transformed now into "thoughts" of the brain, they free themselves and appear in grandiose divine figures. There follows an interpretation of the ancient traditional mythologies in terms, so to speak, of an experimental metaphysics: "I point to the study of mythology, in its essence, as containing the initiation into the powers of our organism; it is the search for a rare science in the possibilities of laying bare a supplementary mystery" (Kremmerz).[5]

Now, if one wishes to refer to operative magic, its essence on this level consists in grafting a certain "efficacious direction," decreed by the integrated personality, onto these energies that pass through it—energies that in given circumstances might also be dramatized in various apparitions, as in their plastic symbols or temporary incarnations. But, directly or indirectly, the "contact" of these subterranean forces with the inner principles of the adept is always necessary: for this contact infuses these forces with a quality of freedom, which

---

[5]. Similarly, Meyrink, taking up ancient ideas such as those of Sebastian Franck, writes, "We see in the Bible not only the chronicle of events in remote times, but also a long path stretching from Adam to Christ, and this is the path that we propose to tread again inside ourselves, from name to name, with the magical virtue of each name, from the expulsion to the resurrection."

permits them to manifest themselves in a different manner to that necessitated by and tied to their nature, by way of which the world has the appearance of a reality governed by physical laws, invariable and automatic.

This is the place for a critical word on ceremonial magic, all the more so since in the school of Kremmerz it played a substantial role. The school of Kremmerz—the Myriam—was in fact constituted as a true and proper magical unity, organized by rites, marked by symbols, degrees of initiation, and ceremonials. It is out of the question that all of this was created ex novo by Kremmerz: we are dealing here rather with the emergence of a vein in a preexisting tradition, whose origin is difficult to identify. This unity aimed at stabilizing a magical force in a community and toward the production through its rites of effects of illumination, or even therapy, in the adherents or for the adherents, similar to what has already been mentioned when speaking of the Catholic Church and its rites. But in this regard it is necessary to make a few observations. The separation of the I from the aggregates of the historical individual by way of the magical rite can occur fragmentarily and, so to speak, experimentally, which leads to vision; other effects, too, might be produced—as, for example, evocations of entities and "divinities," for the purposes of consciousness or else for the imposition of specific goals, and so forth. Here, two points must be kept in mind.

Every effect has its cause. Therefore, when one arrives at a given effect not directly—that is, not through the integrated personality—but rather via a rite, this implies the evocation and employment of something that is the cause of the effect; the rite establishes a relationship between man and this force, which, to whomever follows the path of "ceremonial magic" appears as distinct from his own forces. This creates what in antiquity was called a "pact," for which the Goethean saying holds true, that "from those spirits which you evoke, never can you free yourself." In any case, an energy is grafted onto the personality—an energy that is alien to its form. This procedure might be conscious and deliberate: the voluntary belonging to a "tradition" in which one recognizes the principle of one's own light and one's own power, in magical terms, corresponds precisely to such a case. In evocatory-ceremonial magic in a broad sense, the relationship is not only with those forces determined by a collectivity or condensed into a collectivity; but the principle is the same.

What are we to make of this? It is clear that this path is not without its negative aspects. From the metaphysical point of view, magical evocation is nothing more than an indirect way of making impersonal powers emerge in the consciousness, in forms that have the illusory appearance of individuality—impersonal powers, which ultimately exist in the deeper layers of being. In any "apparition" the process is the same by which a latent tendency or idea might manifest itself in a corresponding symbolic image in a dream. Thus, when the evocator believes these apparitions to be real—and the entire ceremonial situation makes them appear as such—he makes, so to speak, a myth of himself and he divides himself, he places a barrier between one part of himself and another part of himself: the same barrier, basically, that limits his waking consciousness and opposes it to another part hidden by the subconscious. Meyrink puts it this way: "Wretched are they who evoke an idol and are fulfilled. They lose themselves, because they can no longer believe themselves to have been fulfilled by themselves." And in his novel *The Angel of the West Window,* the principal motif is the tragic odyssey lived by whomever has given himself over to this illusion.

This is the limitation of ceremonial magic. In the metaphysically integrated personality, he who commands and he who obeys are in one and the same subject; in ceremonial magic, there are instead two separate subjects, and the practitioner believes that he has in front of himself another being, a "god" or "demon." Such a distinction, like that which is proper to faith and love on theistic basis, presents, to be sure, an advantage: it preserves the sense of one's personality, which in these operative ceremonial forms continues to lean upon the body—but it has the disadvantage of limiting that personality. We have already had occasion to mention a series of experiences and trials that, in certain cases, occur in the post mortem. And according to the Tibetan teaching, in these trials consciousness would experience nothing but itself, all of its real content, and it would only be called to recognize itself in the various apparitions that, so to speak, present it with as many myths of its transcendental nature. Here, what it has established with the objects of its cult plays a fundamental role, it acts as an active force that confirms or destroys the separation; it brings total integration, the "Great Liberation," closer, or it distances it. For whomever puts himself on such a path of magic moved by a spiritual aspiration and not by material ends, the same thing must be said: because the path of awakening is the same for the living and for the dead, the experiences of the post mortem are equivalent with those that the initiate encounters in the course of his trials. But the habit incurred through evocatory ritual actions creates a spiritual barrier: the integration of all the powers in a single center is undermined by it, and one proceeds along the borders of regions where illusion and possession are not ruled out.

Given this danger, we may mention a second one, of an opposite nature, presented by identifications. Having abolished that illusion of appearance as real individualities that the deep forces might assume, and having assumed these forces directly in their "formless" aspect, it is necessary to bear in mind their possible nature. In ceremonial magic, particularly in that of past times, there is often talk of "elementals" and of other entities or forces, which, while not presenting necessary a "demonic" character, also do not have a transcendent character but belong to a world inferior to the one that, in principle, ought to characterize the level of the true man. They even speak of their urge to incarnate. This is moreover the Buddhistic teaching regarding the "gods," conceived, in this doctrine, likewise without a supernatural character. But Éliphas Lévi goes so far as to say that the "angels aspire to make themselves men, and a perfect man, a man-god, stands over all the angels." And Kremmerz: "There is a great host of spirits desirous of immortality; and you are, by a fatal condition of the path, more greatly in contact with them, because they are all elementals of fire, they are thirsty, and you have the water to slake their thirst." Thus, the quality of a being reintegrated in the invisible would act as a magnet and a condenser. Éliphas Lévi specifically speaks of a psychic vertex, which, similarly to one that the waters form by whirling around an immobile and indestructible pillar, is constituted around the mage.[6] And it is a question of having enough strength to not be carried away, to not become the instrument for the desired incarnation of these energies that surround the adept and which flow from his now superconscious body. It is a question of reaching a point of conquering and radically transmuting their mode of being. It is then that these forces might compose, so to speak, the organs and limbs of the incorruptible man. They unite intimately with the nucleus of the renewed soul, which, when necessary, might dispose of them even as it used, and still uses, its organs and physical limbs: to act directly or under the guise of apparently normal phenomena—or to create those "signs," saturated with an illuminating power, of which we have already made mention when speaking of "noble miracles." However, in all this we are speaking of nothing but practical applications, and whoever thinks of these alone is destined to lose track of the essentials, as well as the right path that might lead to their realization. In the traditional teaching, as in the schools in question that have taken up that teaching, the search for "powers" in itself has been considered a deviation and a great danger. We have said at the outset that magic as a spiritual attitude, "high magic" or theurgy, is to be distinguished from magic as an art of powers and of "phenomena." In the magi-

---

[6]. It is for this reason that, according to some, to approach a magical center might be hazardous and that the masters of high magic often practiced it in strict isolation. This regards the influences that remain free, part of which could be likened to the radioactive by-products that are released near places where the artificial fission of atomic nuclei takes place.

cian, in the highest type of the magician, one should essentially see a being who has been released from the two bonds—from the human bond and the divine bond—and who, whatever be the aspect that he assumes externally, resides with his forces and his "form" effectively and stably in a region that lies beyond both this and any other "world." Theoretically, the profane man cannot penetrate the ways, purposes, and the path of such a being.

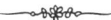

Those who expound doctrines of this kind do not expound anything other than the teachings of a wisdom that runs through the weft of history like a secret vein—the "chain of awakening," as Meyrink calls it—going all the way back to primordial times. And fundamentally linking to this is the highest of the various interpretations—not excluding or contradicting each other, but forming a hierarchy—of which every subject of true traditional spirituality, regardless of time and place, is susceptible. It is the virile aspect of that "primordial tradition" of which we have already spoken.

Today, when there is almost no single form of evocation and evasion that has not found a place in the chaos of the unleashed Western "spirituality," it has been perhaps necessary to cast an almost unveiled light on some parts of this teaching in their entirety. We say "almost," because might not their appearance alongside so many eccentric modern beliefs perhaps be the best way of confounding whomever does not have a right view? In this regard, and by way of a conclusion to these critical considerations, a few clear words are appropriate.

That which has been the soul and axis of every great past civilization cannot be destroyed by a few centuries of modern superstition. Quite differently from an article of faith or as a mere dogma, there exists a supernatural reality, there exists a "kingdom of the heavens," as well as the liminal possibility of transmuting in it the fallen human personality into that of a demigod *participating* in Olympic immortality. But, to express ourselves with traditional symbols, whose sense we hope will be by now clear to the reader, after the "fall" the way to such a region is barred by an angel with a flaming sword, and it is not for everyone—but also not for no one—to make oneself a vanquisher of angels and to use with impunity that violence which, even according to the gospel, the kingdom of heaven may suffer.

The path of high magic has always been the path of the exceedingly few. But nowadays the mentality, the education, the inheritance, the external circumstances and the internal preoccupations, the entire way of feeling, acting, seeing and desiring constitute as in no other epoch an adverse condition with respect to what was, already in the best of times, an exceptional achievement. One should not delude oneself: "power," with which it is easy to confound the theurgic ideal, seems to be the watchword of the day, the "myth" of this century. In reality, things are otherwise. There is an irreducible difference of plane. True magic, in the sense of high magic or theurgy, is a supernatural value. The modern aspiration to power, on the other hand, is naturalistic and profane in every respect. It is a "Luciferian" phenomenon, it manifests in the hubris of the power-abusing man who, without ceasing to be man, which is to say an earthly and animal creature, turns to enslave those forces of the world by which he himself does not cease being constituted and conditioned.

It is thus that the characteristics for which the magical ideal would seem almost to be reflected and anticipated in modern man (so much so that that there has even been a recent book called *The Morning of the Magicians*),[7] and in reality they constitute the most rigid barrier to any one of its realizations. In North America, "the beginning of a new world," as the salon philosopher Count Hermann von Keyserling has called it, yoga and such disciplines have already blossomed regally into the art of "healing by psychic means" in the paltry process of becoming "magnetizers" and "dominating person-

---

7. [Louis Pauwels and Jacques Bergier, *The Morning of the Magicians,* trans. Rollo Myers (New York: Stein and Day, 1963).]

alities," so as to prepare for oneself the surest "road to success" in marriage, business, politics, and so on. Given these developments, tomorrow it could come to pass that certain subtle extranormal forces might even come into current use like others have done, enlisted in the "social service" or else enslaved to the hatreds and profane ends of individuals and of the masses. And thus we will have the worthy "masculine" consort for the mystical, humanitarian, vegetarian, democratic, and feminist "spirituality" overseas.

"Man is something that should be overcome." The principle remains true, but its sense is enclosed in the depths; and, as we have seen, the tragic destiny of the hermit of Sils Maria seals it with a silent admonition for the few who can yet understand. As for the others . . .

To read "spiritualist" works, to associate with theosophist circles, to meditate on the Maeterlinckian "unknown guest," to perform one's twenty minutes of daily concentration like a good child, full of emotional faith in the reincarnation that will permit every soul to continue its "evolution" in a new existence wherein it will gather the fruits of the good humanitarian karma it has accumulated—this is indeed a very comfortable regimen of "overcoming." The original Christian doctrine, according to which one lives a single time and in this single life every fate is decided, including that of an eternal salvation and an eternal damnation—and which does not justify present life without a constant reference to "God"—already sounds like a salutary reveille against such slumbering mediocrity, illusion, and "spiritualistic" languor. And yet here we are still dealing with anything but "religion," although to draw a simple point of comparison from the religious sphere, we might ask: How many "spiritualists" of today would be willing to leave the secular life for the cloister and monastic vows?

Thus, we should not be under any illusions when facing expositions about initiation and "magic." Let them serve as the summit lines, as liminal points of reference—to clearly establish the distances—and not as the instruments of flattery and vanity. Together with these teachings, must always kept in mind the other ones, such as the prohibition against the occult, the saying that "one cannot see God and live," and that he who "has been bitten by the serpent of the spiritual world" was represented as damned. If there exists a right to ask for any higher truth beyond this, such a right is inexorably measured by the capacity for a transfiguring conversion, for detachment, and an absolute overcoming. It is an aristocratic right. This is the only right that the mob never usurp—not today, nor in any other age of the world.

Conclusion

Having reached the end of these critical notes, many will feel disoriented or even disappointed in their desire for a comforting truth and an easy path in the wake of the suggestions offered by so many sects and movements. It is possible that here or there they may even feel disturbed by the traditional doctrines that we have been compelled to examine and explain, so as to set various things aright. Indeed, these traditional doctrines can often serve as a killjoy to both the sectarian spiritualists and their critics alike, for we have no intention of courting the sympathies of either side. Such is notoriously the result if one adheres only to the viewpoint of the truth, without any regard for sentimental and irrational factors, when dealing with questions that are rife with strong internal tensions.

Whoever complains of not having had sufficient positive points of reference should keep in mind the nature of the regions in which we have had to move. To say something that would appear "positive" to most people, we would have had to consider only the values that are applicable to the domain of the visible and the normal (in the conventional sense of these terms), thus the zone that is closed both to the "lower" influences that might arise in the spiritualistic evocations and also to that other sphere: the sphere of the initiatic possibilities and disciplines of a high contemplative ascesis, reserved only to the few.

We would have had to speak of the simple personality in its human form and of whatever might fortify it in relation to the present state of civilization. Essentially, then, it would have been necessary to confront the problem of the *worldview,* because this is the principle of everything. Even within the order of a spiritualism that is itself well oriented, it is a grave error to believe that one might reach something serious through isolated practices without having previously and radically changed the manner of sensing oneself, others, and the world; and without having also changed, consequently, the manner of each one of our reactions. Much has been written in this field since the discussion began concerning the crisis of modern civilization—but almost always without any solid principle. In truth, there exists but a single way for the defense of the personality, and this is the reclamation of the traditional *worldview* and *view* of life, combined with an internal "revolt against the modern world." Now, in that work of ours that bears this selfsame title, we have already given everything that was in our power to give in that direction, without going into specialized fields.

But in the present book our task was different. Here it was essentially a matter of providing the precise sense of the two directions, the one toward the subpersonal, the other toward the superpersonal. This is indeed the indispensable condition for being able to orient oneself vis-à-vis contemporary spiritualism, to be able to ascertain what within it constitutes a mask, and what constitutes a face; to be able to go beyond both the philistine prejudices and the enticements of so many alleged "revelations."

From the start we have recognized that a certain broadening of horizons is now necessary. To insist on prejudices and limitations that even yesterday might have had their pragmatic raison d'être would be imprudent today, and perhaps even dangerous: by contrast, they can produce the opposite effect, as experience itself has demonstrated. Let this be said especially to those who defend a religious tradition in the restricted, habitual, devotional, and conformist sense. These men—let us repeat—should understand that the moment has come for them to awaken, if they wish to prove worthy of the task that falls to them in principle. Once more, something vaster and more universal must be understood as tradition, something considerably less "human" than all that they know and affirm. And this is possible without causing confusion, without weakening their positions—indeed, by strengthening them. Guénon has made this point clear with respect to Catholicism.

The horizons should be broadened not only in this field, but also in all the others we have touched upon in the preceding critical considerations. It is indeed a specific task for whomever has his eyes open to prevent, actively and expeditiously, all that might occur in this sense through the work of uncontrollable influences. But then a test is imposed on modern man: that of knowing how to will the limit that defines and sustains the sense of self before these broadened horizons; of knowing how to calmly close the great many doors that Luciferically stand ajar, or which might open above or below him. Let us say it yet again: in most of these cases, the personality is not a given, but a task. Today, in this era of the irrational and of the demonic realm of the collective, there are already far too many forces against that one must resist and fight in order to approach such a task and to demonstrate a character and a line, without adding to them the hazards of "spirituality."

The "spiritual" has worth today as knowledge, not as a temptation. It must serve to put the claims of all that is science and scientism in their place, to relativize the scope of quite a few values of humanistic civilization, to remove the idées fixes and mental deformations that have established themselves within many disciplines, and thus to enrich their possibility of development. The "spiritual" must also provide a way for us to regain possession of precious parts of a forgotten and disclaimed heritage; it must, that is, give us the possibility of reading through the symbols and myths of the great traditions of the past, which is equivalent to awakening new spiritual senses. What is truly "spiritual" should come to be felt as a present reality, not exceptional but natural, not miraculous or sensational but evident in the context of a sensation of the world that is vaster, freer, and more complete. How far this spirituality then stands apart from man, as something properly "supernatural," is of no importance. What is important is the clarity and the naturalness of the knowledge. To arrive as far as this would already mean a great deal. And yet it would be nothing more than a return to normality. Regarding the degree to which the new spiritualism truly propitiates a revolution of this sort, precisely due to the deviousness that is betrayed behind various of its forms, the Goethean saying holds true: it does good despite willing evil. The only means for favoring this revolution is to keep the traditional teachings clearly in sight, as teachings that act as a rectifying or integrating counterpart to the ideas that are spread today by spiritualism, including those that concern the pseudo-awareness of the "unconscious."

We spoke not long ago of the protective function of the traditional conception of the world. Singular in its essence—that is, in its values and its fundamental categories—this vision however admits various formulations and expressions. One may therefore ask which of these formulations might be of greater aid to the man of today when, with broadened horizons, he comes to consider the supreme things. Most will perhaps think that it is the Christian formulation. We are not of this opinion. Such a formulation for the average man of today is either too much or too little. It is too little if one takes up a diluted Christianity of the confessional and socializing sort, which we have discussed already; it is too much if one takes it in the tragic-desperate direction of the spirit, which we have also discussed—a direction that today either would not be felt or would lead one to dangerous imbalances. It should be expressly underlined that we are not speaking here of doctrinal elements or theology but specifically about what a given formulation might provide for an adequate, comprehensive vision of life.

It is customary to emphasize what Catholicism presents as a defense of the person. And in the preceding chapters we ourselves have had occasion to make, here and there, certain acknowledgments of this. We are dealing, nevertheless, with values that Catholicism did not take from the pure Christianity of the origins, which was characterized by a desperate pathos for redemption and salvation combined with all sorts of emotional suggestions and complexes; the values in question are rather better attested by the best vein of the classical tradition. And the question arises as to whether those values, those elements of a vision of life, are not more fit and effective for the task indicated above, wherever they are freed from a superstructure of faith and dogma and reformulated with a greater adherence to their original root. We hold that this is precisely the case: we think that it is from the classical conception of life that one might draw elements that are simpler, clearer, and more neutral and deprived of "tendencies," which the man of today can make his own toward renovating and broadening his mentality. This can occur autonomously, without reference to a specific religious confession, or to theories and philosophies.

In the classical vision of life, "daemons" and "gods" had their place—the world was thus considered in its totality, comprehending both the subnatural and the supernatural in the sense indicated at the beginning of this book. At the same time, as perhaps in no other civilization, there was a living sense of the personality as a force, form, principle, value, and task. Classical civilization knew the invisible, but at its center it celebrated the ideal of "culture"—that is, of spiritual formation, as it were—to bring to light living and perfect works of art. As is well known, one concept in particular had a primary role in classical ethics, that of the limit, the πέρας [end, goal], which brings us back precisely to what we recently stated; namely, our fundamental need to actively and consciously circumscribe the sphere in which one might truly be oneself and to realize an equilibrium and a "partial perfection," distancing oneself from the enticements of the romantic and mystico-ecstatic paths toward the formless and limitless. Thus, even with regard to the supreme things, one might maintain an Apollinian tranquillity of gaze. If classical man did not have "spiritualistic" illusions, if he therefore knew the double destiny—the way to Hades and the way to the "Isle of Heroes"—just as he knew the law of the inferior world, the eternal "cycle of generation," at the same time as he knew that serenity, for which the beyond creates no vertigo, and "fate" creates no anguish. He knew that intimate bearing of soul that soothes the insatiable thirst for the "fugitive things," and in virtue of which he could even say, with Epicurus: "We have been born once and cannot be born a second time; for all eternity we shall no longer exist"; and he rejects the idea of the gods as caretakers of men. And in leaving, then, he could say that he "regretted not in the least that he should be departing a perfect life."

Essentially, what is most needed today for most people's lives, to prevent these new awarenesses from acting in a negative way, is precisely this sort of clear and calm heroism, combined with self-dominion, with equilibrium and "neutrality" (in the sense we have indicated when speaking of Kremmerz). It is akin to knowing how to sustain oneself without supports, but with an open gaze and a soul that is free from the fetters of "Superman-like" arrogance. It is knowing how to look into the distances, but without vertigo. It is knowing how to form oneself intimately with free activity, without the agitations of hope or fear or the anguish that is betrayed in the various existential "crisis philosophies" that have become fashionable today. It is knowing how to love discipline and limits for oneself, never forgetting that dignity before which we are responsible and without excuse—until that point at which a superior, austere vocation in someone might succeed in gathering all its strength, even to the most intimate, most abyssal roots of life, for the leap that might carry one beyond the human condition.

Index

"active" initiation, 93
Adler, Alfred, 32, 38–39, 47
antarabhāva, 73–74
anthroposophy
   characteristic formation of, 81
   components, 80–81
   contagion, 92
   emergence of, 80
   evolutionist error, 91–92
   evolutionistic obsessions, 90
   first rational development of, 89
   "individual initiation" and, 85, 151
   opposition and, 82
   positive points of, 93
   practice of, 87
   speculations, 84
Apollinism, 142, 143, 148, 194
archetypes, 56
"ascetics of evil," 152, 153
awakening, 177, 185

Bailey, Alice, 65
Besant, Annie, 62–63, 65, 116
Birth of Tragedy, The (Nietzsche), 141, 142
Blavatsky, Helena Petrovna, xi, 13, 62–63, 65
Buddhism, 71, 73, 104, 172, 183

"categorical imperative," 144
catharsis, 51, 150–51
Catholicism
   "blessings," 116
   defense of the person and, 193
   doctrine, 114, 127, 137
   "esoteric" integration of, 117–18
   "integralism" and, 129
   Jesus Christ and, 120–21
   "latent state" in, 120
   magic and, 126–27
   miracles and, 124–25
   monastic orders, 111–12
   morality, 113
   origin, 119–20
   "pastoral care of souls" and, 112, 113
   "primitive revelation" and, 119
   "sacred history" and, 126
   theology claim, 111
   traces of wisdom, 130
ceremonial magic, 181–82
Chévrier, Georges, 65
Christian esotericism, 115
Christianity, 3, 81–84, 112, 114–16, 121–30, 139, 158, 192
Church of Satan, 158–59, 160
"collective unconscious," 28

consciousness
  beyond death, xiii
  "detached," 51
  direct, 54
  higher, 57
  human, new, 73
  "I" and, 8
  impersonal powers and, 182
  inferior forms of, 11
  reduction of, 25
  superconsciousness, xviii, 10, 29, 57–59, 89
  theo-sophic, 65
  "universal," 28
  waking, 55
"conscious neutrality," 178
"coral rock," 177
counter-initiation, 152
Crowley, Aleister, xxi–xxii, 161–67
cyclic conception, 91–92

Darwinism, 11, 59, 132, 136, 159
David-Néel, Alexandra, 25–26
death
  continuum of consciousness and, xiii
  drive, 44
  of God, 3
  "initiatory," 150
  "second," 24
  soul survival of, 21, 22, 23
"deep psychology," 2
demagoguery, 98
demonic force, xvi–xvii, xix, 56
"depth psychology," 2, 31, 52, 58.
  See also psychoanalysis
determinism, 68–69, 81, 121
Dionysism, 46, 142–43
Dostoevsky, Fyodor, 139, 147, 148–49

drugs, 3, 109, 157, 164–66
dualism, 75

ecstasy, 95, 96, 98, 176
Eliade, Mircea, xvi, xxvi, xxxv
escapism, 132
esoteric training, xxvii
"essence," 173
Evola, Julius
  central question and, ix–x
  on contemporary spiritualism, xvi
  on initiation, xxvii, xxviii–xxix
  interpretations, xxxv
  on mask and face of spiritualism, xix–xxiv
  on neo-spiritualism, xix–xxxi
  on psychoanalysis, xvii–xix, xxv
  on search for I, xii–xiii
  on "spiritualistic" organizations, xvii
  on Steiner, x, xxiii
  success of writings, xxxiii
  on the supernatural, xv
"experimental" method, 20
extranormal phenomenology, 21

"familiarization" process, xxxiii
Freud, Sigmund, xviii, 32, 34, 38, 40, 44–45, 136
Freudianism, 35–36, 39–40, 42–46

Gospels, the, 121–22, 125, 126
Great Beast 666, 161, 164, 167
Guénon, René, xi–xii, xiii, xxiii–xxiv, xxvii–xxviii, 24, 51, 116, 120, 135
Gurdjieff, G. I., 171–75, 176

"high magic," 170, 184–85, 186
Holy Spirit, 124, 128, 129

"I," xv, 8
id, 34, 43, 47, 49
Imitation of Christ, 122
immortality, 23, 177–78, 185
"immortal self," 75
"individual initiation," 85, 151
"inferiority complex, 39
inhibitions, removing, 53
"Initiatic Centers," xxvii
initiatic currents, 168
initiation
  "active," 93
  Christian, 115
  "conscious," 84
  counter, 152
  Evola on, xxvii, xxviii–xxix
  "individualistic," 85, 151
  "self," 83, 85, 93
"initiatory death," 150
Integral Tradition, xiii, xxiii, xxix–xxx, xxxi–xxxii
"integral traditionalism," 116
integrationism, 136
"intellectual intuition," 96
intuitive knowledge, xxxiii, xxxiv–xxxv

Jesus Christ, 120–21
Jung, C. G., xxv, xxxv, 28, 32, 49–50

Kant, Immanuel, 144
karma, 67–70, 73, 81
knowledge, intuitive, xxxiii, xxxiv–xxxv
Kremmerz, Giuliano, 171, 175–76, 178, 180, 181, 184, 194
Krishnamurti
  about, 100
  becoming the goal and, 104
  declarations, 100–101
  doctrine, 102–3

  Life and, 102–3, 105, 107
  as "master," 102
  path and, 105
  rejection of authority, 106–7
  "self" and, 103, 104
  "the Unknown" and, 106
KRUR, xiii

La Torre, xiii–xiv, xvi, xvii, xviii, xix
Leadbetter, Charles, 65, 116
Le Bon, Gustave, 33, 38
Left-hand Path, 161
Lévi, Éliphas, 178, 183–84
libido, 35–37, 40–44, 46–47, 50, 55, 59
love, 40, 46, 85, 142, 164

magic
  about, 169–70
  ceremonial, 181–82
  essential aspect of, 170
  facing expositions about, 187–88
  "high," 170, 184–85, 186
  true, 186
Man-God, 148–50
Marcuse, Herbert, 45
Massis, Henri, 1–2
mediums, 13–14, 15, 22
mediumship, 14, 18, 22, 47, 63
Merezhkovsky, Dmitry, 139, 149
messianic phenomenon, 99–100
"metaphysical" state, 56–57
metaphysic research. *See* "psychic research"
metaphysics, xii, 20, 27, 29, 42–43, 180
Meyrink, Gustav, xx, 171, 176, 177–78, 179–80, 182, 185
miracles, 124–25
Myriam, 181

mysticism
  characterization, 95
  Christian, 111
  distancing from, 176
  of instinct and irrationalism, 58
  messianic phenomenon and, 99–100
  of profane things, 97

natural clairvoyance, 8
"naturalistic" theory, 132
"natural law," 135
"natural right," 133
nature, 7, 134, 139
neo-spiritualism
  beginnings of, 3
  defined, xi
  "demonic" danger in, xx–xxi
  Integral Tradition versus, xxix–xxx
  regressive character, 6
  role of, 3
  "second religiosity," 4–5
  ways to transcendence and, xxviii
Nietzsche, Friedrich, 139–47
Nirvana principle, 38, 45

"occult disciple," 89, 91, 151
"One Life," 76, 77
Ordo Templi Orientis (O.T.O.), 162, 166
Ouspensky, P. D., 171, 175

"paganism," 138
pansexualism, 44
"paraphysical" phenomena, 27, 28
personality
  ceremonial magic and, 182–83
  control of "vital" conditions of, 90
  defining essence of, 5–6
  development of, xxv
  integration of, 54
  "second," 21
  spirit as, 72
  spiritualism and, 6
  transfer to "essence," 174
phenomena
  of collective exhilaration, 109
  collectors of, 24
  extranormal, 20
  mediumistic, 18
  metaphysics and, 27
  misleading, 22
  natural, 127–28
  "paraphysical," 27, 28
  psychic research and, 18–19
  Satanic, 22
  transference and, 98
  understanding of, 87
"philosophy of civilization," 84
"phylogenetically regressive" states, 28
positivism, xxviii, 5, 176
Possessed, The (Dostoevsky), 147–48, 150
possession, 17, 109, 157, 183
posthypnotic suggestion, 54
Preface (this book)
  First Edition, xl
  Second Edition, xxxviii
  Third Edition, xxxvii
progressivist myth, 135
"PSI field," 29
"psychic research"
  inadequacy of method, 19
  inauguration of, 14
  phenomena and, 18–19
  spiritualism and, 13–29
psychic researchers, 15
psychic vortex, 184

psychoanalysis
    abdication and, 47
    conceptions, 30–31
    critique of, 30–60
    as cultural phenomenon, 31–32
    as dangerous, 52
    dualism, 33
    id and, 34, 36, 43, 49
    interpretations, 31
    Jewish culture and, 59
    libido and, 35–37, 40–44, 46–47, 50, 55, 59
    penetration into the depths and, 55
    as "positivistic" discipline, 2
    roots of the will and, 51–52
    sexuality and, 41–43, 136
    subconscious and, 32–33, 47, 51
    transference and, 98
    unconscious and, 34–35, 37, 53, 57
purgatory, 74

"reality principle," 48
regression, 6, 7–8, 28
Reich, Wilhelm, 32, 45, 48
reincarnation, 70–73, 75, 81
religions, interpretation of, 137
repression, 36, 45, 48, 108

"sacred pantomime," 175
salvation, xiv, 72, 76, 112, 114, 120, 123, 187
Satan
    about, 155–56
    as "adversary," 159
    as dark and hidden force, 160
    as destructive force, 155
    genealogy of, 154–55
    Great Beast 666 and, 161, 164, 167
Satanic phenomena, 22

Satanic Bible, The, 160
Satanism, xxi, 154–68
"Satan's slaves," 157
Schopenhauer, Arthur, 61, 141
"second death," 24
"second personality," 21
"second religiosity," 4–5
Self, xxiv, 70, 164
self-consciousness, 89
sex magic, 165–66
sexuality, 41–43, 136
"Solar Logos," 82–83
souls, 11, 21, 24–26, 100, 177
Spengler, Oswald, xxviii, 4–5
spiritism, 13–14, 16
"spirits," 14, 20–21, 24, 74
"spiritual," 5–6, 9, 95, 149, 191, 192
spiritualism
    currents of, 12
    danger of, 5
    ideas spread by, 192
    personality and, 6
    as poetry, 176
    "psychic research" and, 13–29
    Steinerian, 82
    theosophism and, 76
    vessel of, 2
"spiritualistic" hypotheses, 20
spirituality
    ancient, 61
    Eastern, 78
    genuine, xiv, xvii, xviii, xxviii
    initiatic, 86
    ladder, descending, 9–10
    measure of, 9
    prepersonal, 84
    pure metaphysics and, xii
    Western, 185
"spiritual science," 86

Steiner, Rudolf, x, xxiii, 76–77, 80, 81–86. *See also* anthroposophy
subconscious, 32–33, 47, 51, 55, 98
"subliminal," 34, 52
subpersonal, xxi, 14, 20, 41–42, 73, 75, 190
sub specie aeternitatis, 58
superconsciousness, xviii, 10, 29, 57–59, 89
superego, 36
Superman, 139, 145–46, 148–49, 150, 194
supernatural, the, xv, 6–7, 10–11, 23, 77, 111, 114, 130
superstition, 27, 75, 81, 117, 137–38

Tao Te Ching, x, xxxv
Theosophical Society, xix, 64–66
theosophism
    aimless roving of, 66
    critique of, 61–79
    current form of, 62
    doctrine of, 66–67
    "great Guardians of Humanity" and, 63
    "invisible" origin of, 78
    karma and, 67–70, 73
    limitation of man and, 70
    "One Life" and, 76, 77
    reincarnation and, 70–73, 75
    role of, 61–62
    spiritual East and, 78
    spiritualism and, 76
    "teaching of ancient knowledge" and, 70
    validity versus negativity and, 64
    "World Teacher" and, 100
thoughts, 6, 8, 20, 89, 177, 179–80

Tibetan Book of the Dead, xxvi, 23
Tillich, Paul, xvi–xvii, 96–97
traditional method
    knowledge gained through, xxxii–xxxiii
    as objective, xxxii
    spiritual content and, xxxii
    as universal, xxxiv
traditional teachings
    cyclic conception, 91–92
    esoteric sense of, 71
    "initiatory death," 150
    keeping in sight, 192
    recurrent idea in, 23
    root of "natural" life and, 43
    search for powers and, 184
    study and comprehension of, 27
transcendence, xxi, xxix, 3, 10, 42, 112, 130
transference, 51, 53, 98, 99
True Will, 163
"truth," xxxiii, 133

unconscious, 33–34, 37, 53, 57
"unknown guest," 187
"Unknown, the," 106
UR Group, xii, xiii
UR/KRUR monographs, xxv

"value," 144
Vedānta, 70–71, 90–93

"waking sleep," 172, 173
WITCH, 156
"World Teacher," 100
worldview, 190

Zen, 106, 108